The Visual Miscellaneum

The Visual Miscellaneum

A Colorful Guide to the World's Most Consequential Trivia

David McCandless

COLLINS DESIGN

An Imprint of HarperCollinsPublishers

HarperCollins books may be purchased for educational, business, or
sales promotional use. For information, please write: Special Markets
Department, HarperCollins Publishers, 10 East 53rd Street, New York, NY
10022.

Written and designed by David McCandless
http://www.davidmccandless.com

Library of Congress Cataloging-in-Publication Data is available upon
request.

ISBN 978-0-06-6174836-3

10 9 8 7 6 5 4 3 2

to the beautiful internet

Introduction

This book started out as an exploration. Swamped by information, I was searching for a better way to see it all and understand it. Why not visually?

In a way, we're all visual now. Every day, every hour, maybe even every minute, we're looking and absorbing information via the web. We're steeped in it. Maybe even lost in it. So perhaps what we need are well-designed, colourful and – hopefully – useful charts to help us navigate. A modern day map book.

But can a book with the minimum of text, rammed with diagrams, maps and charts, still be exciting and readable? Can it still be fun? Can you make jokes in graphs? Are you even allowed to?

So I started experimenting with visualizing information and ideas in both new and old ways. I went for subjects that sprang from my own curiosity and ignorance – the questions I wanted answering. I avoided straightforward facts and dry statistics. Instead, I focused on the relationship between facts, the context, the connections that make information meaningful.

So, that's what this book is. Miscellaneous facts and ideas, interconnected visually. A visual miscellaneum. A series of experiments in making information approachable and beautiful. See what you think.

David McCandless

POP

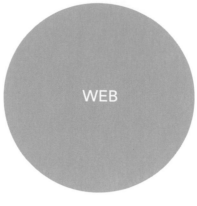

WEB

THOUGHT

NATURE

SCIENCE

HEALTH

FOOD

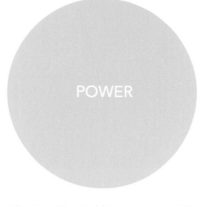

POWER

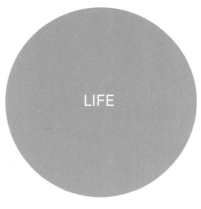

LIFE

FILM

MEDIA

MUSIC

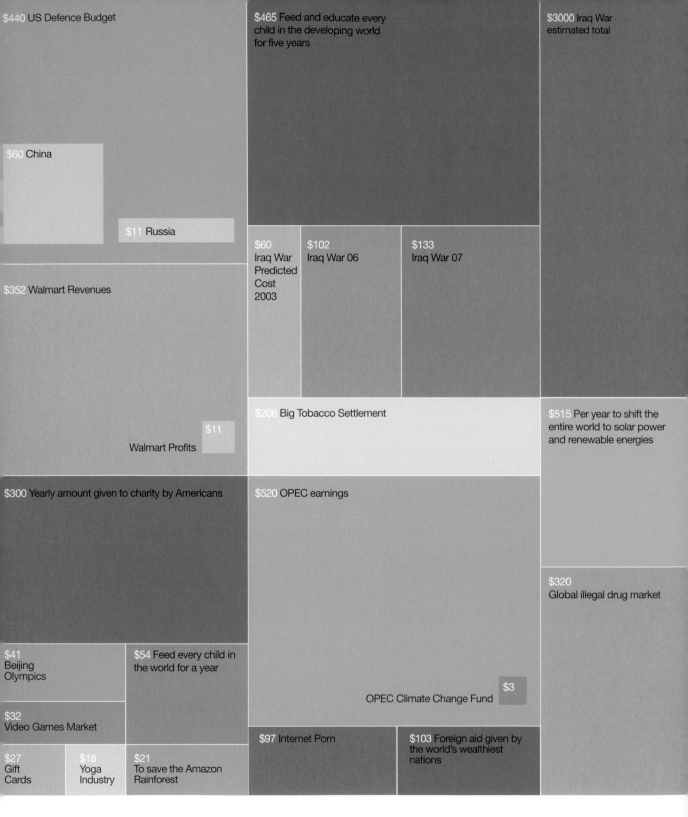

$440 US Defence Budget

$60 China

$11 Russia

$352 Walmart Revenues

$11 Walmart Profits

$300 Yearly amount given to charity by Americans

$41 Beijing Olympics

$32 Video Games Market

$27 Gift Cards

$18 Yoga Industry

$21 To save the Amazon Rainforest

$54 Feed every child in the world for a year

$465 Feed and educate every child in the developing world for five years

$60 Iraq War Predicted Cost 2003

$102 Iraq War 06

$133 Iraq War 07

$206 Big Tobacco Settlement

$520 OPEC earnings

OPEC Climate Change Fund $3

$97 Internet Porn

$103 Foreign aid given by the world's wealthiest nations

$3000 Iraq War estimated total

$515 Per year to shift the entire world to solar power and renewable energies

$320 Global illegal drug market

Billion-Dollar-O-Gram

Billions spent on this. Billions spent on that. It's all relative, right?

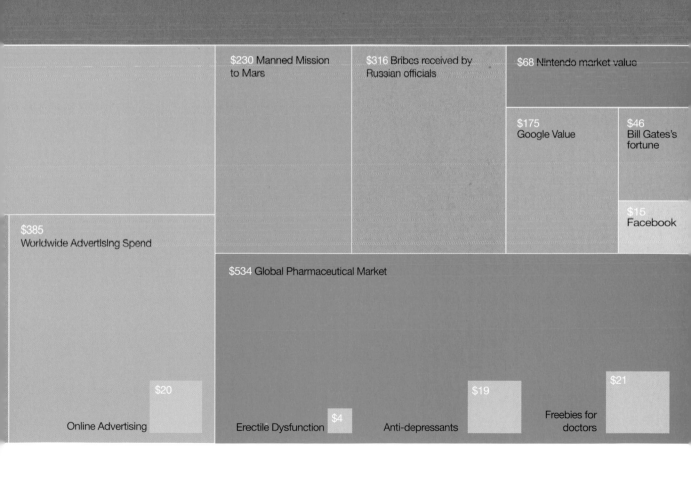

$230 Manned Mission to Mars

$316 Bribes received by Russian officials

$68 Nintendo market value

$175 Google Value

$46 Bill Gates's fortune

$15 Facebook

$385 Worldwide Advertising Spend

$20 Online Advertising

$534 Global Pharmaceutical Market

$4 Erectile Dysfunction

$19 Anti-depressants

$21 Freebies for doctors

■ spending ■ earning ■ giving ■ fighting ■ losing ■ illin'

source: MSNBC, Guardian, Washington Post, Forbes, UNODC, BBC News. All figures 2006–07 unless otherwise stated.

$7800 'Worst case' scenario cost of financial crisis to US Government

$2800 Total cost of financial crisis to US Government to date (Aug 09)

$500 The New Deal, the US recovery package after the Great Depression of 1933 (in today's dollars)

$823 NASA's total all time budget (1958-)

$115 The Marshall Plan to rebuild Europe after WWII (in today's dollars)

$238 UK government bailouts

$570 Chinese government stimulus package, Nov 08

$67 German gov bailout Jan 09

$35 French gov bailout Dec 08

$24 Wall St bonuses 2006

$36 Wall St bonuses 2007

$18 Wall St bonuses 2008

$200 Africa's entire debt to Western nations

■ Spending ■ Wincing ■ Giving ■ Crying

source: Wikipedia, Guardian, Business Week, Ritzholtz.com

Left

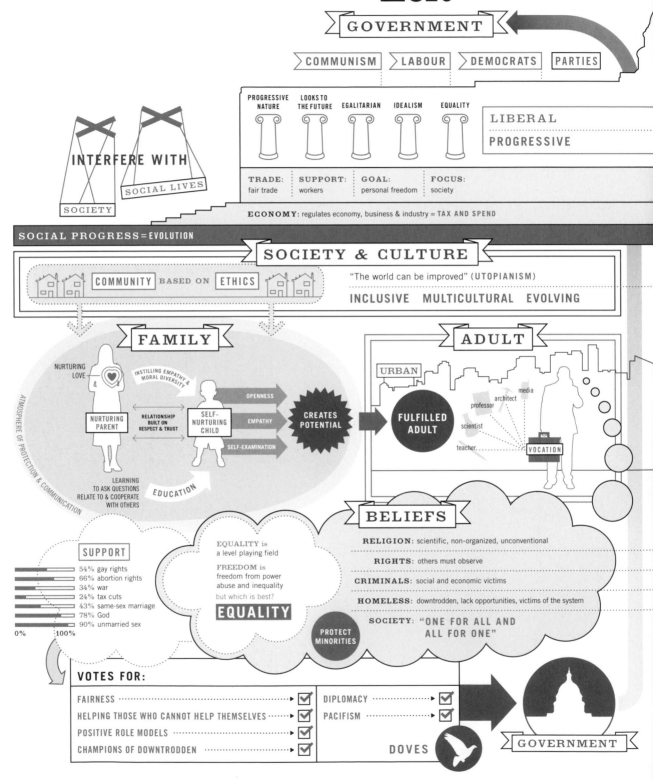

GOVERNMENT

COMMUNISM | LABOUR | DEMOCRATS | PARTIES

PROGRESSIVE NATURE | LOOKS TO THE FUTURE | EGALITARIAN | IDEALISM | EQUALITY

LIBERAL
PROGRESSIVE

TRADE: fair trade | SUPPORT: workers | GOAL: personal freedom | FOCUS: society

ECONOMY: regulates economy, business & industry = TAX AND SPEND

INTERFERE WITH SOCIAL LIVES
SOCIETY

SOCIAL PROGRESS = EVOLUTION

SOCIETY & CULTURE

COMMUNITY BASED ON ETHICS

"The world can be improved" (UTOPIANISM)

INCLUSIVE MULTICULTURAL EVOLVING

FAMILY

ATMOSPHERE OF PROTECTION & COMMUNICATION

NURTURING LOVE

INSTILLING EMPATHY & MORAL DIVERSITY

NURTURING PARENT

RELATIONSHIP BUILT ON RESPECT & TRUST

SELF-NURTURING CHILD

OPENNESS
EMPATHY
SELF-EXAMINATION

CREATES POTENTIAL

LEARNING TO ASK QUESTIONS RELATE TO & COOPERATE WITH OTHERS

EDUCATION

ADULT

URBAN

media
architect
professor
scientist
teacher

FULFILLED ADULT

VOCATION

BELIEFS

RELIGION: scientific, non-organized, unconventional

RIGHTS: others must observe

CRIMINALS: social and economic victims

HOMELESS: downtrodden, lack opportunities, victims of the system

SOCIETY: "ONE FOR ALL AND ALL FOR ONE"

SUPPORT

54% gay rights
66% abortion rights
34% war
24% tax cuts
43% same-sex marriage
78% God
90% unmarried sex

0%   100%

EQUALITY is a level playing field

FREEDOM is freedom from power abuse and inequality but which is best?

EQUALITY

PROTECT MINORITIES

VOTES FOR:

FAIRNESS ·········▶ ☑   DIPLOMACY ·········▶ ☑

HELPING THOSE WHO CANNOT HELP THEMSELVES ·········▶ ☑   PACIFISM ·········▶ ☑

POSITIVE ROLE MODELS ·········▶ ☑

CHAMPIONS OF DOWNTRODDEN ·········▶ ☑

DOVES

GOVERNMENT

Right

PARTIES REPUBLICAN CONSERVATIVE NATIONALIST

CONSERVATIVE

TRADITIONAL

EQUITY	LAW OF THE JUNGLE	SURVIVAL OF THE FITTEST	LOOKS TO THE PAST	CONSERVATIVE NATURE

FOCUS: individual	GOAL: economic freedom	SUPPORT: employers	TRADE: free trade

ECONOMY: de-regulated economy, business & industry = **DON'T TAX AND SPEND**

DON'T INTERFERE WITH

SOCIETY

SOCIAL LIVES

SOCIAL PROGRESS = STATUS QUO

SOCIETY & CULTURE

"The world is fine as it is" (PRESERVATION)

EXCLUSIVE ESTABLISHED NATIONALISTIC

COMMUNITY BASED ON MORALS

ADULT

RURAL

police
military
stockbroker
sales
judge

SELF-RELIANT ADULT

VOCATION

FAMILY

INSTILLING MORAL STRENGTH & ABSOLUTES

TOUGH LOVE

BUILDS CHARACTER

SELF-DEFENCE
MORAL STRENGTH
SELF-DISCIPLINE

SELF-RELIANT CHILD

RELATIONSHIP BUILT ON RESPECT & FEAR

STRICT PARENT

EDUCATION

SKILLS TO SUCCEED TO COMPETE INDIVIDUALISM

BELIEFS

RELIGION: theistic, organized, conventional

RIGHTS: others must not interfere

CRIMINALS: choose to be criminals

HOMELESS: no work ethic, no values, no sense of shame

SOCIETY: **"SURVIVAL OF THE FITTEST"**

IMMIGRATION CONTROL

EQUALITY is opportunity

FREEDOM is the chance to achieve or fail

but which is best?

FREEDOM

SUPPORT

gay rights	44%
abortion rights	43%
war	91%
tax cuts	84%
same-sex marriage	12%
God	87%
unmarried sex	80%

0%   100%

VOTES FOR:

AGGRESSION ☑
MILITANCY ☑

UPHOLDING ORDER ☑
HELPING THOSE WHO HELP THEMSELVES ☑
STRONG ROLE MODELS ☑
CHAMPIONS OF OPPORTUNITY ☑

GOVERNMENT

HAWKS

note: colour with your country's colours for left and right // source: Wikipedia, Britannica.com, New Scientist, Conservative-resources.com.

ULTRA PARADOX!
The Terminatrix encounters Evan from *Butterfly Effect* pursued by *Timecop* Max Walker

Austin Powers: The S

Star Trek TOS: Assignment Ear

Austin Powers in Goldmember

Buck Rogers in the 25th Century

Star Trek TOS: Tomorow is Yesterday

Trek: The Voyage Home

ntor

Planet of the Apes

Twelve Monkeys

Terminator 2

Timecop

Star Trek TNG: Times Arrow 2

Star Trek: First Contact

Twelve Monkeys

Terminator 3

1990

2000

Kate & Leopold

Back to the Future 2

Back to the Future 3

Sleeper

2050

2100

The Time Machine (2,300)

The Time Machine (802,701)

The Time Machine (30,000,000)

2500

3000

2400

4000

2300

2200

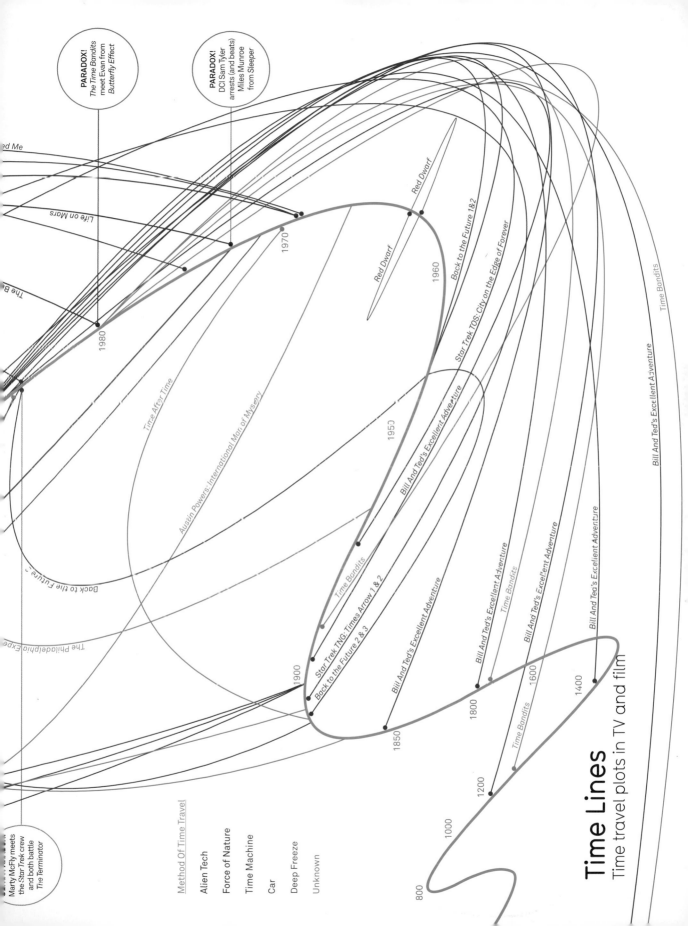

Time Lines
Time travel plots in TV and film

PARADOX! *The Time Bandits* meet Evan from *Butterfly Effect*

PARADOX! DCI Sam Tyler arrests (and beats) Miles Munroe from *Sleeper*

Marty McFly meets the *Star Trek* crew and both battle *The Terminator*

Method Of Time Travel

Alien Tech

Force of Nature

Time Machine

Car

Deep Freeze

Unknown

Life on Mars

Red Dwarf

Red Dwarf

Back to the Future 1 & 2

Star Trek TOS: City on the Edge of Forever

Bill And Ted's Excellent Adventure

Time After Time

Austin Powers: International Man of Mystery

Back to the Future

The Philadelphia Expe…

Time Bandits

Star Trek TNG: Times Arrow 1 & 2

Back to the Future 2 & 3

Bill And Ted's Excellent Adventure

Bill And Ted's Excellent Adventure

Bill And Ted's Excellent Adventure

Bill And Ted's Excellent Adventure

Bill And Ted's Excellent Adventure

Time Bandits

Time Bandits

Time Bandits

1980

1970

1960

1950

1900

1850

1800

1600

1400

1200

1000

800

Snake Oil?

Scientific evidence for popular dietary supplements showing tangible health benefits when taken orally by an adult with a healthy diet.

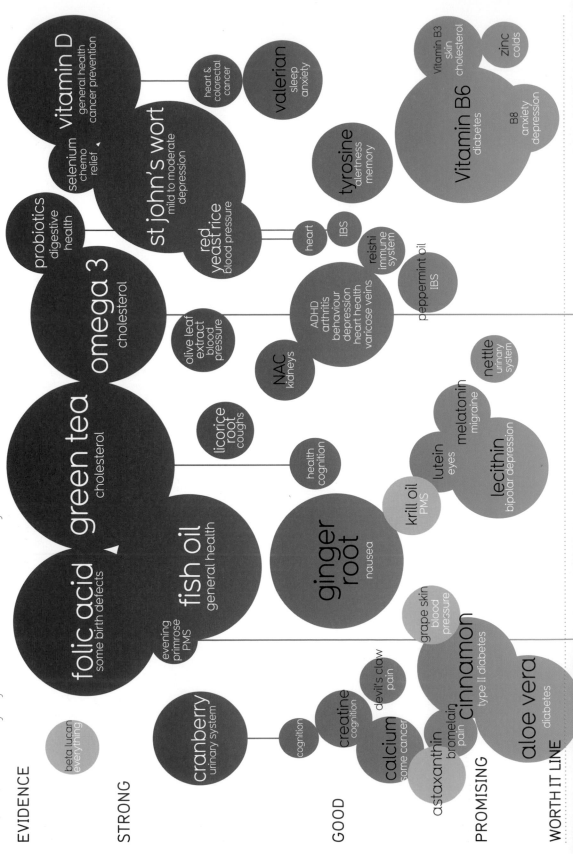

Popularity

Promising

EVIDENCE

STRONG

GOOD

PROMISING

WORTH IT LINE

beta lucan
everything

vitamin D
general health
cancer prevention

selenium
chemo
relief

heart &
colorectal
cancer

valerian
sleep
anxiety

Vitamin B3
skin
cholesterol

zinc
colds

Vitamin B6
diabetes

B8
anxiety
depression

st john's wort
mild to moderate
depression

red
yeast rice
blood pressure

tyrosine
alertness
memory

probiotics
digestive
health

omega 3
cholesterol

heart

IBS

reishi
immune
system

peppermint oil
IBS

olive leaf
extract
blood
pressure

ADHD
arthritis
behaviour
depression
heart health
varicose veins

NAC
kidneys

green tea
cholesterol

licorice
root
coughs

health
cognition

nettle
urinary
system

folic acid
some birth defects

fish oil
general health

evening
primrose
PMS

ginger
root
nausea

krill oil
PMS

lutein
eyes

melatonin
migraine

lecithin
bipolar depression

cranberry
urinary system

cognition

creatine
cognition

devil's claw
pain

calcium
some cancer

astaxanthin

bromelain
pain

grape skin
blood
pressure

cinnamon
type II diabetes

aloe vera
diabetes

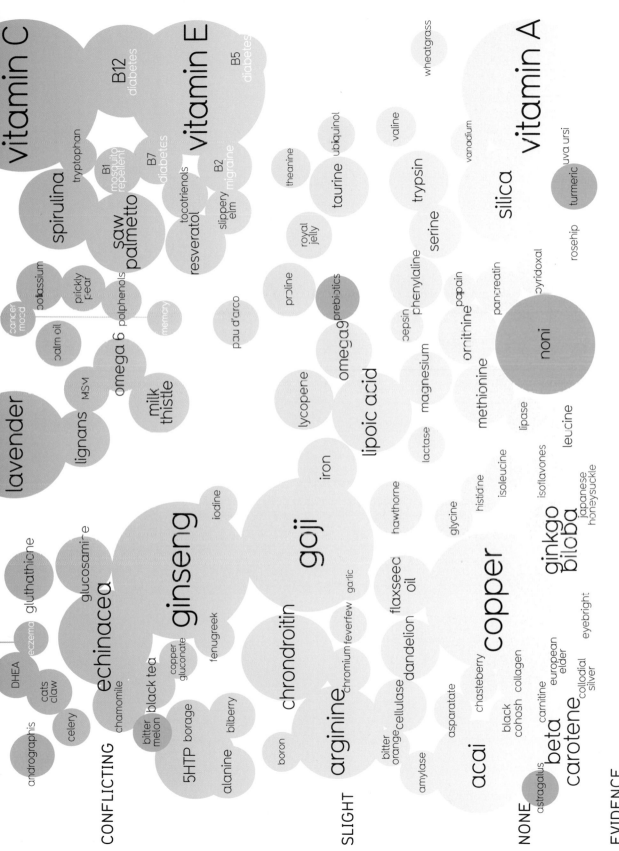

EVIDENCE

source: English language placebo-controlled double-blind human trials on PubMed.org, The US Office of Dietary Supplements, Herbmed.org, European Medicines Agency

Creationism vs Evolutionism
Where did everything come from?

Circle size = approximate number of believers (this side only)

BUDDHISM
The creation of humanity unknowable, therefore irrelevant. What is, is.

FLAT EARTHERS
The Earth is flat because the Bible says it is. Flat like a coin. Or perhaps a plate.

MOST MUSLIMS

POSITION OF THE CATHOLIC CH

GEOCENTRICISM
Earth is centre of the universe. All modern science is bunk.

PROGRESSIVE CREATIONISM
God created man and the animals. Everything else evolved.

THEISTIC EVOLUTION
God creates through evolution

Evolution is fine. But God intervenes at critical moments in the history of life. The Hand of God is also necessary for the creation of the human soul.

YOUNG EARTH CREATIONISM
The Earth is 6000 years old. Humans are not related to animals. And you will burn in Hell if you don't believe this.

INTELLIGENT DESIGN
Because things are so well designed, they could not have evolved. Therefore God must've created them.

GAP CREATIONISM
The world and mankind created in 7 days, but then there was a gap of a billion years or so.

DEISM
God created Earth and man but has been silent since.

SCIENTOLOGY
Galactic ruler Xenu gathered the disembodied spirits of alien beings called Thetans into human form.

HINDU EVOLUTION
God *is* evolution
Evolution is a spiritual process. Humanity is God incarnate, evolving towards a realization of this living truth.

ONE EXTREME

UNIVERSAL DARWINISM

All universal processes, yep all, are governed by Darwinian evolution.

CO-EVOLUTION

Co-operation, not competition, between organisms accelerates evolution. "Survival of the nicest."

DARWINIAN EVOLUTION
Survival of the fittest

Random mutations give certain organisms a survival advantage in their environment. This adaptation is passed on to their offspring over hundreds of generations ("natural selection"). No God necessary.

GROUP SELECTIONISM

Entire species are actually higher-level organisms in their own right. Natural selection affects species differently.

CONVERGENT EVOLUTION

Complex elements like eyes have evolved more than twice. Huh? Exactly. Deeper structures are at play.

NEO LAMARCKISM

Not as random as we think. Genes show some capacity to "choose" mutations.

PUNCTUATED EQUILIBRIUM

Evolution is essentially static until sudden dramatic events shift it into a higher gear.

NEO DARWINISM

Selfish genes in DNA evolve slowly over time taking us, the host organisms, with them.

LAMARCKISM

Traits acquired by parents during lifetime can be passed on to their offspring. Proven incorrect.

source: Wikipedia, BBC.com, Skeptic.com

INTENSITY (NUMBER OF STORIES)

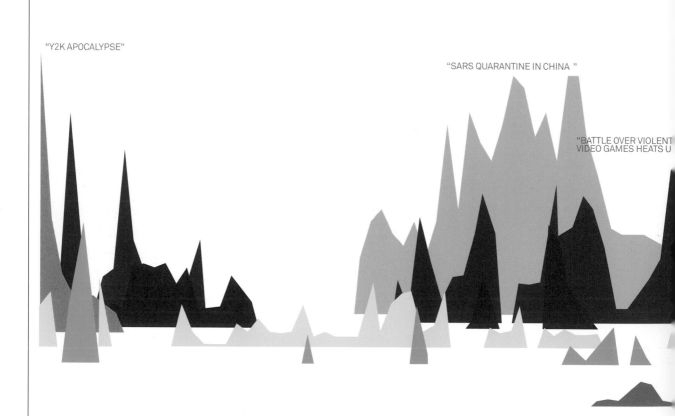

"Y2K APOCALYPSE"

"SARS QUARANTINE IN CHINA "

"BATTLE OVER VIOLENT
VIDEO GAMES HEATS U

2000   2001   2002   2003   2004

Story (approximate worldwide deaths)

Killer Wasps (1000)   Autism Vaccinations (0)   Mad Cow Disease (204)   Bird Flu (262)

Killer Wifi (0)   Asteroid Collision (0)   Violent Video Games (Unknown)   Swine Flu (702)

Mobile Phones & Tumours (0)   Millennium Bug (0)   SARS (774)

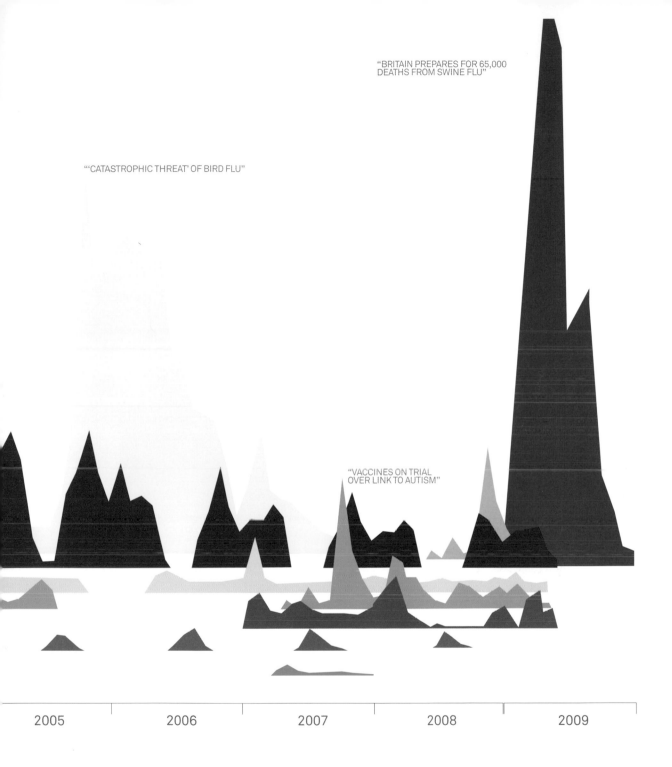

"'CATASTROPHIC THREAT' OF BIRD FLU"

"BRITAIN PREPARES FOR 65,000 DEATHS FROM SWINE FLU"

"VACCINES ON TRIAL OVER LINK TO AUTISM"

2005   2006   2007   2008   2009

Mountains Out of Molehills
A timeline of global media scare stories

source: Google News (worldwide deaths at time of print)

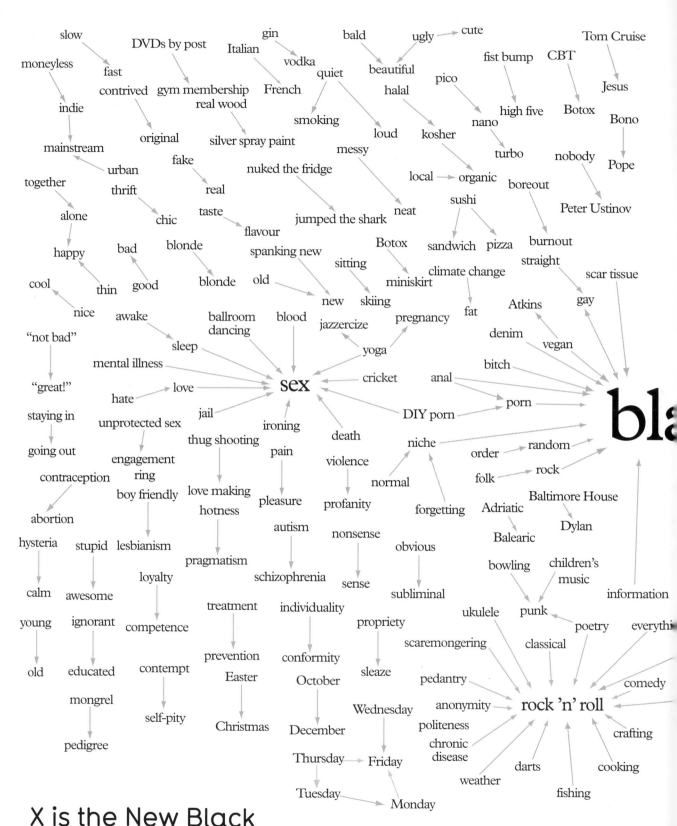

X is the New Black

A map of clichés

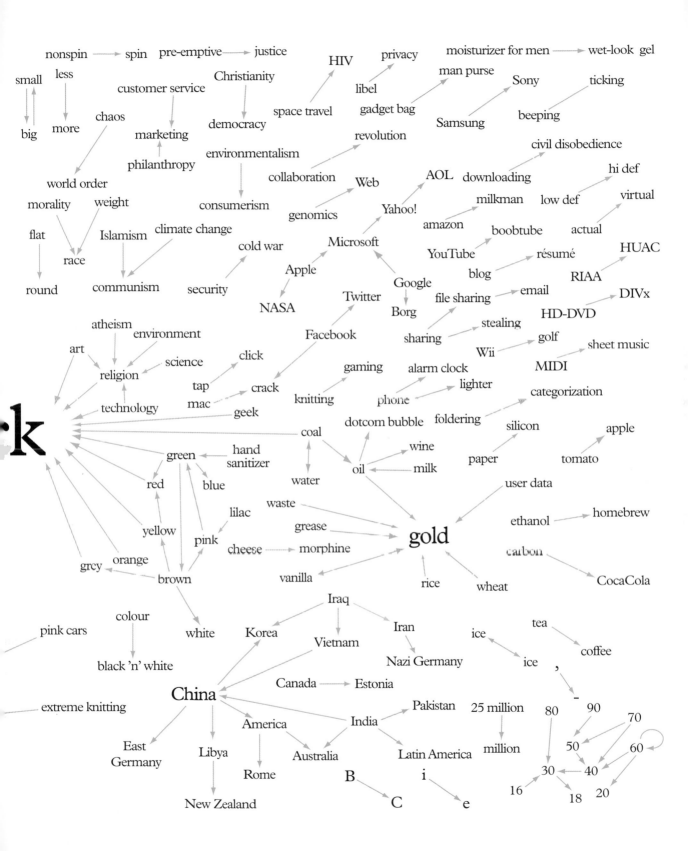

Searches for the phrase 'is the new' on various media outlet websites.

idea: Randall Szott // source: Google, Guardian.co.uk, NewScientist.com, Wired.com, Nytimes.com

Tons Of Carbon
Per year unless otherwise stated

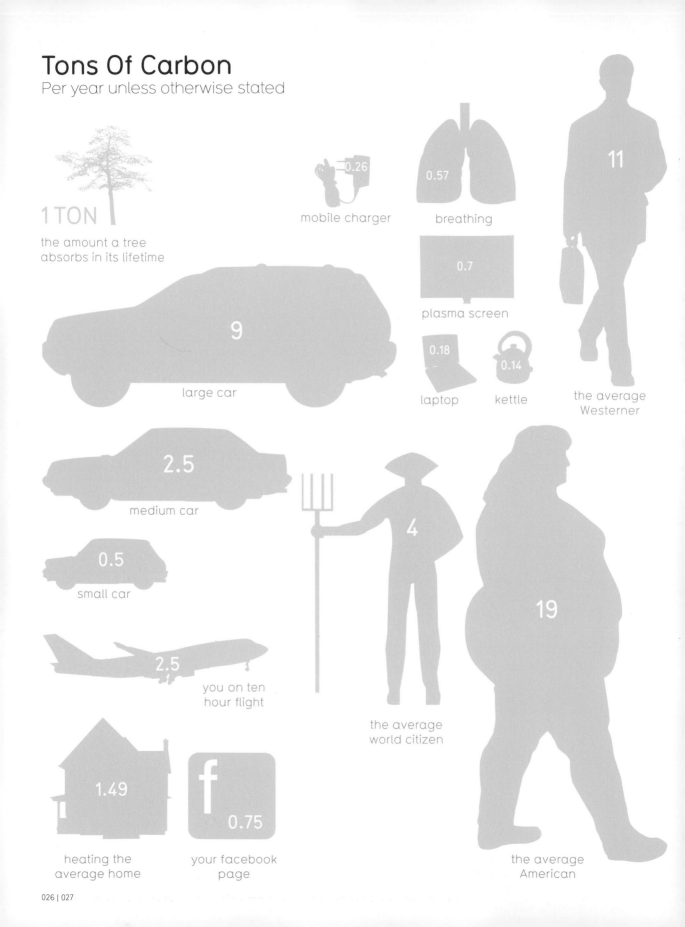

1 TON
the amount a tree
absorbs in its lifetime

mobile charger
0.26

breathing
0.57

plasma screen
0.7

11
the average
Westerner

9
large car

0.18
laptop

0.14
kettle

2.5
medium car

0.5
small car

4
the average
world citizen

2.5
you on ten
hour flight

19
the average
American

1.49
heating the
average home

f
0.75
your facebook
page

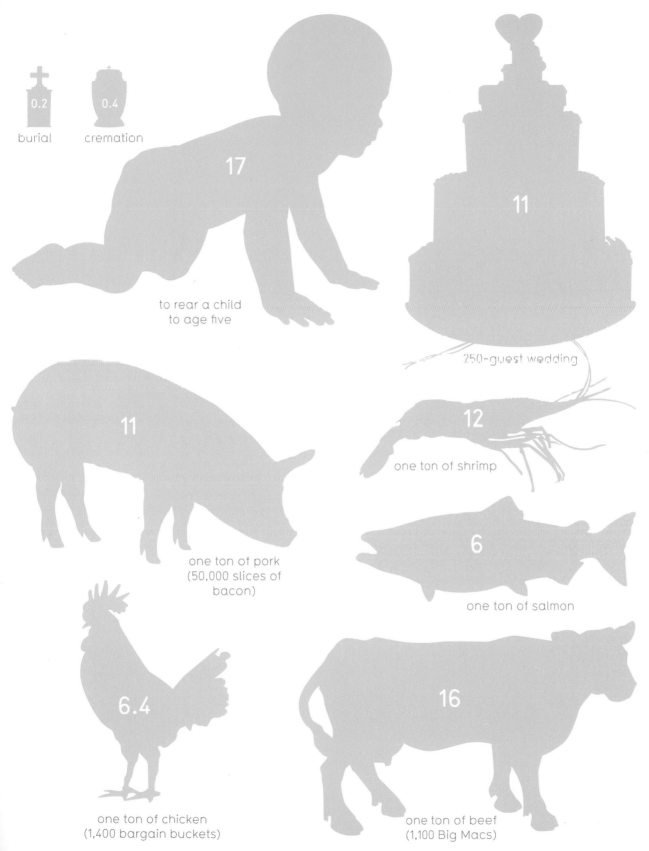

0.2
burial

0.4
cremation

17
to rear a child
to age five

11
250-guest wedding

11
one ton of pork
(50,000 slices of
bacon)

12
one ton of shrimp

6
one ton of salmon

6.4
one ton of chicken
(1,400 bargain buckets)

16
one ton of beef
(1,100 Big Macs)

source: New York Times, Environmental Protection Agency, IPCC, Energy Information Administration. UNESCO

Books Everyone Should Read

A consensus cloud

OfTracyBeaker

'Urbervilles

heGalaxy TomSawyer TheAmazingAdventuresOfKavalierAndClay

New World AChristmasCarol

LeavesOfGrass InSearchOfLostTime TheColorPurple Middlemarch

ToKillAMockingbird

ield ThePillarsOfTheEarth TheLifeOfPi TheLordOfTheRings

d Prejudice TheCorrections Midnight'sChildren

Walden The PickwickPapers WarAndPeace

Regeneration

heFury CatcherInTheRye

OfMiceAndMen JaneEyre

GreatGatsby CaptainCorelli'sMandolin 1984

rgarita DonQuixote TheRoad

ahrenheit451 ForWhomTheBellTolls

ndredYearsOfSolitude

1 ThingsFallApart HuckleberryFinn

hePoisonwoodBible VanityFair

CountOfMonteCristo

source: Desert Island Discs, Pulitzer Prize, AskMetafilter.com, World Day Book Poll, Booker Prize,
BBC Big Reads, Oprah's Book Club List & the author's own top five

Which Fish are Okay to Eat?

Crashing fish stocks. Pollution. Over-exploitation. Near-extinction.

FARMED

ATLANTIC

YES

Arctic Char

Barramundi

Catfish

Trout

Striped bass

Tuna (Albacore)

Sturgeon

King Mackerel

Tilapia

Skipjack Tuna

OK

Basa

Shrimp
(US farmed)

Sardines

Herring

Anchovies

Hake

Swordfish

NO

Salmon

Shrimp

Eel

Bluefin Tuna

Haddock
(trawler)

Atlantic Cod

Yellowfin & Albacore Tuna
(longline)

Monkfish

Halibut

Sturgeon

Sole

Hake
(trawler)

Shrimp
(any)

FARMED

ATLANTIC

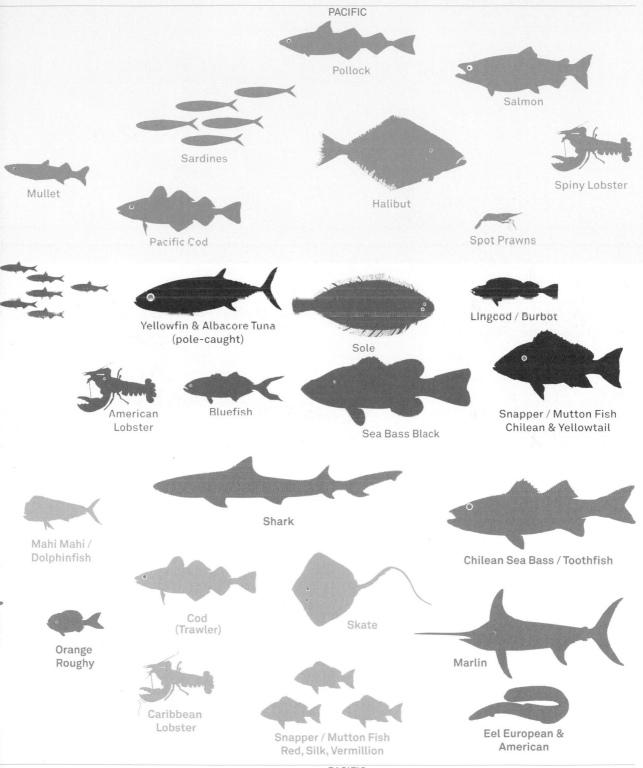

Dioxins & Mercury — low, high

PACIFIC

Pollock

Salmon

Sardines

Spiny Lobster

Mullet

Halibut

Spot Prawns

Pacific Cod

Yellowfin & Albacore Tuna
(pole-caught)

Sole

Lingcod / Burbot

American
Lobster

Bluefish

Sea Bass Black

Snapper / Mutton Fish
Chilean & Yellowtail

Shark

Chilean Sea Bass / Toothfish

Mahi Mahi /
Dolphinfish

Cod
(Trawler)

Skate

Orange
Roughy

Marlin

Caribbean
Lobster

Snapper / Mutton Fish
Red, Silk, Vermillion

Eel European &
American

PACIFIC

source: Marine Stewardship Council

SUMMER | WINTER

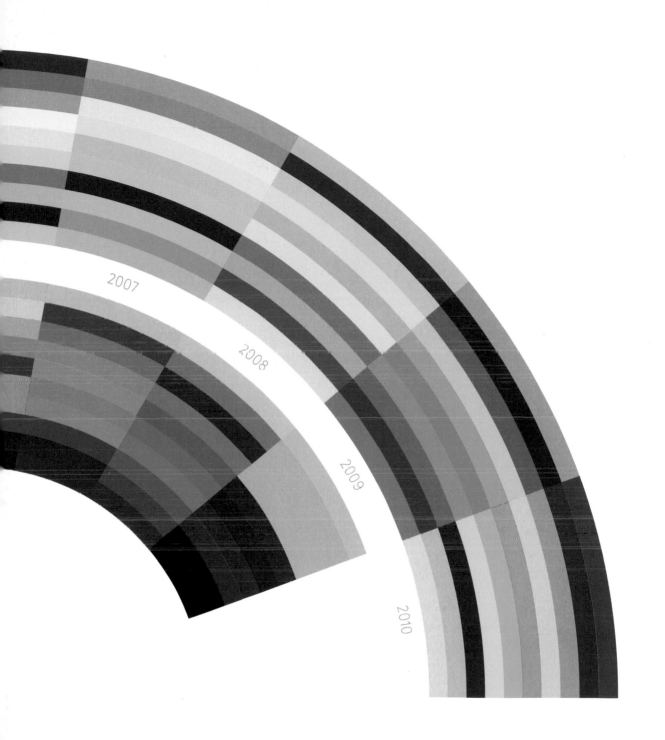

2007

2008

2009

2010

The "In" Colours
Women's fashion colours

source: pantone.com

The "Interesting" Colours
Selected women's fashion colours

SUMMER

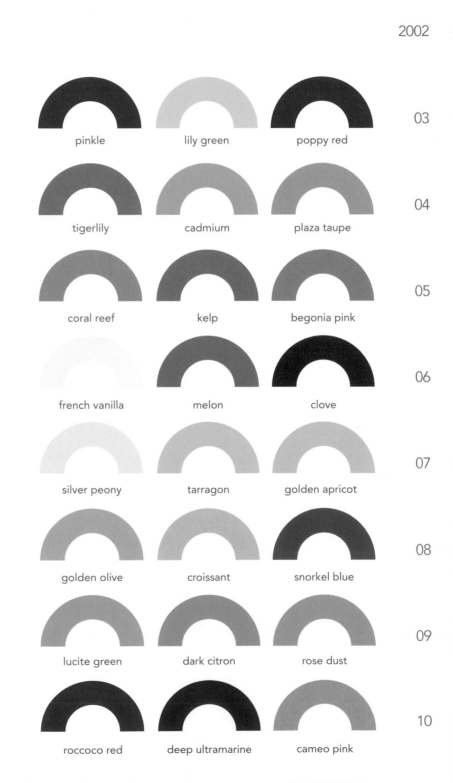

pinkle	lily green	poppy red
tigerlily	cadmium	plaza taupe
coral reef	kelp	begonia pink
french vanilla	melon	clove
silver peony	tarragon	golden apricot
golden olive	croissant	snorkel blue
lucite green	dark citron	rose dust
roccoco red	deep ultramarine	cameo pink

03
04
05
06
07
08
09
10

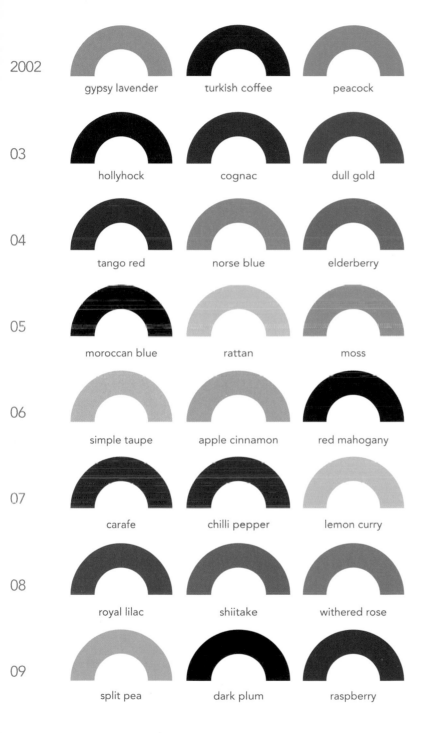

2002
gypsy lavender   turkish coffee   peacock

03
hollyhock   cognac   dull gold

04
tango red   norse blue   elderberry

05
moroccan blue   rattan   moss

06
simple taupe   apple cinnamon   red mahogany

07
carafe   chilli pepper   lemon curry

08
royal lilac   shiitake   withered rose

09
split pea   dark plum   raspberry

10

WINTER

Three's a Magic Number

BIZARRE LOVE TRIANGLES

hmmmmm

leia

han   luke

70s

cough

diana

charles   camilla

80s

wha—?

woody

mia   soon

90s

THREE THINKING

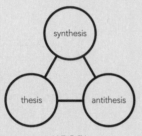

dialectics

synthesis

thesis   antithesis

HEGEL

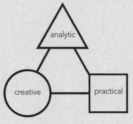

types of thinking

analytic

creative   practical

APPARENTLY

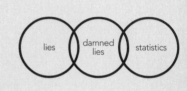

journalistic

lies   damned lies   statistics

MARK TWAIN

THE THREE DOMAINS OF LIFE

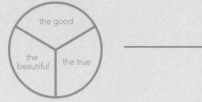

the domains

the good

the beautiful   the true

PLATO

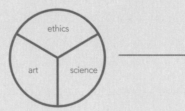

their disciplines

ethics

art   science

their types of truth

justness

integrity   fact

CHRISTIAN TRINITIES

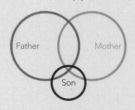

God is a happy family

Father   Mother

Son

GNOSTIC (100 AD)

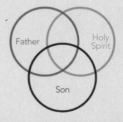

1 god, 3 persons

Father   Holy Spirit

Son

EARLY (200 AD)

all separate

Father

Son   Holy Spirit

NICENE (325 AD)

HEALTHREE

life essentials

exercise   diet

sleep

COMMON SENSE

types of fitness

stamina   flexibility

strength

SHAWN PHILIPS

relationship essentials

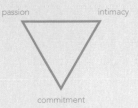

passion   intimacy

commitment

GOOD LUCK!

3 part mind

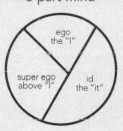

ego
the "I"

super ego
above "I"   id
the "it"

FREUD

3 part brain

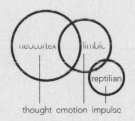

neocortex   limbic

reptilian

thought emotion impulse

PAUL D MACLEAN

3 voices in the mind

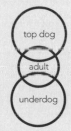

top dog

adult

underdog

FRITZ PERLS

THREEDOM

pre-modern values

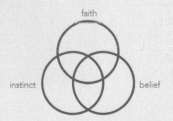

faith

instinct   belief

PRE 1700

modern values

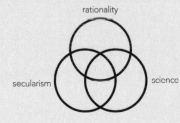

rationality

secularism   science

1700–1945

post-modern values

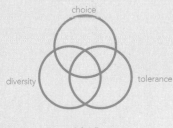

choice

diversity   tolerance

1945+

no, son both human & divine

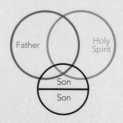

Father   Holy Spirit

Son
Son

CALCEDON (451 AD)

er, son created by union

Father   Holy Spirit

Son

ORIENTAL ORTHODOXY (451 AD)

I know! Father creates *both*

Father

Son   Holy Spirit

EASTERN ORTHODOXY (1054 AD)

source: Wikipedia, The Gale Encyclopedia Of Religion

Who Runs the World?

▲ 192 countries united to promote peace and security.

▲ Settles disputes between countries.

INT. COURT OF JUSTICE

SECRETAF

▲ Punishes genocide, war atrocities and crimes against humanity.

INT. CRIMINAL COURT

NATO

▲ Worldwide intelligence agency. Anti-terrorism, trafficking, and organized crime. James Bond stuff basically.

INTERPOL

NATION STATES

ASEAN

AF
U

NGOs

NATIONS

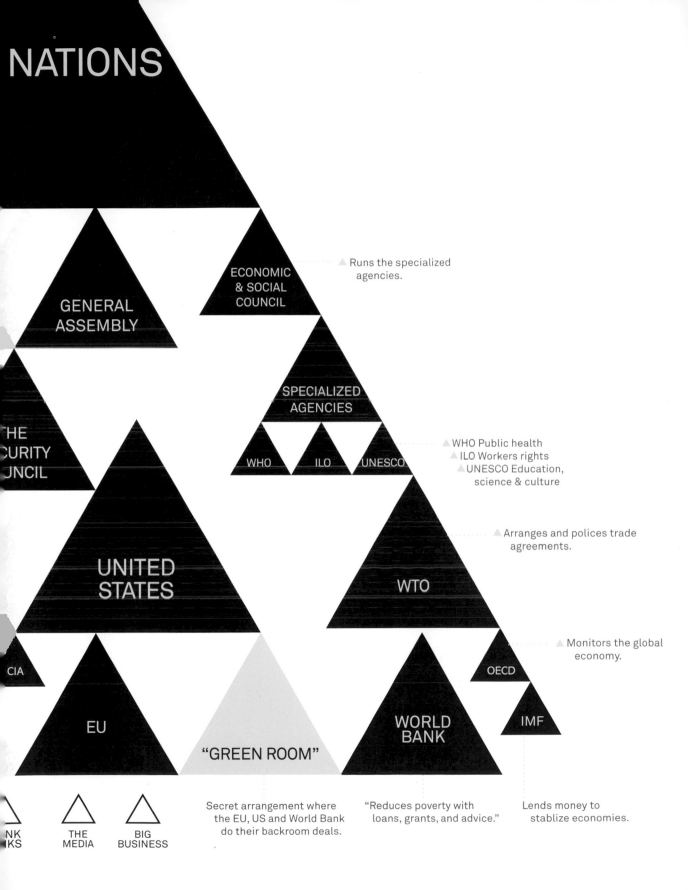

GENERAL ASSEMBLY

ECONOMIC & SOCIAL COUNCIL

▲ Runs the specialized agencies.

SPECIALIZED AGENCIES

THE SECURITY COUNCIL

WHO   ILO   UNESCO

▲ WHO Public health
▲ ILO Workers rights
▲ UNESCO Education, science & culture

UNITED STATES

WTO

▲ Arranges and polices trade agreements.

CIA

OECD

▲ Monitors the global economy.

EU

"GREEN ROOM"

WORLD BANK

IMF

NK KS   THE MEDIA   BIG BUSINESS

Secret arrangement where the EU, US and World Bank do their backroom deals.

"Reduces poverty with loans, grants, and advice."

Lends money to stablize economies.

source: Wikipedia, UN.org

Who *Really* Runs the World?
Conspiracy theory

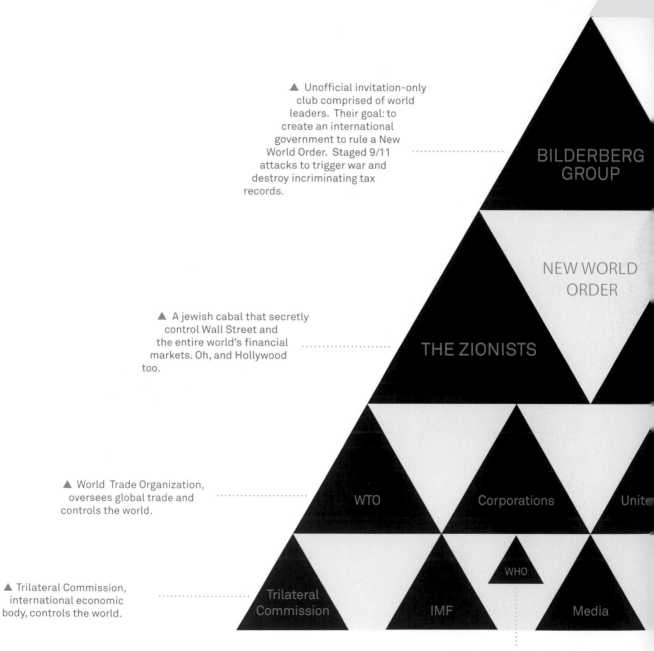

▲ Secret group, similar to Freemasons, who mastermind world events and control governments for their own purposes.

▲ Unofficial invitation-only club comprised of world leaders. Their goal: to create an international government to rule a New World Order. Staged 9/11 attacks to trigger war and destroy incriminating tax records.

▲ A jewish cabal that secretly control Wall Street and the entire world's financial markets. Oh, and Hollywood too.

▲ World Trade Organization, oversees global trade and controls the world.

▲ Trilateral Commission, international economic body, controls the world.

▲ Invents disorders like ADHD to market drugs.

BILDERBERG GROUP

NEW WORLD ORDER

THE ZIONISTS

WTO

Corporations

Unite

Trilateral Commission

IMF

WHO

Media

ILLUMINATI

SATAN

SHAPESHIFTING LIZARDS

▲ Reptilian humanoids. The Babylonian Brotherhood controls the world. Its ranks include George Bush, Queen Elizabeth and Kris Kristofferson.

The Anti-Christ

...TED ...TES

ALIENS

s

CIA

UFOs

Black Ops

▲ Contrails are chemicals.
▲ Fluoride in water is mind-control juice.
▲ AIDS/HIV/Bird Flu/SARS – all man-made.
▲ Invented crack cocaine to shackle underclass.
▲ Global warming a fraud.
▲ Evidence of WMDs in Iraq faked to justify war.
Err...

▲ Aliens routinely abduct and experiment on humans. US government knows this but hides the truth.

source: Wikipedia, Skeptic.com

Stock Check
Estimated remaining world supplies of non-renewable resources

Metals

	Zinc	musical instruments	10 years
	Titanium	aircraft, armour	12 years
	Indium	solar panels, LCD screens	13 years
	Lead	bullets, car batteries	14 years
	Silver	bandages, medals, jewellery	14 years
	Gold	jewellery, bullion	14 years
	Hafnium	nuclear power, computer chips	17 years
	Chromium	plating, paint	20 years
	Tin	food cans, industry	23 years
	Uranium	nuclear weapons	23 years
	Copper	brass, wires, piping	26 years
	Tantalum	mobile phones	28 years
	Antimony	drugs, batteries	29 years
	Nickel	coins, plating	31 years
	Platinum	fuel cells, catalytic converters, more jewellery	39 years
	Cadmium	rechargeable batteries, TV screens	54 years

assuming a 1%–2.5% increase in demand every year depending on resource

Oil

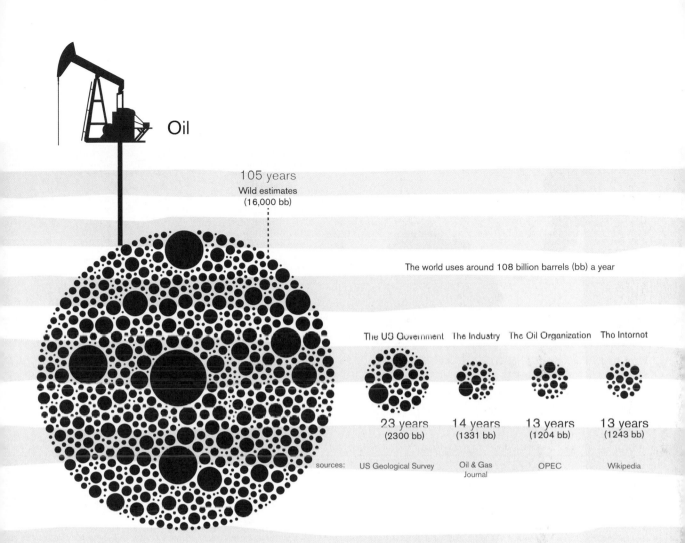

105 years
Wild estimates
(16,000 bb)

The world uses around 108 billion barrels (bb) a year

The US Government	The Industry	The Oil Organization	The Internet
23 years (2300 bb)	**14 years** (1331 bb)	**13 years** (1204 bb)	**13 years** (1243 bb)
sources: US Geological Survey	Oil & Gas Journal	OPEC	Wikipedia

Coal

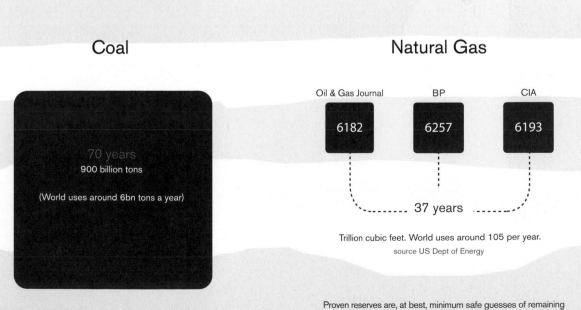

70 years
900 billion tons

(World uses around 6bn tons a year)

assuming a 1% increase in demand every year

Natural Gas

Oil & Gas Journal	BP	CIA
6182	6257	6193

37 years

Trillion cubic feet. World uses around 105 per year.
source US Dept of Energy

Proven reserves are, at best, minimum safe guesses of remaining and easy-to-access resources. More reserves are likely to be found.

source: Wikipedia, OPEC, Environmental Investigation Agency, USGS, CIA Factbook, Oil & Gas Journal, World Energy Council, World Coal Institute, BP

30 Years Makes A Difference

1978

COLOMBIA

AMAZON

PERU

BOLIVIA

BRAZIL

2008

source: Global Forest Watch

Creation Myths
How did it all start?

Ex Nilhilo (Out Of Nothing)

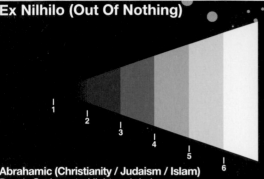

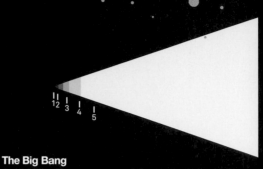

Abrahamic (Christianity / Judaism / Islam)
Day 1. God created light and darkness.
Day 2. He created water and sky.
Day 3. Separated dry ground from oceans, created all vegetation.
Day 4. Created sun, moon and stars.
Day 5. Created all water-dwelling creatures and birds.
Day 6. Created all creatures of the world.
Day 7. Have a nice rest.

The Big Bang
1. 15,000 million years ago all the matter in the Universe burst out from single point. **2.** Inflates from the size of an atom to the size of a grapefruit in a microsecond. **3.** Three minutes in, the universe is a superhot fog, too hot for even light to shine. **4.** 300,000 years later, everything is cool enough to form the first atoms. Light shines! **5.** After a billion years, clouds of gas collapse. Gravity pulls them in to form the first galaxies and stars.

Primordial "Soup"

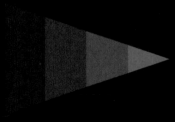

Hinduism
In a dark vast ocean, Lord Vishnu sleeps. A humming noise trembles. With a vast "OM!" Vishnu awakes. From his stomach blossoms a lotus flower containing Brahma. Vishnu commands him to create the world, then vanishes. Brahma splits the lotus flower into heaven, earth & sky.

Chinese (Taoist)
There was a mist of chaos. The mist separated and the light rose to heaven and the heavy sank and formed the earth. From heaven and earth came yin and yang, masculine and feminine. Together they keep the world in harmony.

Infinite Universe / Continuous Creation

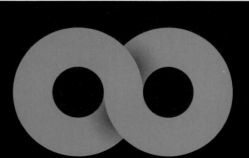

Steady state theory
Matter is generated constantly as the universe expands.
No beginning, no end.

Buddhism
The universe is not fixed in a state of 'being', but of 'becoming'.
At any moment some stars and galaxies are born while others die.

Infinite Universe / Cyclical

Big Bangs Big Crunches
Endless cycles of big bangs and big crunches, with each cycle lasting about a trillion years. All matter and radiation is reset, but the cosmological constant is not. It gradually diminishes over many cycles to the small value observed in today's universe.

Involution / Evolution (Hinduism, Theosophy)
Infinite number of universes in an infinite cycle of births, deaths and rebirths. Each cycle lasts 8.4 billion years. The universe involves (in breath) gathers all the material then 'evolves' (out breath) and expands. This cycle repeats infinitely.

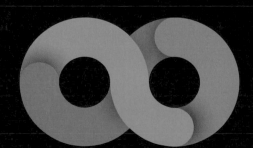

Quasi Solid State (QSS)
The cosmos has always existed. Explosions, of all different sizes, occur continuously, giving the impression of a big bang in our locality.

Bubble Universe
Our universe is a bubble spawned off a larger "foam" of other universes. Each bubble is different. Ours is finely tuned to support life.

source: Wikipedia, NewScientist.com

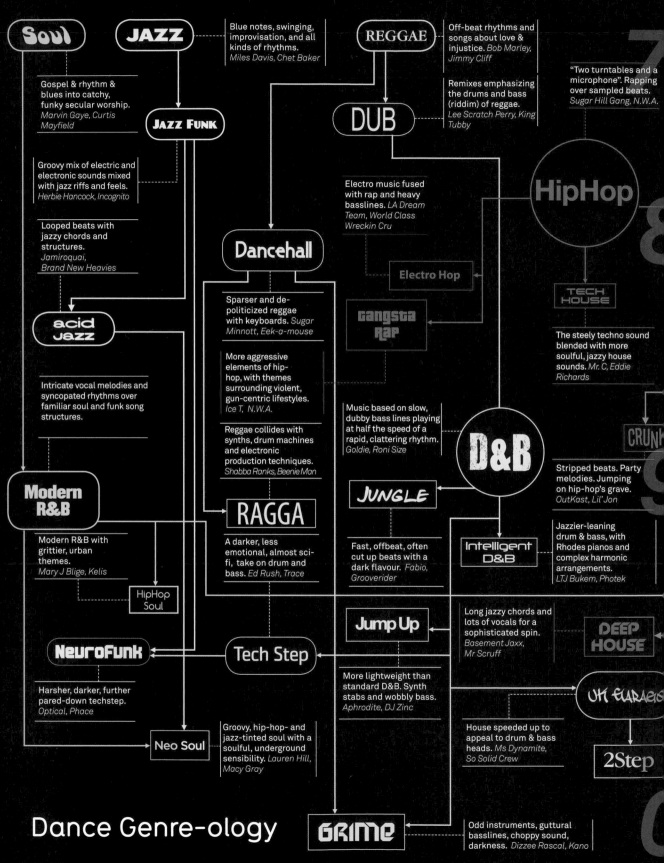

Soul

JAZZ

Blue notes, swinging, improvisation, and all kinds of rhythms. *Miles Davis, Chet Baker*

REGGAE

Off-beat rhythms and songs about love & injustice. *Bob Marley, Jimmy Cliff*

"Two turntables and a microphone". Rapping over sampled beats. *Sugar Hill Gang, N.W.A.*

Gospel & rhythm & blues into catchy, funky secular worship. *Marvin Gaye, Curtis Mayfield*

JAZZ FUNK

Remixes emphasizing the drums and bass (riddim) of reggae. *Lee Scratch Perry, King Tubby*

DUB

HipHop

Groovy mix of electric and electronic sounds mixed with jazz riffs and feels. *Herbie Hancock, Incognito*

Electro music fused with rap and heavy basslines. *LA Dream Team, World Class Wreckin Cru*

Looped beats with jazzy chords and structures. *Jamiroquai, Brand New Heavies*

Dancehall

Electro Hop

TECH HOUSE

acid jazz

Gangsta Rap

The steely techno sound blended with more soulful, jazzy house sounds. *Mr. C, Eddie Richards*

Sparser and de-politicized reggae with keyboards. *Sugar Minnott, Eek-a-mouse*

Intricate vocal melodies and syncopated rhythms over familiar soul and funk song structures.

More aggressive elements of hip-hop, with themes surrounding violent, gun-centric lifestyles. *Ice T, N.W.A.*

Music based on slow, dubby bass lines playing at half the speed of a rapid, clattering rhythm. *Goldie, Roni Size*

D&B

CRUNK

Reggae collides with synths, drum machines and electronic production techniques. *Shabba Ranks, Beenie Man*

Stripped beats. Party melodies. Jumping on hip-hop's grave. *OutKast, Lil' Jon*

Modern R&B

RAGGA

JUNGLE

Jazzier-leaning drum & bass, with Rhodes pianos and complex harmonic arrangements. *LTJ Bukem, Photek*

Modern R&B with grittier, urban themes. *Mary J Blige, Kelis*

A darker, less emotional, almost sci-fi, take on drum and bass. *Ed Rush, Trace*

Fast, offbeat, often cut up beats with a dark flavour. *Fabio, Grooverider*

Intelligent D&B

HipHop Soul

Jump Up

Long jazzy chords and lots of vocals for a sophisticated spin. *Basement Jaxx, Mr Scruff*

DEEP HOUSE

NeuroFunk

Tech Step

UK GARAGE

Harsher, darker, further pared-down techstep. *Optical, Phace*

More lightweight than standard D&B. Synth stabs and wobbly bass. *Aphrodite, DJ Zinc*

Neo Soul

Groovy, hip-hop- and jazz-tinted soul with a soulful, underground sensibility. *Lauren Hill, Macy Gray*

House speeded up to appeal to drum & bass heads. *Ms Dynamite, So Solid Crew*

2Step

Dance Genre-ology

GRIME

Odd instruments, guttural basslines, choppy sound, darkness. *Dizzee Rascal, Kano*

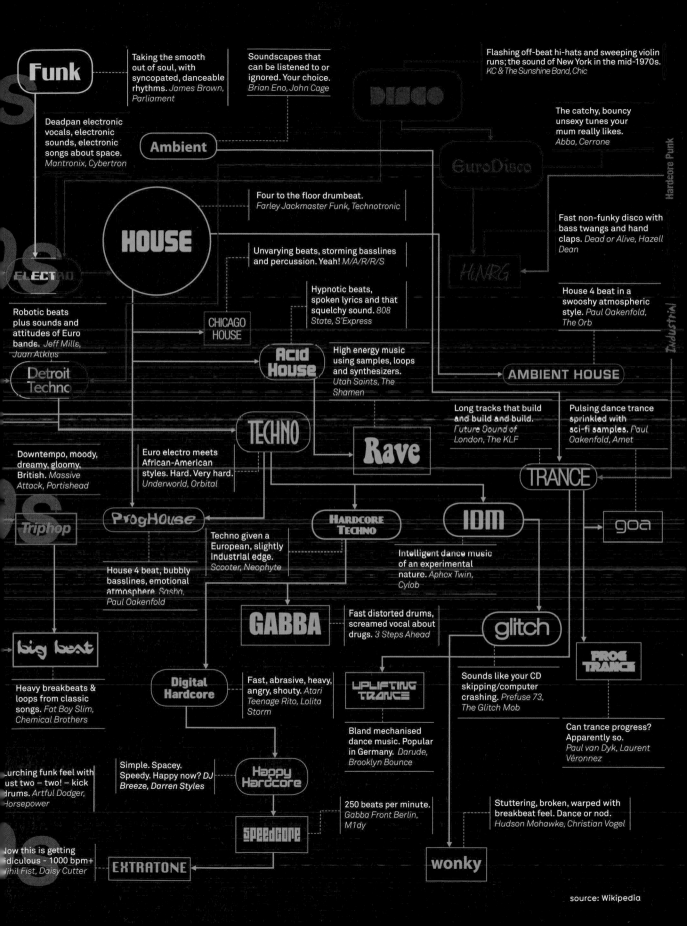

Funk — Taking the smooth out of soul, with syncopated, danceable rhythms. *James Brown, Parliament*

Soundscapes that can be listened to or ignored. Your choice. *Brian Eno, John Cage*

DISCO — Flashing off-beat hi-hats and sweeping violin runs; the sound of New York in the mid-1970s. *KC & The Sunshine Band, Chic*

The catchy, bouncy unsexy tunes your mum really likes. *Abba, Cerrone*

Deadpan electronic vocals, electronic sounds, electronic songs about space. *Mantronix, Cybertron*

Ambient

EuroDisco

Hardcore Punk

HOUSE — Four to the floor drumbeat. *Farley Jackmaster Funk, Technotronic*

Unvarying beats, storming basslines and percussion. Yeah! *M/A/R/R/S*

Fast non-funky disco with bass twangs and hand claps. *Dead or Alive, Hazell Dean*

ELECTRO

HiNRG

Hypnotic beats, spoken lyrics and that squelchy sound. *808 State, S'Express*

House 4 beat in a swooshy atmospheric style. *Paul Oakenfold, The Orb*

Robotic beats plus sounds and attitudes of Euro bands. *Jeff Mills, Juan Atkins*

Detroit Techno

CHICAGO HOUSE

Acid House

High energy music using samples, loops and synthesizers. *Utah Saints, The Shamen*

AMBIENT HOUSE

Industrial

Downtempo, moody, dreamy, gloomy, British. *Massive Attack, Portishead*

Euro electro meets African-American styles. Hard. Very hard. *Underworld, Orbital*

TECHNO

Rave — Long tracks that build and build and build. *Future Sound of London, The KLF*

Pulsing dance trance sprinkled with sci-fi samples. *Paul Oakenfold, Amet*

Triphop

ProgHouse

HARDCORE TECHNO

IDM

TRANCE

goa

Techno given a European, slightly industrial edge. *Scooter, Neophyte*

Intelligent dance music of an experimental nature. *Aphex Twin, Cylob*

House 4 beat, bubbly basslines, emotional atmosphere. *Sasha, Paul Oakenfold*

GABBA — Fast distorted drums, screamed vocal about drugs. *3 Steps Ahead*

glitch

PROG TRANCE

big beat

Heavy breakbeats & loops from classic songs. *Fat Boy Slim, Chemical Brothers*

Digital Hardcore — Fast, abrasive, heavy, angry, shouty. *Atari Teenage Riot, Lolita Storm*

UPLIFTING TRANCE

Sounds like your CD skipping/computer crashing. *Prefuse 73, The Glitch Mob*

Can trance progress? Apparently so. *Paul van Dyk, Laurent Véronnez*

Bland mechanised dance music. Popular in Germany. *Darude, Brooklyn Bounce*

...urching funk feel with ...ust two – two! – kick ...drums. *Artful Dodger, ...orsepower*

Simple. Spacey. Speedy. Happy now? *DJ Breeze, Darren Styles*

Happy Hardcore

250 beats per minute. *Gabba Front Berlin, M1dy*

Stuttering, broken, warped with breakbeat feel. Dance or nod. *Hudson Mohawke, Christian Vogel*

Speedcore

...ow this is getting ...idiculous - 1000 bpm+ ...ihil Fist, Daisy Cutter

EXTRATONE

wonky

source: Wikipedia

The Book of You

A copy in every one of your 10,000,000,000 cells

The Book
Your complete DNA (or "genome") – 3 billion words

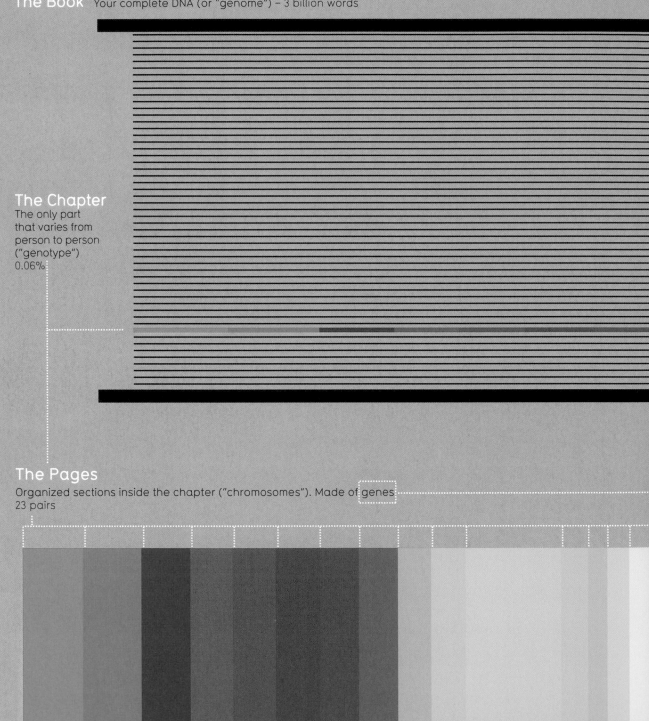

The Chapter
The only part
that varies from
person to person
("genotype")
0.06%

The Pages
Organized sections inside the chapter ("chromosomes"). Made of genes
23 pairs

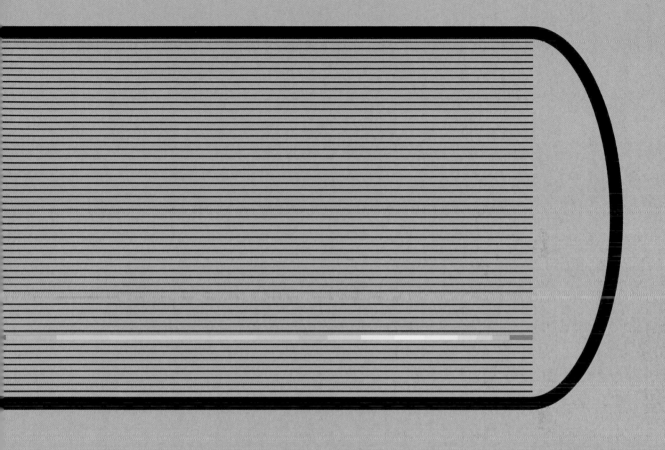

The Paragraphs
Genes are clumps of DNA
made up of basepairs
20 – 25,000

The Words
Individual two letter
"words" of DNA
2 million

The Letters
Letters made of
individual molecules
4

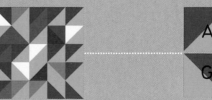

A   C

G   T

Responsible for all your physical characteristics, susceptibility to certain diseases, and even earwax
We have identified the effects of around 5000 out of 2,000,000 (0.25%)

source: Decodeme.com, Wikipedia

folate metabolism & several cancers

The Book of Me
My chromosomes sequenced (2 million letter combinations)

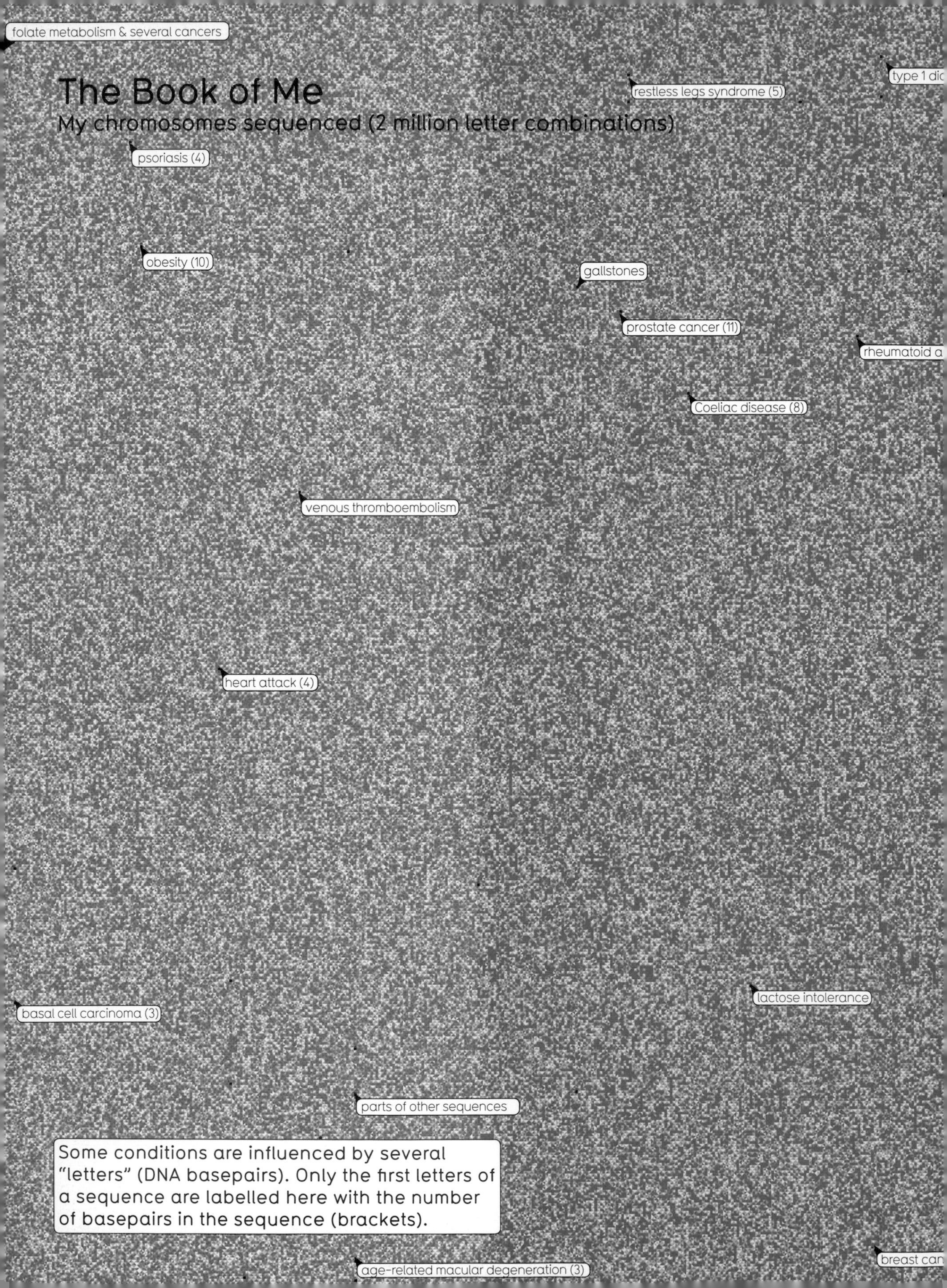

restless legs syndrome (5)

type 1 dia

psoriasis (4)

obesity (10)

gallstones

prostate cancer (11)

rheumatoid a

Coeliac disease (8)

venous thromboembolism

heart attack (4)

lactose intolerance

basal cell carcinoma (3)

parts of other sequences

Some conditions are influenced by several
"letters" (DNA basepairs). Only the first letters of
a sequence are labelled here with the number
of basepairs in the sequence (brackets).

age-related macular degeneration (3)

breast can

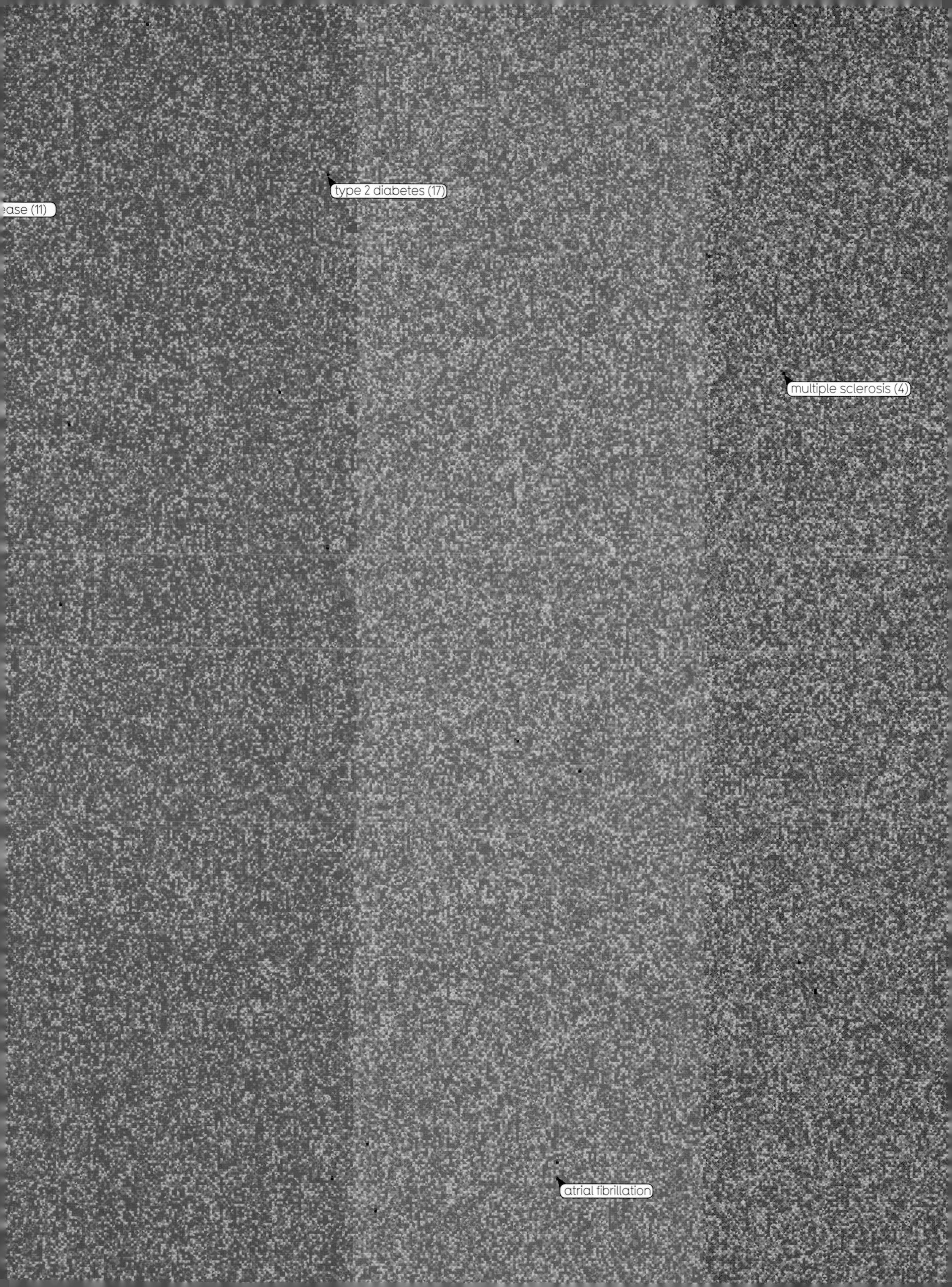

type 2 diabetes (17)

...ease (11)

multiple sclerosis (4)

atrial fibrillation

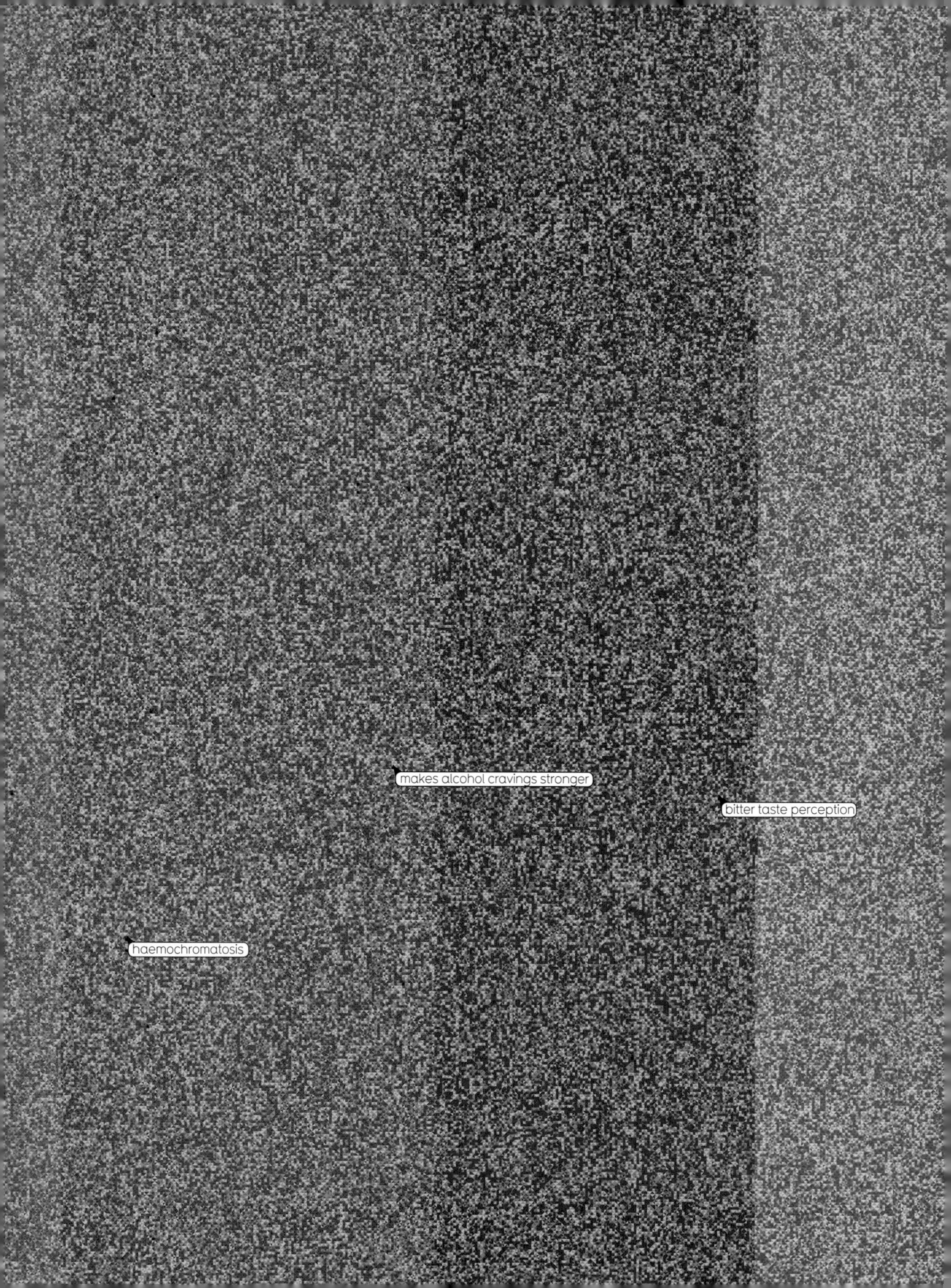

makes alcohol cravings stronger

bitter taste perception

haemochromatosis

intercranial aneurysm

sensitivity to pleasure

endurance athletics

warfarin metabolism (3)

bladder cancer

colorectal cancer (6)

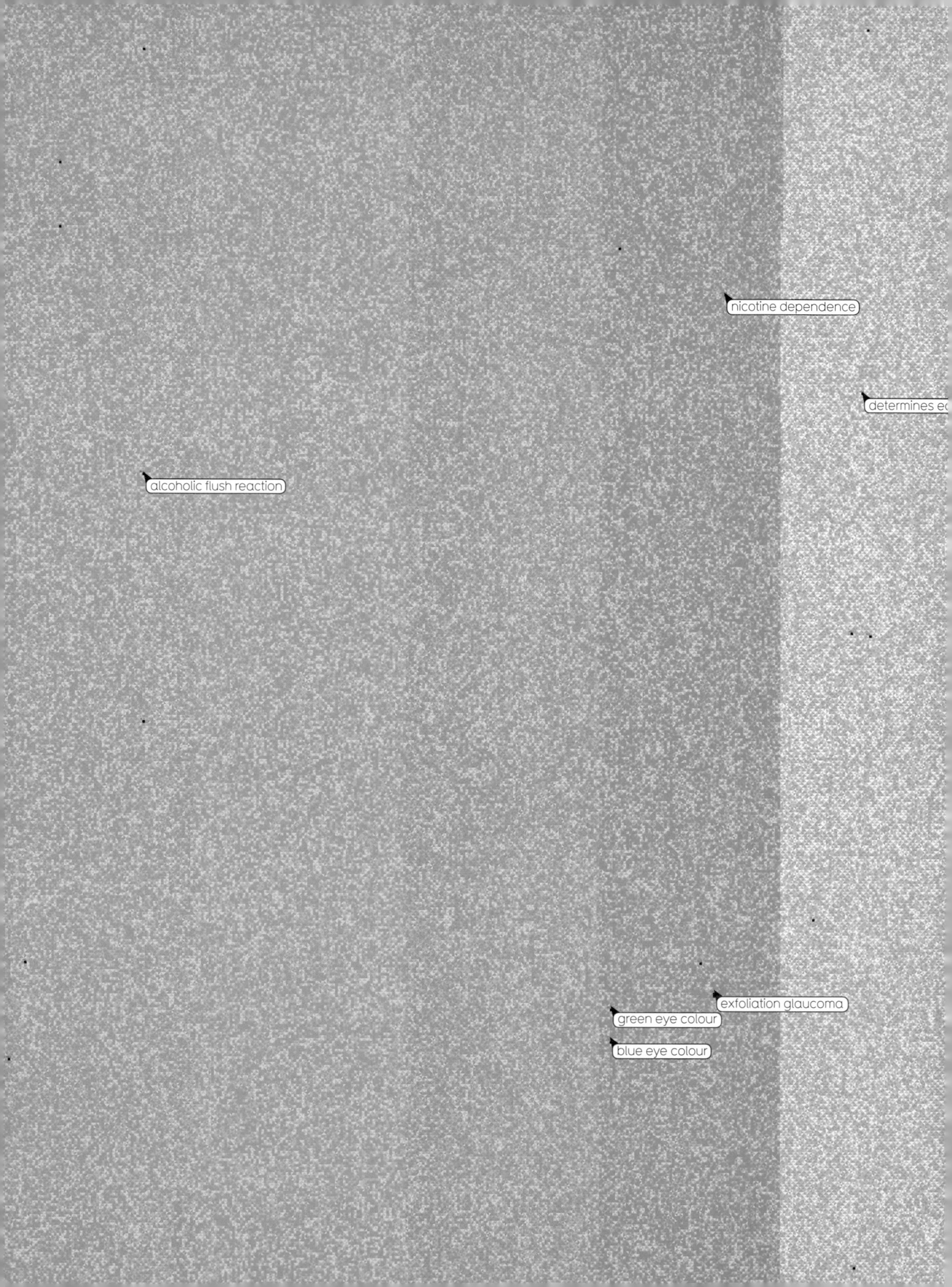

nicotine dependence

determines e

alcoholic flush reaction

exfoliation glaucoma

green eye colour

blue eye colour

asthma
increased Alzheimer's risk (3)
baldness
source: Decodeme.com // programming : Mattias Gunnerås
varied cognitive effects

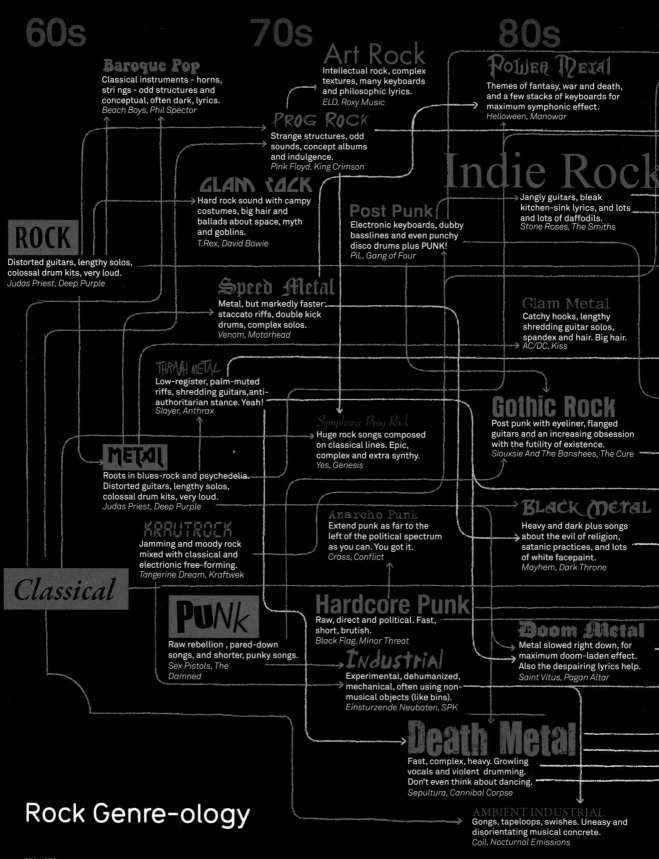

Baroque Pop
Classical instruments - horns, strings - odd structures and conceptual, often dark, lyrics.
Beach Boys, Phil Spector

Art Rock
Intellectual rock, complex textures, many keyboards and philosophic lyrics.
ELO, Roxy Music

PROG ROCK
Strange structures, odd sounds, concept albums and indulgence.
Pink Floyd, King Crimson

POWER METAL
Themes of fantasy, war and death, and a few stacks of keyboards for maximum symphonic effect.
Helloween, Manowar

GLAM ROCK
Hard rock sound with campy costumes, big hair and ballads about space, myth and goblins.
T.Rex, David Bowie

Post Punk
Electronic keyboards, dubby basslines and even punchy disco drums plus PUNK!
PiL, Gang of Four

Indie Rock
Jangly guitars, bleak kitchen-sink lyrics, and lots and lots of daffodils.
Stone Roses, The Smiths

ROCK
Distorted guitars, lengthy solos, colossal drum kits, very loud.
Judas Priest, Deep Purple

Speed Metal
Metal, but markedly faster: staccato riffs, double kick drums, complex solos.
Venom, Motorhead

Glam Metal
Catchy hooks, lengthy shredding guitar solos, spandex and hair. Big hair.
AC/DC, Kiss

THRASH METAL
Low-register, palm-muted riffs, shredding guitars,anti-authoritarian stance. Yeah!
Slayer, Anthrax

Gothic Rock
Post punk with eyeliner, flanged guitars and an increasing obsession with the futility of existence.
Siouxsie And The Banshees, The Cure

Symphonic Prog Rock
Huge rock songs composed on classical lines. Epic, complex and extra synthy.
Yes, Genesis

METAL
Roots in blues-rock and psychedelia. Distorted guitars, lengthy solos, colossal drum kits, very loud.
Judas Priest, Deep Purple

Black Metal
Heavy and dark plus songs about the evil of religion, satanic practices, and lots of white facepaint.
Mayhem, Dark Throne

KRAUTROCK
Jamming and moody rock mixed with classical and electrionic free-forming.
Tangerine Dream, Kraftwek

Anarcho Punk
Extend punk as far to the left of the political spectrum as you can. You got it.
Crass, Conflict

Classical

Hardcore Punk
Raw, direct and political. Fast, short, brutish.
Black Flag, Minor Threat

Doom Metal
Metal slowed right down, for maximum doom-laden effect. Also the despairing lyrics help.
Saint Vitus, Pagan Altar

PUNK
Raw rebellion , pared-down songs, and shorter, punky songs.
Sex Pistols, The Damned

Industrial
Experimental, dehumanized, mechanical, often using non-musical objects (like bins).
Einsturzende Neubaten, SPK

Death Metal
Fast, complex, heavy. Growling vocals and violent drumming. Don't even think about dancing.
Sepultura, Cannibal Corpse

Rock Genre-ology

AMBIENT INDUSTRIAL
Gongs, tapeloops, swishes. Uneasy and disorientating musical concrete.
Coil, Nocturnal Emissions

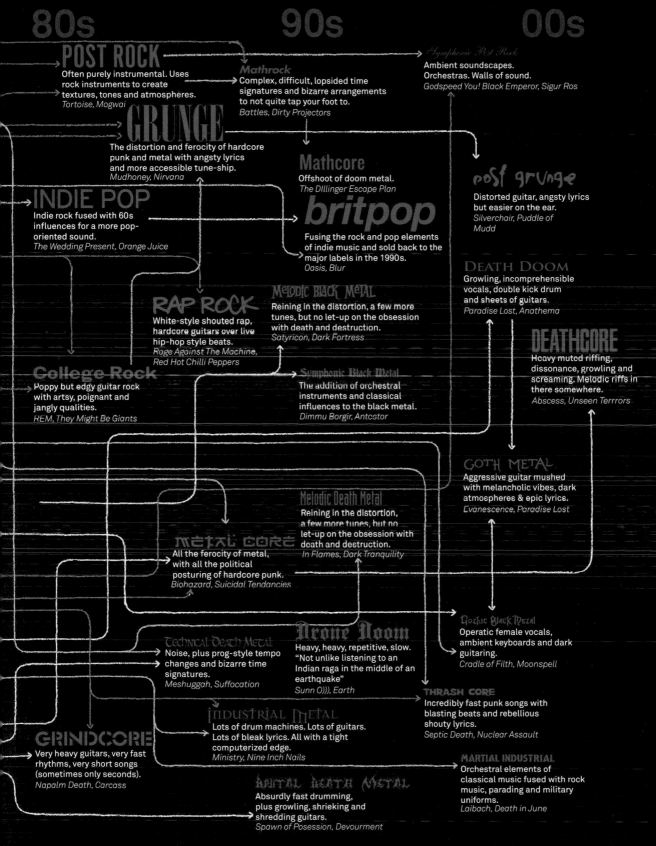

80s

90s

00s

POST ROCK
Often purely instrumental. Uses rock instruments to create textures, tones and atmospheres.
Tortoise, Mogwai

Mathrock
Complex, difficult, lopsided time signatures and bizarre arrangements to not quite tap your foot to.
Battles, Dirty Projectors

Symphonic Post Rock
Ambient soundscapes. Orchestras. Walls of sound.
Godspeed You! Black Emperor, Sigur Ros

GRUNGE
The distortion and ferocity of hardcore punk and metal with angsty lyrics and more accessible tune-ship.
Mudhoney, Nirvana

Mathcore
Offshoot of doom metal.
The Dillinger Escape Plan

britpop
Fusing the rock and pop elements of indie music and sold back to the major labels in the 1990s.
Oasis, Blur

post grunge
Distorted guitar, angsty lyrics but easier on the ear.
Silverchair, Puddle of Mudd

INDIE POP
Indie rock fused with 60s influences for a more pop-oriented sound.
The Wedding Present, Orange Juice

RAP ROCK
White-style shouted rap, hardcore guitars over live hip-hop style beats.
Rage Against The Machine, Red Hot Chilli Peppers

Melodic Black Metal
Reining in the distortion, a few more tunes, but no let-up on the obsession with death and destruction.
Satyricon, Dark Fortress

DEATH DOOM
Growling, incomprehensible vocals, double kick drum and sheets of guitars.
Paradise Lost, Anathema

DEATHCORE
Heavy muted riffing, dissonance, growling and screaming. Melodic riffs in there somewhere.
Abscess, Unseen Terrrors

College Rock
Poppy but edgy guitar rock with artsy, poignant and jangly qualities.
REM, They Might Be Giants

Symphonic Black Metal
The addition of orchestral instruments and classical influences to the black metal.
Dimmu Borgir, Antestor

GOTH METAL
Aggressive guitar mushed with melancholic vibes, dark atmospheres & epic lyrics.
Evanescence, Paradise Lost

Melodic Death Metal
Reining in the distortion, a few more tunes, but no let-up on the obsession with death and destruction.
In Flames, Dark Tranquility

METAL CORE
All the ferocity of metal, with all the political posturing of hardcore punk.
Biohazard, Suicidal Tendancies

Technical Death Metal
Noise, plus prog-style tempo changes and bizarre time signatures.
Meshuggah, Suffocation

Drone Doom
Heavy, heavy, repetitive, slow. "Not unlike listening to an Indian raga in the middle of an earthquake"
Sunn O))), Earth

Gothic Black Metal
Operatic female vocals, ambient keyboards and dark guitaring.
Cradle of Filth, Moonspell

THRASH CORE
Incredibly fast punk songs with blasting beats and rebellious shouty lyrics.
Septic Death, Nuclear Assault

INDUSTRIAL METAL
Lots of drum machines. Lots of guitars. Lots of bleak lyrics. All with a tight computerized edge.
Ministry, Nine Inch Nails

MARTIAL INDUSTRIAL
Orchestral elements of classical music fused with rock music, parading and military uniforms.
Laibach, Death in June

GRINDCORE
Very heavy guitars, very fast rhythms, very short songs (sometimes only seconds).
Napalm Death, Carcass

BRUTAL DEATH METAL
Absurdly fast drumming, plus growling, shrieking and shredding guitars.
Spawn of Posession, Devourment

Simple Part I

Think of the Children
% of children living in poverty

Denmark France Germany UK / Canada United States

8 2 10 16

source UNICEF 2007. Numbers rounded up.

Farty Animals
Annual methane emissions in equivalent CO2

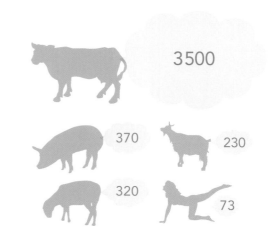

3500

370

230

320

73

source: UN Environmental Programme, theregister.co.uk

Who Reads the Most?
Amazon book stock as % of population size

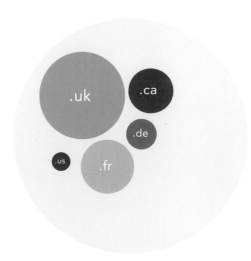

.uk .ca .de .us .fr

source: Data scraped from Amazon websites.

Wave Of Generosity
% of promised tsunami aid money actually paid

Greece 100%
New Zealand
Iceland UK Norway
Japan 90%
Australia Canada 75%
Portugal Netherlands
Italy France 50%
USA 35%
Germany 26%

source: OECD

Celebrities with Issues
Number of celebs behind each cause

Mostly male celebs

Equal men & women

Mostly female celebs

idea: Richard Rogers @ govcom.org // source: looktothestars.org

How Rich?
Yearly earnings of world's wealthiest nations as combined earnings of US states

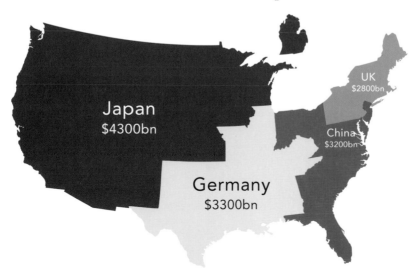

source: WorldBank 2007, ASecondHandConjecture.com.

Sex Education

% virgin students by university subject

0%   50%   100%

Studio Art

Anthropology

Neuroscience

Art History

Computer Science

Spanish

English

French

Philosophy

History

Economics

Undecided

Psychology

International Relations

Biology

Political Science

Biochemistry

Mathematics

0%   50%   100%

source: MIT/Wellesley college magazine, *Counterpoint 2001*.

Godless Swedes

% of atheists, agnostics & non-believers

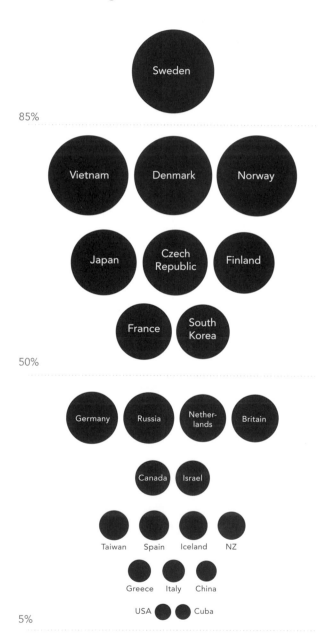

85%

50%

5%

source: Adherents.com [via Swivel.com]. Upper limits in ranges used.

Net Increase
Internet traffic growth

Entire internet per year
1993

Internet per second
2008

Internet per year, 2000

YouTube per month, 2008

source: Cisco.

Left Hand Path
Increased wealth of left-handed men

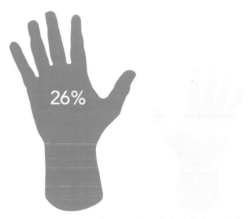

26%

Does not apply to left-handed women.

source: Lafayette College and Johns Hopkins University study.

Bottoms Up
% of world's wealth owned by...

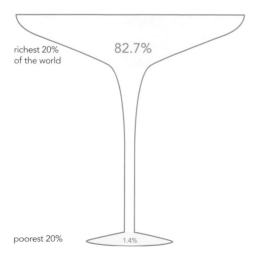

richest 20%
of the world

82.7%

poorest 20%

1.4%

source: UN

Clear Cut
Drop in HIV transmission in circumcised males

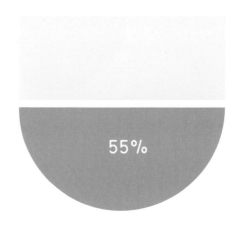

55%

source: University Of Melbourne, BBC News

Excuse Us
Reasons for divorce

Debt

Financial disagreements

Over focus on children

Alcohol/drug abuse

Gambling

Empty nest

Partner's infidelity

Their infidelity

Runaway hobbies

Boredom

Life changing event

Their career

Commuting

My career

Lack of sex

Abuse

⬤ top reason for women   ⬤ top reason for men

source: Insidedivorce.com

National Hypochondriacs Service

Top health searches

UK

Sciatica Shingles
IBS Thyroid Back pain
Pregnancy
Kidney Infection Ringworm
Chickenpox
Thrush Anaemia
Glandular Fever
Diabetes

source: NHS Direct

USA

Stroke Asthma
Flu ADHD Hepatitis
Pregnancy
Headache Arthritis
Cancer
Herpes HIV
HPV

source: About.com.

France

Arthritis Migraine
Endometriosis Back pain
Anorexia
Hepatitis Hemorrhoids
Cancer
Thrush STDs
Hypertension

source: Doctissimo.fr

For Cod's Sake

Stocks of cod in the North Atlantic (100,000 tons)

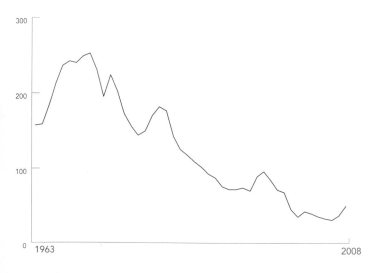

source: Fisheries Research Service

Ups and Downs

Cover vs. coverage

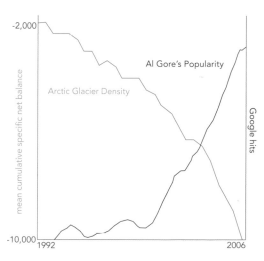

Al Gore's Popularity

Arctic Glacier Density

mean cumulative specific net balance

Google hits

source: Google Insights

What is Consciousness?

Make up your own mind

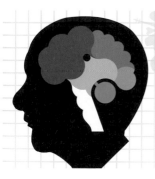

A field that exists in its own parallel "realm" of existence outside reality so can't be seen.
(Substance Dualism)

A sensation that "grows" inevitably out of complicated brain states.
(Emergent Dualism)

A physical property of all matter, like electromagnetism, just not one the scientists know about.
(Property Dualism)

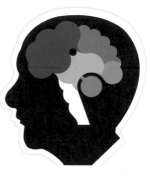

All matter has a psychic part. Consciousness is just the psychic part of our brain.
(Pan Psychism)

Simply mental states are physical events that we can see in brain scans.
(Identity Theory)

Consciousness and its states (belief, desire, pain) are simply functions the brain performs.
(Functionalism)

Literally just behaviour. When we behave in a certain way, we appear conscious.
(Behaviourism)

An accidental side-effect of complex physical processes in the brain.
(Epiphenomenalism)

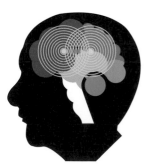

Not sure. But quantum physics, over classical physics, can better explain it.
(Quantum Consciousness)

The sensation of your most significant thoughts being highlighted.
(Cognitivism)

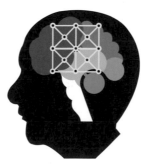

Consciousness is just higher order thoughts (thoughts about other thoughts).
(Higher Order Theory)

A continuous stream of ever recurring phenomena, pinched like eddies into isolated minds.
(Buddhism)

Carbon Conscious

Tweak your day

Unaware (kg)		Aware (kg)	
Thermostat on 25	5.75	Thermostat on 24	5.7
Snack of strawberries	2.4	Snack on an apple	0.5
Heavy meat diet	9.5	Vegetarian diet	9
Commute by car	2.8	Commute by train	0.01
Having a shower	3.5	with a water-saving shower head	3.2
Tumbledryer	1.3	Clothesline	0
Desktop computer	1.3	Laptop	0.2
Laundry 90°	0.9	Laundry 60°	0.5
Bottle of imported wine	1	Carton of local wine	0.5
Dishwasher (D class)	0.8	Dishwasher (A class)	0.5
Breathing	1	Not breathing	0
Computer on overnight	0.5	Computer off	0
Treadmill	0.4	Run outside	0
Fridge (A)	0.4	Fridge (A++)	0.25
Regular light bulbs	0.4	Energy saving bulbs	0.1
Phone charger plugged in	0.03	Phone charger unplugged	0
Leaving TV on standby	0.05	TV unplugged	0
Hairdrying hair	0.19	Natural dry	0
Smoking 20 cigarettes	0.02	Quitting	0

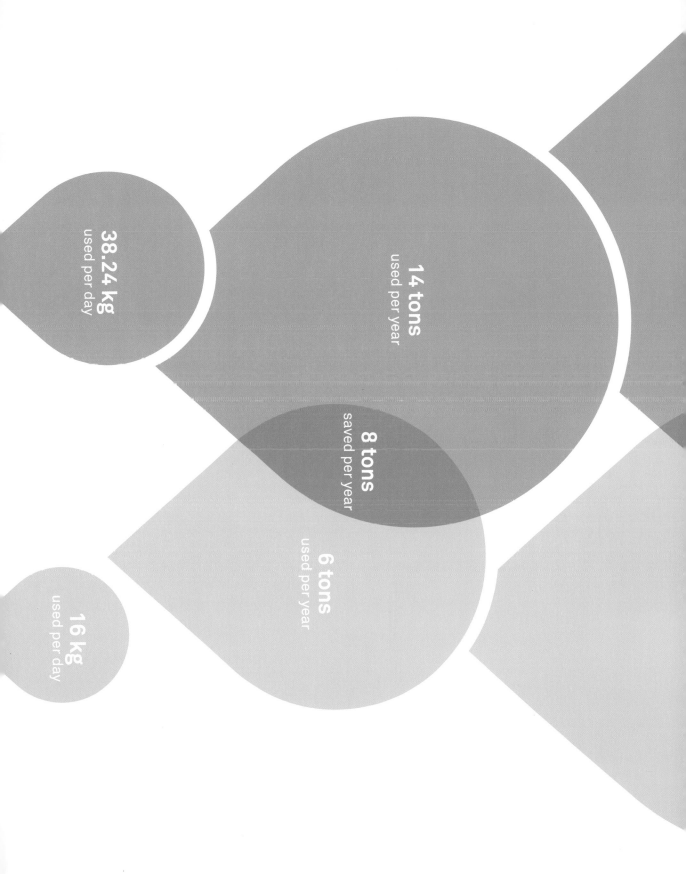

38.24 kg
used per day

14 tons
used per year

8 tons
saved per year

6 tons
used per year

16 kg
used per day

source: UNESCO, Environmental Protection Agency, Energy Information Administration

including everyone in the UK & USA

4,187,280,000 tons

including everyone in the UK

907,244,000 tons
used per year

527,644,000
tons saved

including everyone in the UK & USA

1,752,000,000 tons
(Equivalent to Japan's annual
CO_2 emissions)

including everyone in the UK

379,600,000 tons
used per year

2,435,280,000 tons
saved
(equivalent to Russia & Japan's
total combined emissions per year)

Looking for Love Online
"I want..."

my night in shinning armour to come and sweep me off my feet

a strong, passionate, independent man who is healthy and fit

a man who is confide

to laugh and walk in the rain

to find a good man for

a special guy. I like em kinda chubby

someone I can watch footb

a guy that will give me what if they no what i mean

someon

someone to walk that beach with me   a man that loves science fiction, fantasy, speculative fiction en general

a gentle giant to accompany me on wilderness adventures

to scream

a partner, not a project please

someone that wants to be with me & me only yo

for a real assertive man with a mischivous streak but a good heart

my mr darcy!

som

a country boy who knows how to respect a woman   someone who's fun, honest, loyal and who is just as much sick of the club scene a

A LOVE MAN TO TAKE CARE OF ME AND I WILL BE A GOOD WIFE   a guy who is loving kind   someone like me

a man who is going to treat me like the princess that I am!   someone taller than me   a he

r someone who has the same interest in tattoos and piercings and music   to find myself a man who isn't consumed by women

a guy who is loving kind   LOVE   FRIENDSHIP,

someone to go crazy

the butterflies, the holding hands, the chasing each other up the stairs   someone who will love me for all the things I am

a tall, non smoking, non drug using, single, man with brain and peronsality who can use them all at once...

someone who knows at least how to spell che

SOMEONE REAL THAT HAS LEARNED FROM HIS MISTAKES   my man to be secure and not jealous

to find the one in my life that could fill in the emptiness inside me   you to feel the unbearable lack of

someone thats good as me in bed   someone who can make me laugh,

someone who wont mind if my kids come along

for a gentleman with a certain je ne sais quoi   a redneck who can handle me, I'm a wild one, and full of life

someone who is funny, outgoing yet kind and considerate   someone who is ready to settle down and is involved heavily in churc

a God fearing man with good looks too   someone who can naturally do a lot of silly

someone with a brain

a boy who will move the hair away from my eyes, and then kiss me   to hold hands and kiss for hours

someone in my life to keep me on the edge of my seat but in a good way!   the spark and the tinkling   to be inspired and feel safe

a boy to ride ride ride   to share something great with someone   someone to walk me home because im scared o

for someone with good shoes   someone who I can talk to for hours without getting bored

mess and chaos a lover and a fighter   someone sympathetic to my feminism   someone who fits with me

to hold hands and kiss for hours   to be inspired and fee

someone who looks fancy, and knows what that means   passionate playmates with verve

to know a nice man w

to be intellectually, emotionally and physically stimulated   to co-create a conscious committed LTR with a like minded

Colin Firth diving into a lake   pure love that will form a family

a guy that'll take me to the movies and wont spend his life on video ga

someone to hang out with and sing to   SOMEONE WHO WOULD CALL ME 3 TIMES A DAY IF

to settle down with someone who give me the space to fly away and a reason to come back   someone who has t

someone with whom I can share demented laughter with for no apparent reason

someone who birngs out the best in m

a slim athletic or muscular femail who likes to work out

to find a person who thinks the way I do   someone who likes walking

it all   someone who is loyal, genuine, and can enjoy herself in any situation   to be me w

a friend first and a love secor

a woman who will make me feel inspirated to do great thing's   a "normal" woman if there is such a person

a caring, honest, passionate women to complete my life   someone who doesn't make me think about what I want

the kind of soulmate who can challenge me intellectually   a woman who is slim or curvy   passsion

hot chicks   for a girly girl   someone between a thrill-seeker and a couch potato   warm re

to try everything... bring it on!   tall for a girl who's ready to come out of the that tiny little closet

someone to butt hug with   a girl who is riding it high a stunner   to find a sexy and intelligent lady who is sure of

what people have in the movies   an explorer   to get out more

to meet someone who is down to earth, proud of their accomplishments and caring   a woman who is self sufficient and is

for a lovely professional woman to love and to care for

someone who is loyal, genuine, and can enjoy herself in any situation   an outgoing gal who ain't affriad to try any

meet a waman for sex end maiby more

a girl to treat like a princess and who will treat me like her prince   a woman who won't be always pestering for sex and st

o know what you ache for, and if you dare to dream of meeting in heart's longing   to be that thought in your head that brings a

the sort of person who could be a close friend as well as all the rest of the ro

a highly educated and pretty French women   someone to make dinner for   her to be as pretty inside as

someone who doesn't weigh more than me   a woman to caress and adore

to make you laugh   for someone with a rubbish sense of humour a girl who doesnt have ne extra luggage

a lady to slow down with   to be cherished, but not owned   someone who is into football nas

My main interest in life is garage sales and flea markets and Jeebus

an asian girl who only love me seriously who

someone who loves and respects music as much as me   for a maternal, nurturing person, someone who will like to baby me!

ra heart of gold to find friend her in UK whom i can normal speak

someone who enjoys good conversation not only the random things about your day

for someone to spend the days with and eventually the nights also   I am only interested in attactive women therefore very shall

a girl who loves God, is willing to support me in my ministry but have fun also man not a boy u should know by now what u want and who u are in life so lest talk if u tired of games

high maintenance fake girls, enjoys books and parties

ct me   a man that is romantic and will surprise me at work with a flower

, while having beer and pizza, and the next night, dress up for an elegant dinner

tremely open minded in everything he does

                                        to be on a date with foreigner   my very own Tour Guide

someone to appreciate and work my senses (all 5)   a positive outgoing person!!!   someone with good/pure heart.

man to meke me a wife   someone to have an adventure with   friends to play with me in Petawawa

will love me for all the things I am   her to be honest and true to me

guy who will tell his mother I have beautiful eyes   to find a woman who knows what she want   friends to play with me

one with style and determination   an affectionate ladie friend. Who doesn't mind a hug and kiss once twice or 3 times a day   a man or a woman

, AND HUMOUR.   or someone that's not scared to let her self go

e highest passion   someone who knows how to have fun and is laid back and adventerous.

                    some company. Someone I can trust and talk to openly, someone I feel comfortable with

man or a woman. I'm ready to settle down and start a family

                                        someone who enjoys spending alot of time behind closed doors

for someone who wont get mad if I don't talk to them for three weeks

                        someone to walk beside me, not behind me or infront of me

                                    A PERSON THAT IS NOT SCARED TO BE FREAKY!!

a woman who knows what she wants out of life   someone who is loving and caring

to make friends with foreigners, no matter what kind of people, but I only can speak English

a woman that doesn't want a serious committed relationship we can just get together when it's convenient for both of us

someone to show me the ropes. try anything at least once.

to be loved and love you all night long   strength, protection and heart   help

SOMEONE WHO CAN FILL MY EMPTINESS   someone that is interested in taking control

to have you in my life because you want me   someone to get me motivated

somcone that is secure in themselves and not afraid to be in an alternative relationship as I am not your typical guy

a lovely, sexy man   it to be really hard and aggressive

nt mentality   spirituality and eternity   to realize my fantasy to satiate my curiosity   attention and praise

                                    No public humiliation please   someone to take it easy with me

serious minded men only, no fantasy seakers   a top muscle man

            a guy that will protect me when I am in danger and love me and hold me when I am sad and down   to find some one that can make me happy

T AWAY

values   money for medicine, books, school fees and funerals

        a good man in my life   richness but not only in the bank   some one really bad, are you really bad?

HELP WITH A FIRST TIME   to be seen all dressed up   somebody with a HUMAN TOUCH someone to teach me

to be careful and to be able to trust you

a Masculine non panty wearing man   someone to show me the other side of excitement

to make my Master happy sir.   discretion and a bit of extra understanding

someone to teach me   someone with a sense of humour

to show myself off wearing my bunny ears and letting guys tell me what to   someone to introduce me to the game

            a daddy type to keep me company   SO MUCH

someone who isn't looking for a "daddy" or wanting to be one   that adult someone to make my life complete

        a man that's may best friend as well as my love

                someone to be very discreet and i hate to say it but you might have to teach me a thing or to

I don't like to be rude or judge other people, but if you're over 35 that's too old for me   a pampering

        to take my time and really have some fun

stuff   A WOMAN OF MY OWN, MY BLOOD. SHE SHOULD BE LOVING, CARING AND ABOVE ALL GOD FEARING

tside   someone who is playful, and sensual, and who I can't get enough of

e a matador   you to love me as a poet loves his sorrowful thoughts

shing a 6ft tall brunette supermodel, with lots of money in the bank

't mind critters and knows how to handle a horse, rope, gun

e a highway banditt, and rob things

Searches for phrases beginning 'I want' on popular dating sites

straight women   straight men   gay women   gay men

source: Match.com, Guardian Soulmates, Matchmakers.com, Outpersonals.com

Rising Sea Levels
How long have we got?

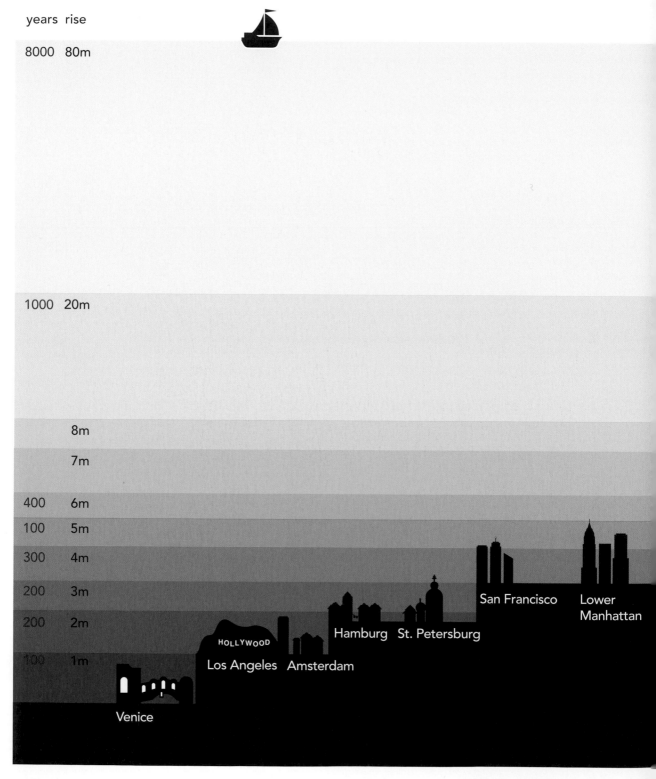

years	rise
8000	80m
1000	20m
	8m
	7m
400	6m
100	5m
300	4m
200	3m
200	2m
100	1m

San Francisco

Lower Manhattan

Hamburg

St. Petersburg

HOLLYWOOD

Los Angeles

Amsterdam

Venice

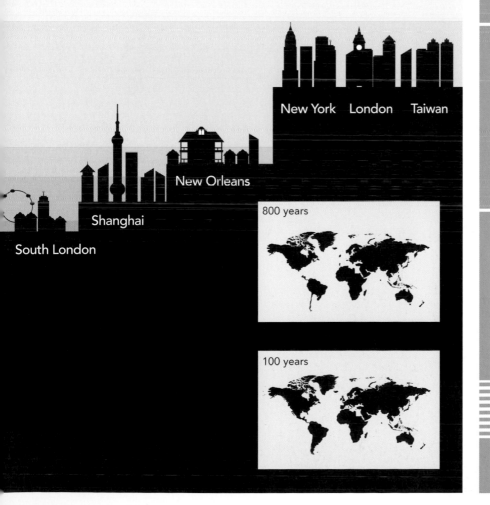

total contributions

Antarctic ice sheet
(S. Pole) 61m

8000 years

Greenland ice sheet
7m

New York   London   Taiwan

New Orleans

W. Arctic ice sheet 6m

Shanghai

800 years

South London

Heating ocean expanding
1m per century

100 years

Already happened

source: IPCC, UN Sea Levels Report, Realclimate.org, Telegraph.co.uk

Colours and Culture
The meanings of colours around the world

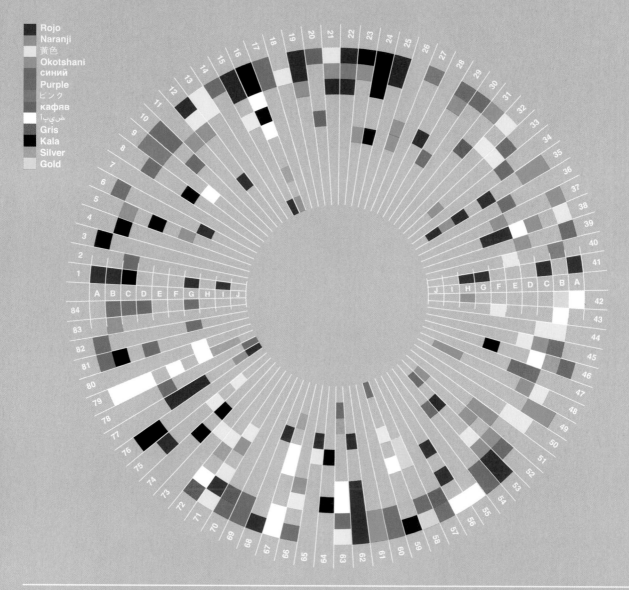

Legend (colours):
- Rojo
- Naranji
- 黄色
- Okotshani
- синий
- Purple
- ピンク
- кафяв
- ضياء
- Gris
- Kala
- Silver
- Gold

A American	1 Anger	18 Deceit	35 Good Luck	52 Life	69 Rationality
B Japanese	2 Art / Creativity	19 Desire	36 Gratitude	53 Love	70 Reliability
C Hindu	3 Authority	20 Earth	37 Growth	54 Loyalty	71 Repelling Evil
D Native American	4 Bad Luck	21 Energy	38 Happiness	55 Luxury	72 Respect
E Chinese	5 Balance	22 Eroticism	39 Healing	56 Marriage	73 Royalty
F Asian	6 Beauty	23 Eternity	40 Healthiness	57 Modesty	74 Self-cultivation
G Eastern European	7 Calm	24 Evil	41 Heat	58 Money	75 Strength
H Muslim	8 Celebration	25 Excitement	42 Heaven	59 Mourning	76 Style
I African	9 Children	26 Family	43 Holiness	60 Mystery	77 Success
J South American	10 Cold	27 Femininity	44 Illness	61 Nature	78 Trouble
	11 Compassion	28 Fertility	45 Insight	62 Passion	79 Truce
	12 Courage	29 Flamboyance	46 Intelligence	63 Peace	80 Trust
	13 Cowardice	30 Freedom	47 Intuition	64 Penance	81 Unhappiness
	14 Cruelty	31 Friendliness	48 Religion	65 Political Power	82 Virtue
	15 Danger	32 Fun	49 Jealousy	66 Personal Power	83 Warmth
	16 Death	33 God	50 Joy	67 Purity	84 Wisdom
	17 Decadence	34 Gods	51 Learning	68 Radicalism	

source: Wikipedia, general web

Stages of You
Children grow in phases. Do adults too? If so, what are the stages? Some theories...

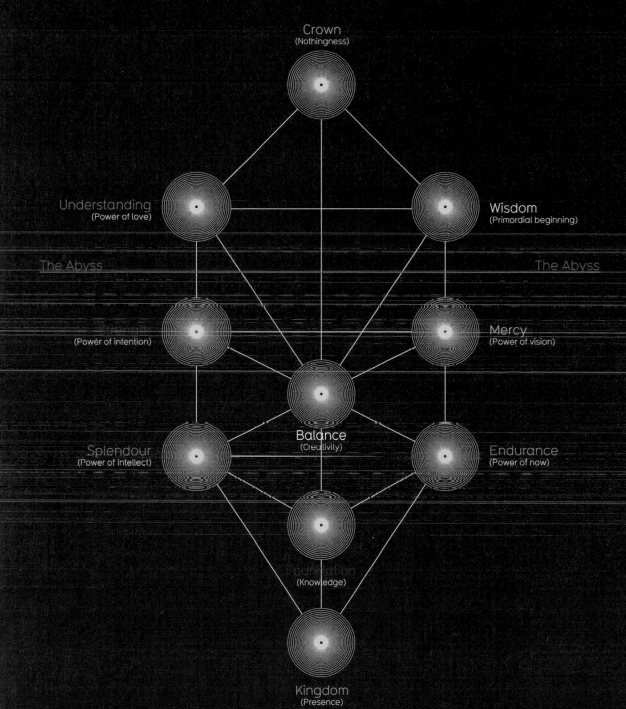

Crown
(Nothingness)

Understanding
(Power of love)

Wisdom
(Primordial beginning)

The Abyss

The Abyss

(Power of intention)

Mercy
(Power of vision)

Balance
(Creativity)

Splendour
(Power of intellect)

Endurance
(Power of now)

Foundation
(Knowledge)

Kingdom
(Presence)

The Tree Of Life
In Jewish Kabbalah, these are the ten stages through which the universe was created and also the ten qualities of God. As an adult grows, they ascend the tree and acquire these qualities for themselves.

CRITICS SAY: "Where's the evidence?"

Sufism

In the mystical form of Islam, the soul or self (nafs) has seven degrees of development, each with increasing purity.

The Pure Self

Self is entirely transcended. No ego or separate self left. Only the Divine exists. Any sense of individuality or separateness is an illusion.

The Self Pleasing to God

Inner marriage of self and soul. All power to act comes from God. You can do nothing by yourself. You no longer fear anything nor ask for anything. Genuine inner unity and wholeness.

The Pleased Self

You are content with your lot, and pleased with even the difficulties and trials of life, realizing that these difficulties come from God. Very different from the usual way of experiencing the world (i.e. focused on seeking pleasure and avoiding pain).

The Contented Self

The struggles of the earlier stages are basically over. The self is at peace. Old desires and attachments still exist but are no longer binding. Grateful, trusting, and adoring. One accepts difficulties in the same way one accepts benefits. The ego-self begins to let go, allowing the individual to come more closely in contact with the Divine.

The Inspired Self

Beginning to taste the joys of spiritual experience. Genuine pleasure from prayer, meditation and other spiritual activities, motivated by compassion, service and morals. Though not free from desires and selfishness, their power is significantly reduced. Emotional maturity is dawning.

The Regretful Self

Insight dawns. The negative effects of a habitually self-centred approach to the world become apparent. Wants and desires still dominate. But now you can see your faults. Regret and a desire for change grow. Attempts to follow higher impulses follow – not always successfully.

The Commanding Self

A false personality created by parents, school and culture. Selfish, controlling and lacking compassion. Must be recognized and bypassed (not destroyed) to grow.

The Arc Of Ascent

CRITICS SAY
"Says who?"

Source: Sufi (Laleh Bakhtair), Sufi.org, Wikipedia, Idries Shah

The Seven Chakras

In this Eastern system, you develop by mastering life-force energy expressed through certain energy centres or "chakras" (roughly centred on various glands and organs). Imbalances in these energy wheels create feelings of blockage and dissatisfaction.

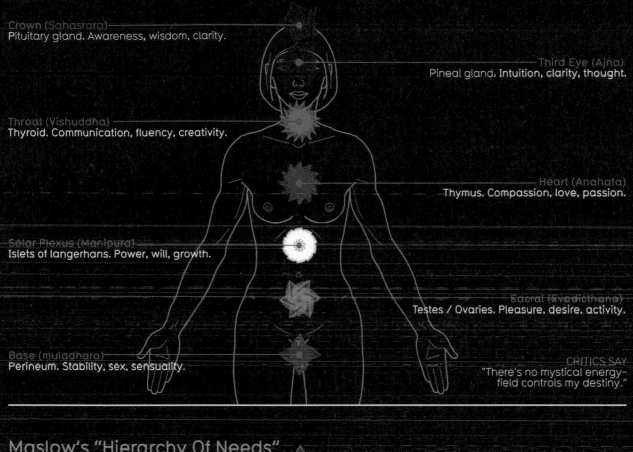

Crown (Sahasrara)
Pituitary gland. Awareness, wisdom, clarity.

Third Eye (Ajna)
Pineal gland. Intuition, clarity, thought.

Throat (Vishuddha)
Thyroid. Communication, fluency, creativity.

Heart (Anahata)
Thymus. Compassion, love, passion.

Solar Plexus (Manipura)
Islets of langerhans. Power, will, growth.

Sacral (Svadisthana)
Testes / Ovaries. Pleasure, desire, activity.

Base (muladhara)
Perineum. Stability, sex, sensuality.

CRITICS SAY
"There's no mystical energy-field controls my destiny."

Maslow's "Hierarchy Of Needs"

Psychologist Abraham Maslow believed that adult growth occurs in seven stages. But only after certain needs are fulfilled in your life.

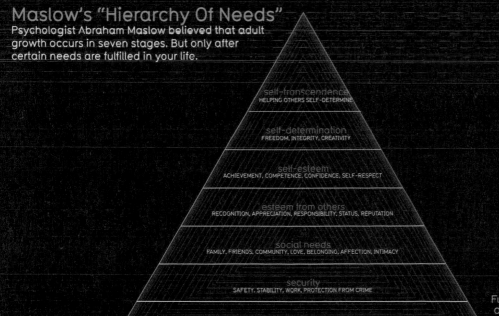

self-transcendence
HELPING OTHERS SELF-DETERMINE

self-determination
FREEDOM, INTEGRITY, CREATIVITY

self-esteem
ACHIEVEMENT, COMPETENCE, CONFIDENCE, SELF-RESPECT

esteem from others
RECOGNITION, APPRECIATION, RESPONSIBILITY, STATUS, REPUTATION

social needs
FAMILY, FRIENDS, COMMUNITY, LOVE, BELONGING, AFFECTION, INTIMACY

security
SAFETY, STABILITY, WORK, PROTECTION FROM CRIME

physical
FOOD, SHELTER, WATER, WARMTH, HEALTH

CRITICS SAY
"Little evidence. Fundamental human needs don't change over time and certainly can't be ranked in a hierarchy."

source: Wikipedia, Sufi.org, IdriesShah.com

Spiral Dynamics

Measures how people think. The intensity with which you embrace or reject each coloured value system reveals how high you are up the development spiral. Can also be applied to societies and cultures.

Developed by Professor Clare Graves, Dr Don Beck and Chris Cowan

Yellow Autonomous

Behaviour Ecological thinking. **Embraces** Change and chaos. Self-directed. **Attitude** See the big picture. Life is learning. **Decision-making** Highly principled. Knowledge based. **Admire** The Competent. **Seek** Integrity. **Love** Natural systems, knowledge, multiplicity. **Want** Self-knowledge. **Hide** Attachment. **Good side:** Free. Wise. Aware. **Bad side:** Overly intellectual, excessively sceptical, angst ridden.

Orange Achiever

Behaviour Strategic. Scientific thinking. Competes for success. Driven. Competitive. **Attitude** Goal orientated. Play to win. Survival of the fittest. **Decisions** Bottom line. Test options for best results. Consult experts. **Admire** The successful. **Seek** Affluence. Prosperity. Rational truth. **Love** Success, status. **Wants** Self-expression. **Hide** Lies **Good side:** Great communication and creativity. Risk taking. Optimistic. **Bad side:** Workaholic. Babbling. Fearful.

Red Egocentric

Behaviour Self-centred. **Attitude** Do what you want, regardless. Live for the moment. The World is a jungle. Might makes right. **Decisions based on** what gets respect, what feels good now. **Admire** The powerful. **Seek** Power, glory and revenge. **Love** Glitz, conquest, action. **Want** Self-definition. **Hide** Shame. **Good side:** Spontaneous, purposeful. **Under pressure:** Dominating, blaming, aggressive. **Bad side:** Passive, sluggish fearful.

Beige Instinctive

Behaviour Instinctive. Materialistic. Greedy. Fearful. **Attitude** Do what you can to stay alive. **Seek** Food, water, warmth, security.

Turquoise Whole View

Behaviour Holisic intuitive thinking. **Attitude** Global. Harmonious. An ecology of perspectives. **Decision-making** Flow. Blending. Looking up and downstream. Long range. **Admire** Life! **Seek** Interconnectedness. Peace in an incomprehensible world. **Love** Information. Belonging. Doing.

Green Communitarian

Behaviour Consensus-seeking. Harmony within the group. Accepting. Dialogue. **Attitude** Everybody is equal. **Decision-making** Consensus. Collaborative. Accept everyone's input. **Admires** The charismatic. **Seeks** Inner peace with caring community. **Love** Affection, good relationships, beneficial resolution. **Want** Self-reflection. **Hide** Doubts. **Good side:** Listens well. Receptive. Perceptive, imaginative. **Bad side:** "Politically correct", inauthenticity.

Blue Absolutist

Behaviour Authoritarian. Cautious. Careful. Fit in. Discipline. Faith. **Attitude** Only one right way. **Decision-making** based on obeying rules, following orders, doing "right". **Admire** The righteous. **Seek** Peace of mind. **Love** Everything in its right place. **Want** Self-acceptance. **Hide** Grief. **Good side:** Balanced, compassionate. **Bad side:** Needy, possessive, jealous, bitter, critical.

Tribal

Behaviour Impulsive. Honour the "old ways". **Attitude** Self-gratifying. **Decision-making** Based on custom and tradition. **Seek** Safety, security. **Admire** The clan. **Hide** Guilt. **Good side:** Fluid with a healthy sexuality. **Bad side:** Overly emotional, obsessive, frigid, impotent, numb.

CRITICS SAY: "Says who? Exact characteristics for advance stages are unclear and speculative."

source: spiraldynamics.net, wikipedia

Loevinger's Stages of Self Development

Psychologist Loevinger's system emphasizes the maturing of conscience. Social rules govern most people's personal decisions
But if differences appear between social rules and your behaviour, you must adapt to resolve the conflict, i.e. you have to grow

	Opportunist	Diplomat	Expert
DEFINED BY	mistrust & manipulation	the group (tribe, family, nation)	knowledge
POSITIVES	energetic	dependable	ideas & solutions
SELF DEFINITION	self-centred	self-in-group	self-autonomy
ACTION	whatever	obeying	doing
INTERESTS	domination, control	neatness, status, reputation	efficiency, improveme perfection
THINKING	black & white	concrete	watertight
BEHAVIOUR	opportunistic	controlled	superior
WORLD VIEW	hostile, dangerous place	conformist, fundamentalist	rational, scientific
LOOKING FOR	rewards	acceptance	perfection
MORALITY	for self-interest only	given by the group	self-righteous
LANGUAGE HABITS	polarities: good/bad, fun/boring	superlatives, platitudes, clichés	"yes but..."
COMMON FLAWS	selfish	hostility to "outsiders"	selfish
FEAR OF	being overpowered	disapproval, rejection	loss of uniqueness
DEFENCES	blaming, distortion	suppression, projection, idealization	intellectualizing, host humour, blaming tool
SOCIALLY	two-faced, hostile	facilitator, socialite	seek to stand out from crowd
RELATIONSHIPS	exploitative, volatile	useful for status	useful or not?
WHEN OPPOSED	tantrums, harsh retaliation	meekly accept	argumentative, belittl opinionated

Achiever	Individualist	Strategist	Alchemist
independence	unconventionality	strength & autonomy	complexity, authenticity
conviction, fairness, enthusiasm	inspiring & spontaneous	insightful, principled, balanced	charismatic authentic leaders
self-in-society	self as individual	self-determination	transparent self
perfecting	being & feeling	integrating	playing, reinventing
reasons, causes, goals, effectiveness	unique personal achievements	patterns, trends, processes, complexity	problems of language and meaning
rational, sceptical	holistic	visionary	intuitive
challenging, supportive	creative	highly collaborative, spontaneous	free
postmodern, scientific	paradoxical, no need to explain everything	multi-faceted, ambiguous	chaotic
root causes	uniqueness	authenticity	truths
self-chosen	non-judgement, almost amoral	deeply principled, will sacrifice self for values	very high moral standards
ask lots of "why" questions	contrasting ideas, vivid language	complex, lyrical	fluid orators
exhaustion, over-extension, self-criticism	can appear aloof & unapproachable	impatient with theirs & others development	feeling better than others
failure, loss of control	self-deception	not fulfilling their potential	fearless
rationalization, self-criticism	sublimation, spiritualization	suppression, humour, altruism	sublimation, humour
genuinely friendly	fun!	great communicators	can talk to anyone
diverse, intense & meaningful	intense & mutually rewarding	vital for intimacy & growth	deeply empathic
"we agree to differ"	respectful, differences are celebrated	tolerant, insightful, responsive	empathetic

CRITICS SAY: The "self" is a complex of developing parts, not governed by a single factor.

source: Susanne Cook-Greuter, Ego Development: Nine Levels Of Increasing Embrace, Wikipedia

K10

Core Duo

Sony JS160

Playstation III

TP X300

Wii

TP Z60

Sony FW

Alienware ALX

VAIO XL2

Core

Xbox 360

TP X41

VIAO C1

Shuttle SV24

Gamecube

TP 570

Presario 5000

Pavillion 6835

Pentium IV

ThinkPad 770

Xbox

K7 "Athlon"

Compaq Deskpro 4000

Gateway TV/PC

Pentium III

Dreamcast

Playstation II

Toshiba Satellite

Pentium II

ThinkPad 300

AMD K5

IBM Aptiva

IBM PC 300

Sega Saturn

PS/2 L40SX

Toshiba 3400

SuperH

Hitachi

Jaguar

N64

Compaq Presario

Pentium Mini Tower

PS2 / 25   PS2 / 65

PS/2 70

gameboy pocket

Playstation

RIM

CDi

IBM 5140

PS/2 30

Amstrad PCW

ZX88

PC Engine

lynx

Compaq Deskpro 386

IBM PS/2 60

gameboy

megadrive

neogeo

STE

Amiga 3000

HP 110

XT 286

Amstrad 1512

128

mastersystem

SNES

ST2

Amiga 2000

MSX2

IBM 5155

IBM AT

Amstrad CPC 464

Spectrum+

QL

7800

1040 ST

compaq portable

MSX

NES

130XE

C128

Atari ST

IBM 5150

Timex 1000

ZX81

Spectrum

Timex 2068

1200XL

Commodore C64

IBM XT

ColecoVision

5200

ZX80

MZ80B

Atari 400/800

VIC 20

MZ80K

Atari 2600

Commodore PET

8086

Intel

Z80

Zilog

6502

MOS

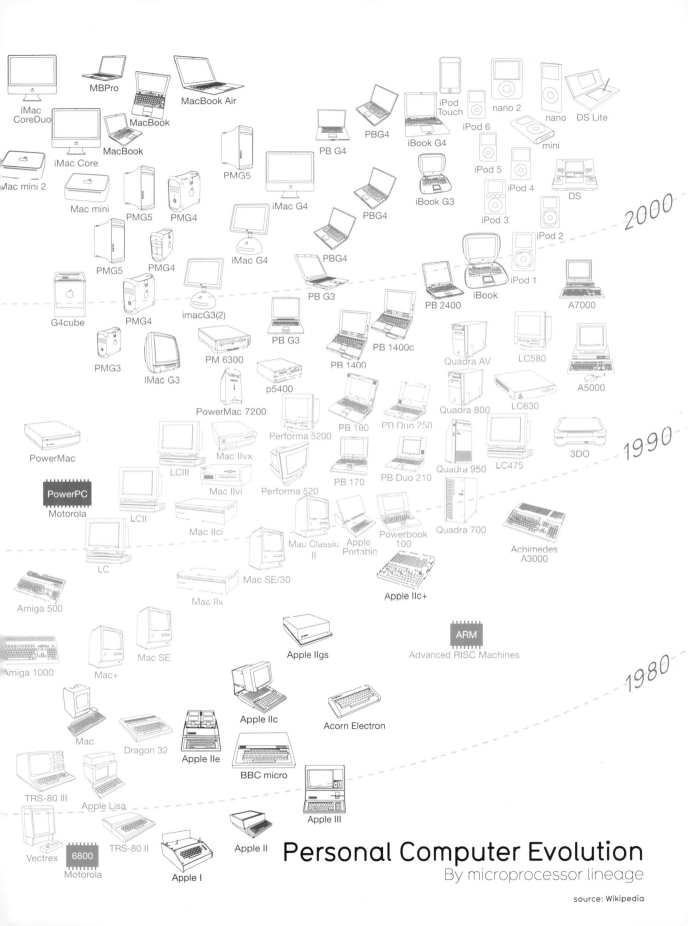

Personal Computer Evolution
By microprocessor lineage

source: Wikipedia

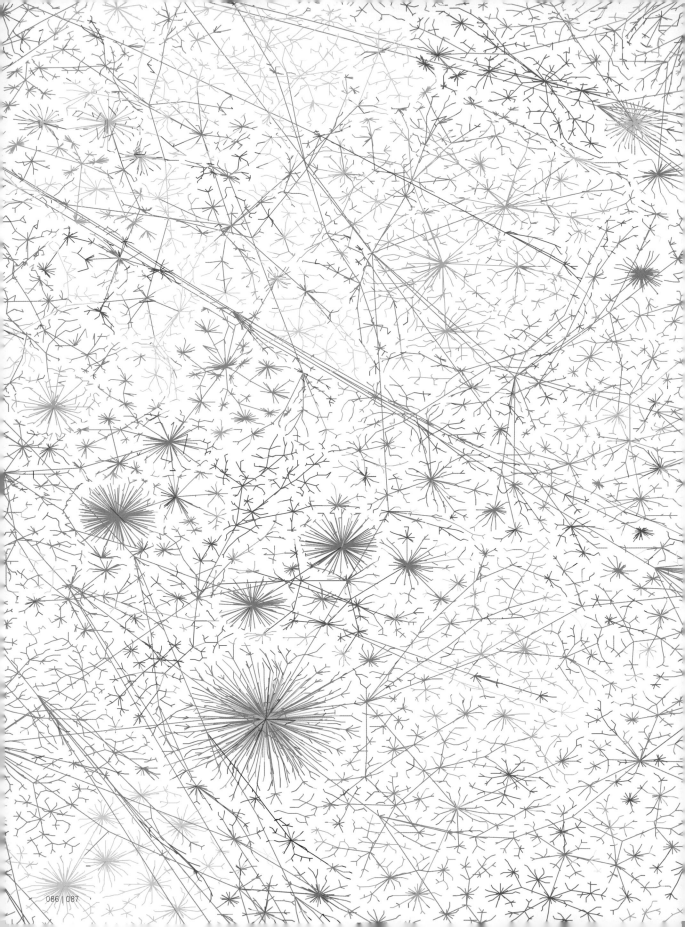

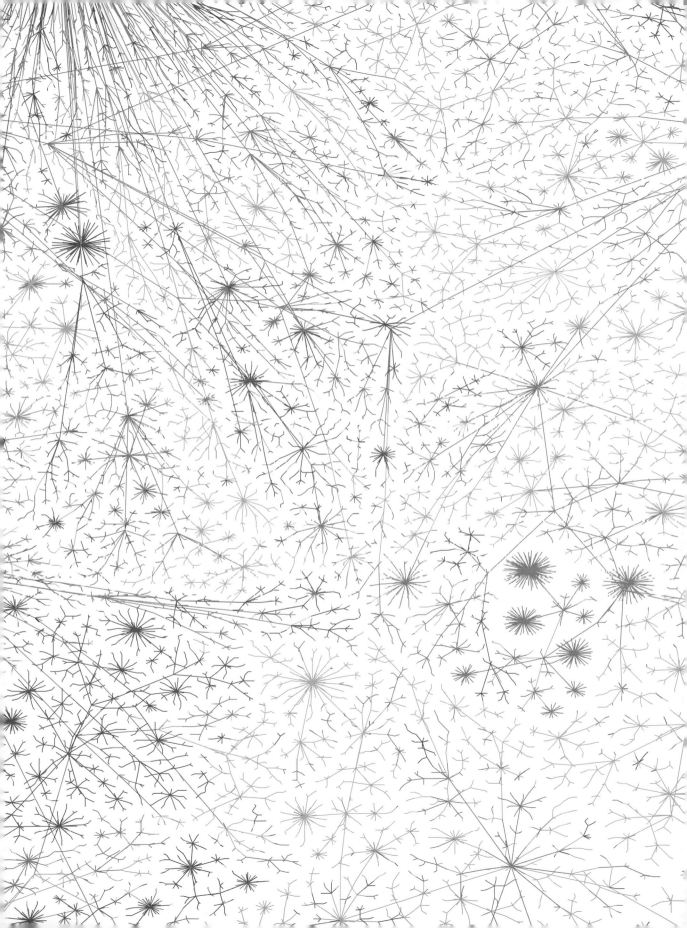

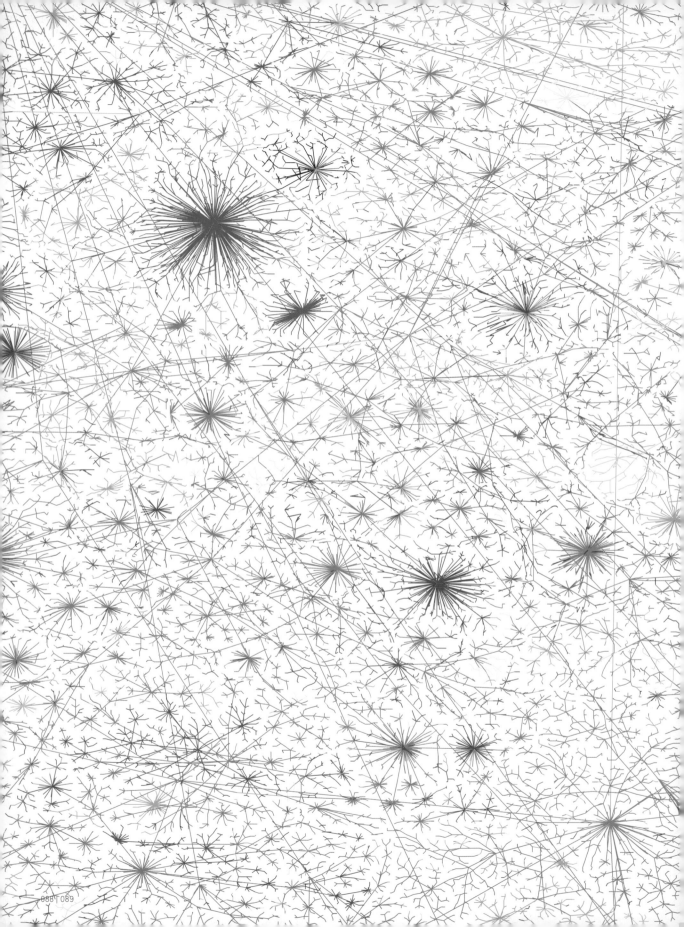

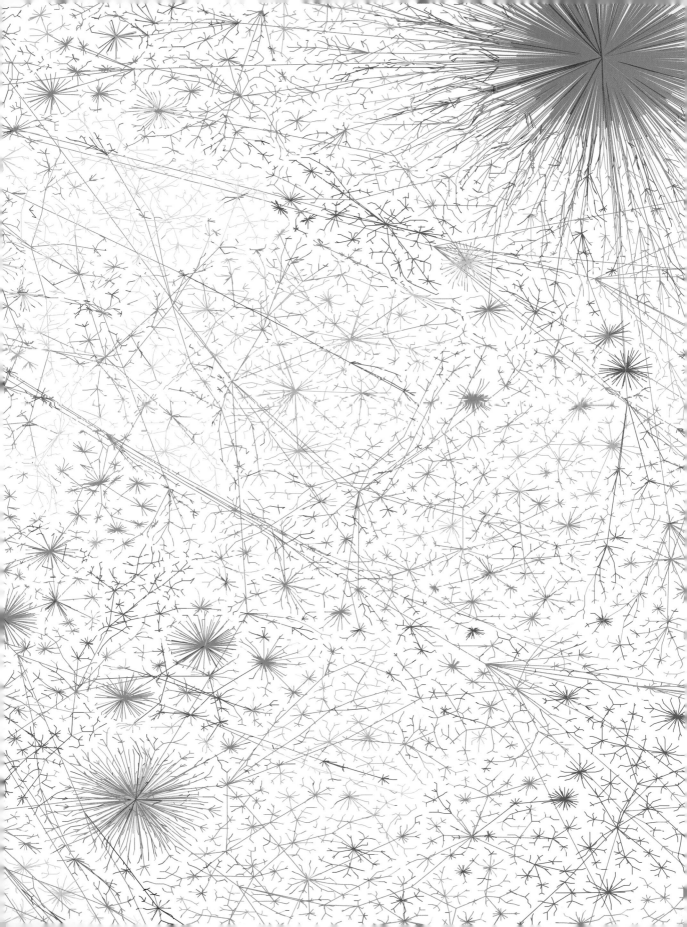

The One Machine
Map of the internet

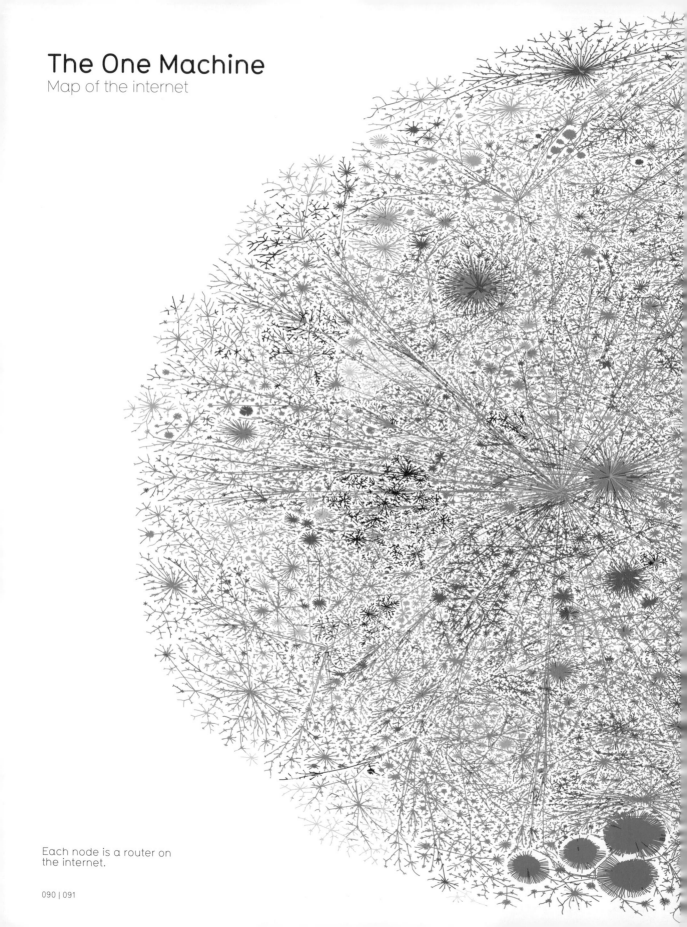

Each node is a router on
the internet.

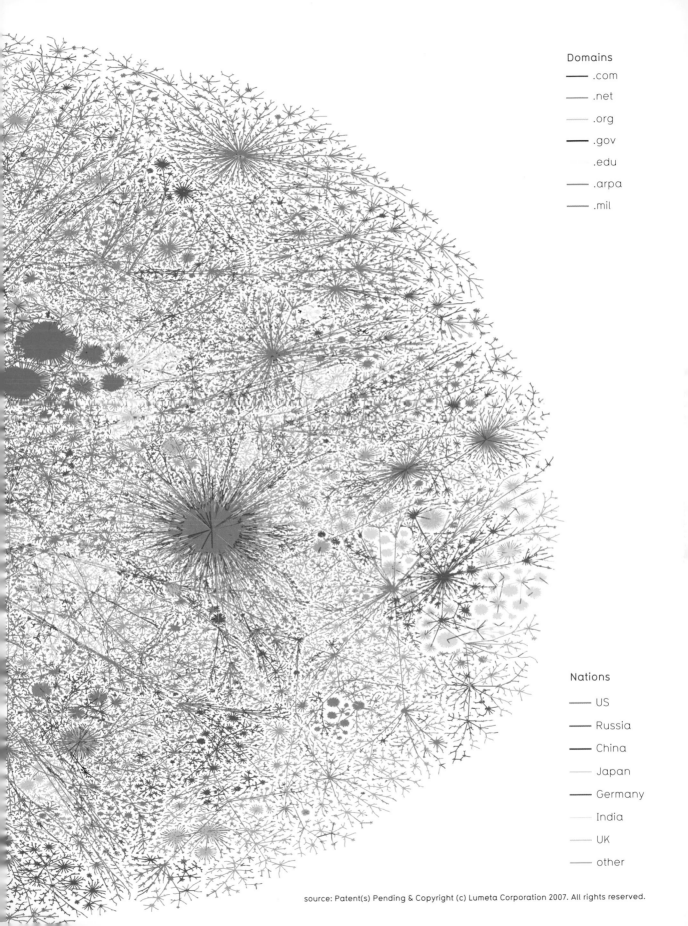

Domains

— .com
— .net
— .org
— .gov
— .edu
— .arpa
— .mil

Nations

— US
— Russia
— China
— Japan
— Germany
— India
— UK
— other

Internet Virals
How many you seen?

1996

MR T
A-Team star embarks on ironic post career with risible rap.

The Oracle of Bacon
Six degrees of separation applied to unremarkable actor.

Loose Change
Convincingly well-made 9/11 conspiracy documentary is alarmingly popular.

MySpace: The Movie
Tiresome spoof of social networking vagaries. Ten minutes too long.

Chad Vader
Darth's younger brother Chad w at a supermark

2005

Man vs. Bear
Orange-trousered man fights bear for tinned salmon.

YouTube Launched

JenniCAM
19-year-old girl installs webcam. Inspires millions of pornographers.

Hot or Not
Simple human rating concept anticipates online dating craze.

Xiao Xiao
Stick men kick each other about.

Evolution of Dance
Rubber-legged slaphead performs history of dance in six minutes.

99m
views

1997

TimeCube.com
Ranting racist homophobe claims the world is a cube.

All Your Base Are Belong To Us
Video game dialogue lost in translation.

1998

The Maze Game
Linda Blair booby trap scares millions of players.

Bert is Evil
Good name of **Sesame Street** stalwart besmirched in worrying detail.

2004

The Show / Ze Frank
Manic American talks crap for a year.

Mullets Galore
Billy Ray Cyrus to Bill Hicks. Two haircuts, zero dignity.

Peter Pan Guy
Man models homemade Peter Pan costumes for no discernible reason.

2000

Y2K
Glad you filled your cellar with batteries and bottled water?

End of the World
Rudimentary animation explains global nuclear policy with comedy voiceover.

Diet Coke and Mentos
Oversized mints added to fizzy drinks with explosive results. Science.

Ask a Ninja
Stream of consciousness from man in a burka.

Bonsai Kitten
Miniature cat spoof taken seriously by the hard of thinking.

We're Not Afraid
We're actually absolutely terrified. Please don't kill us, terrorist scum.

Real Ultimate Power
A boy called Robert who can't stop thinking about ninjas.

Demotivators
The power of negative thinking.

I Kiss You
Low-rent simpleton's homepage that allegedly provided inspiration for Borat.

2003

One Red Paperclip
Gurning redneck turns paperclip into house via grossly improbable trades.

Crank That Soulja Boy
It's not music, it's just noise.

40.7m
views

6 Years of Noah
Unhappy-looking narcissist takes picture of self every day for six years.

Blair Witch Project
Pioneering website promotes low budget film, inadvertently sets industry template.

Million Dollar Homepage
Clever sod pays way through university by selling pixels.

2006

Dancing Baby
Symbolized Ally McBeal's body clock, and enthralled tiresome office dullards.

Hampster Dance
Rudimentary animation of dancing rodents pre-empts a billion wasted hours.

Fred
Hyperactive six-year-old boy video blogs super-maniacally.

2002

2001

Troops
Star Wars met **Cops**.

Robot Dance
Imagine if Napoleon Dynamite had discovered robotic dancing instead.

Chuck Norris Facts
Fact-based deification of bearded action star.

Black Dorm Boys
Two Chinese boys mime banal pop song. Friend ignores them.

tendo
ty-FOOOUR
s go feral upon
eiving underper-
ming games
asole.

Hasselhoff's "Hooked on a Feeling"
In Germany this is considered high art.

Snakes on a Plane
Internet hype fails to prevent box-office flop.

Little Superstar
He's small, he's Indian and he's dancing.

Leeroy Jenkins
Online roleplayer shouts his character's name. Rest of society remains oblivious.

Free Hugs Campaign
Do-gooder invades personal space. Don't touch me.
33.3m views

Star Wars Kid
Fat kid throws himself into enthusiastic lightsabre routine, ruins life.

Sneezing Panda
Baby panda causes mother to buck with man-sized sneeze.

2007

I Can Haz Cheezburger?
Kittens plus illiterate slogans excite world.

Beatbox Flute
Handsome beatboxing flautist chooses dire track to debut superpowers.

Daft Hands
Daft Punk song dubbed by tattooed hands. Yes, you read that correctly.
25.6m views

Charlie bit my finger
Charlie bit me!
60.7m views

Rick Roll
Pete Waterman reminds us again how he invented music.

Drunk Hasselhoff
Baywatch star wrestles with burger. Where's KITT now?

Stephen Colbert at White House Dinner
US comedian Colbert makes Bush squirm.

Chocolate Rain
Po-faced song about racism is hilarious.
29.9m views

300 PG Version
Modified **300** trailer promotes dental hygiene.

Otters Hold Hands
Otters hold hands while floating. Entire world stops to watch.

I Like Turtles
Random kid at fair proclaims love for turtles.

Will it Blend?
iPhone destroyed in modern take on baby in a blender.

Thriller
Murderers and rapists re-enact seminal Wacko Jacko video.
19.2m views

Benny Lava
Indian Michael Jackson dances hilariously on high mountain range.

Miss Teen South Carolina
Miss Teen USA 2007 displays limited grasp of geography.
30.7m views

Leave Britney Alone!
Eye-linered Britney fan wrapped in sheet.

Don't tase me, bro!
Nobody likes students but this may have been an over-reaction.

Dramatic Chipmunk
Prairie dog turns menacingly towards the camera.

Weezer's Pork & Beans
Music video features every single viral reference since 1990.

Hot for Words
Hot Russian philologist gets lots of hits talking about 'word origins'.
Loads of views

Kicking a Wall
Essex boy kicks wall, breaks ankle, queries evolution.

Big Dog
Eerie robot dog frightens entire world.

I'm F**king Matt Damon
Comedienne Sarah Silverman sings about her sexual relations with a celebrity.

Evil look baby
Baby gives evil look.

2008

Hahaha
Small baby laughs like Satan with a head cold.
66.3m views

The Last Lecture
Respected professor gives final lecture before dying. Powerful stuff.

celebs
crazies
cute
funny
irony
kittens
mash-up
one-offs
ninjas
scary
sexxxxy
song/dance
star wars
wow!

source: Wikipedia, diplty.com/tatercaxes/Internet_Memes

You Tubes
Your personal info online

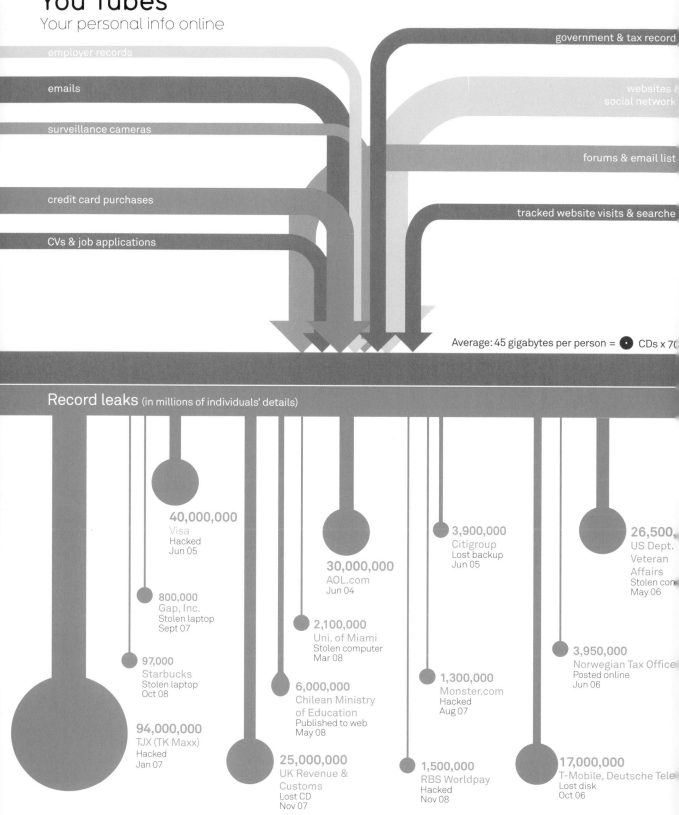

employer records

emails

surveillance cameras

credit card purchases

CVs & job applications

government & tax record

websites &
social network

forums & email list

tracked website visits & searche

Average: 45 gigabytes per person = ● CDs x 7(

Record leaks (in millions of individuals' details)

40,000,000
Visa
Hacked
Jun 05

800,000
Gap, Inc.
Stolen laptop
Sept 07

97,000
Starbucks
Stolen laptop
Oct 08

94,000,000
TJX (TK Maxx)
Hacked
Jan 07

30,000,000
AOL.com
Jun 04

2,100,000
Uni. of Miami
Stolen computer
Mar 08

6,000,000
Chilean Ministry
of Education
Published to web
May 08

25,000,000
UK Revenue &
Customs
Lost CD
Nov 07

3,900,000
Citigroup
Lost backup
Jun 05

1,300,000
Monster.com
Hacked
Aug 07

1,500,000
RBS Worldpay
Hacked
Nov 08

26,500,
US Dept.
Veteran
Affairs
Stolen com
May 06

3,950,000
Norwegian Tax Office
Posted online
Jun 06

17,000,000
T-Mobile, Deutsche Tele
Lost disk
Oct 06

Hotspots (be especially careful in these nations)

Digital blackmarket prices

$1	**email address**	for spamming and phishing
$12	**credit card**	without CVV security number
$25	**credit card**	with CVV security number
$25	**full identity**	name, address, ID numbers, DOB etc
$30	**email password**	very valuable
$250	**full bank account**	with all details

Leaky routes

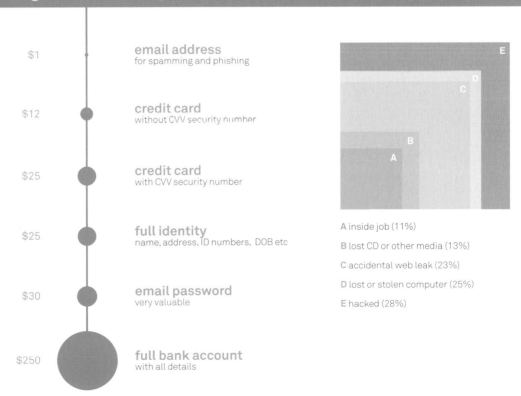

A inside job (11%)

B lost CD or other media (13%)

C accidental web leak (23%)

D lost or stolen computer (25%)

E hacked (28%)

source: Infowatch.com, Datalossdb.org, ITRC, Forbes, Wikipedia

In 25 Words or Less

Most common words used by (in)famous columnists

George Monbiot
Guardian

change government
every nations now
just
people
world power
new even
also last global much
climate years
means public companies

a mention of "I" every 246 words

Richard Littlejohn
Daily Mail

new police government
people Gordon got
like now years time
last Britain Labour way
know get even just go
back home

117 words

Oh the Agony

Most common words used by noted advice specialists

Pamela Stephenson Connolly
Guardian

intercourse well
try feel good life
therapy make sex often may
experience sexual many
seek need
relationship way men
ask partner
people help
women

Dear Abby
syndicated

right person time
now go know
feel life make people
sure thank tell
may like someone
however
also please parents much
one better
husband might family
two

Data scrape of columns from Jan 1st 2007–Dec 2008. Common words ("and", "to", "were", "there" etc) and duplicate political terms excluded. Wordle.net used to establish word freq

Christopher Hitchens
Freelance

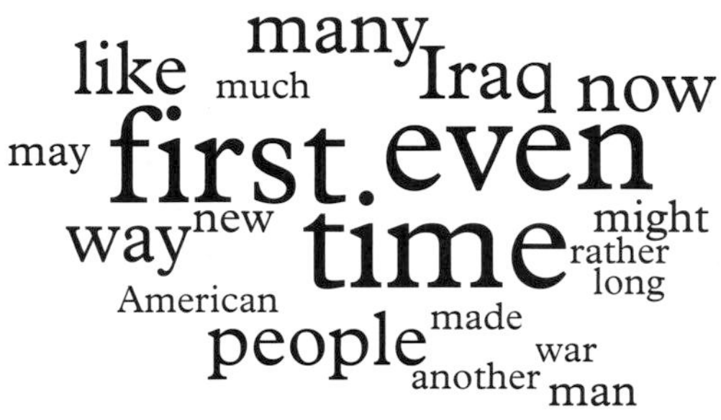

many
like
much
Iraq
now
may
first
even
way
new
time
might
rather
long
American
made
people
war
another
man

271 words

Thomas Friedmann
New York Times

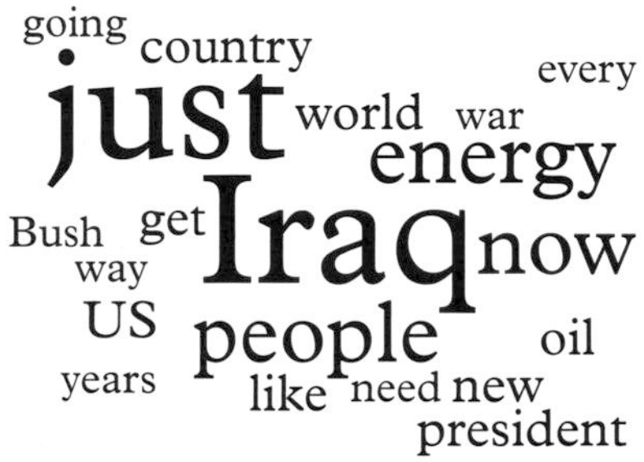

going
country
every
just
world
war
energy
Bush
get
way
Iraq
now
US
people
oil
years
like
need
new
president

103 words

Miriam Stoppard
Daily Mirror

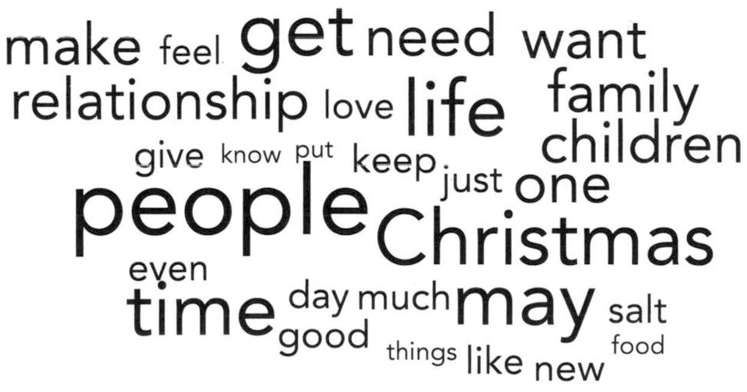

make
feel
get
need
want
relationship
love
life
family
children
give
know
put
keep
just
one
people
Christmas
even
time
day
much
may
salt
good
things
like
new
food

Self Help
Book titles & subtitles

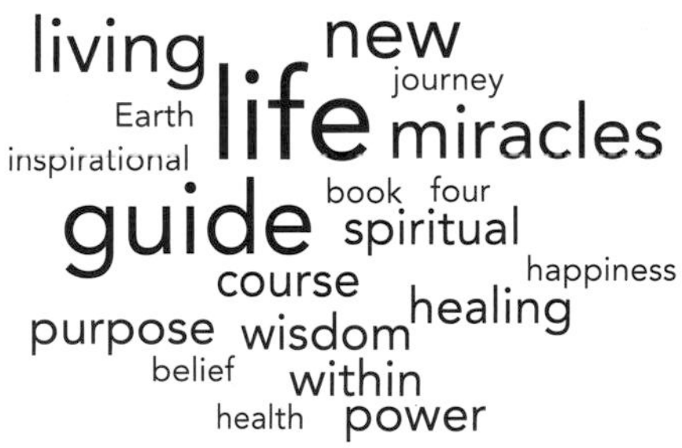

living
new
journey
Earth
life
miracles
inspirational
book
four
guide
spiritual
course
happiness
purpose
wisdom
healing
belief
within
health
power

source: Guardian.co.uk, NYTimes.com, DailyMail.co.uk, DailyMirror.co.uk, ChristopherHitchens.com, Wordle.net

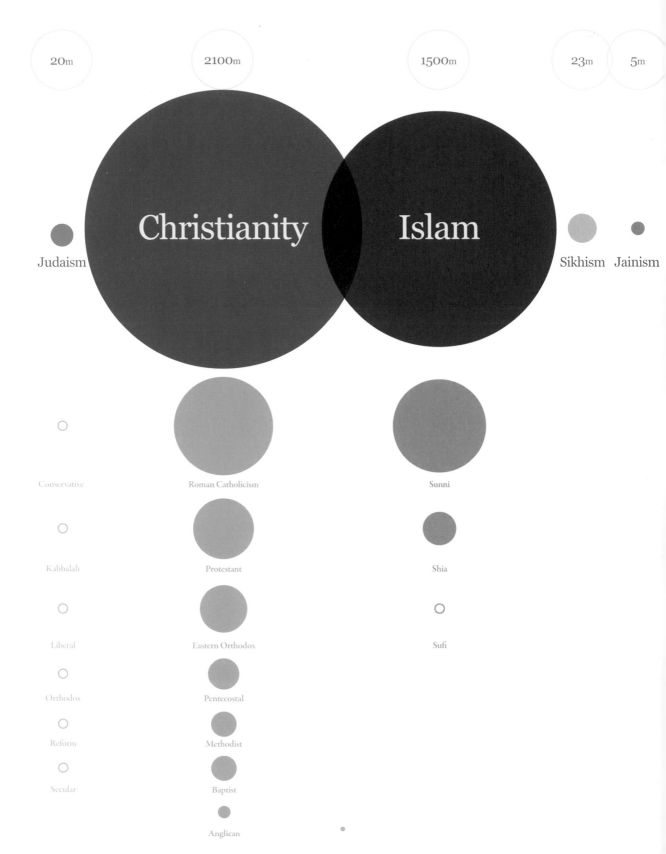

20m

2100m

1500m

23m

5m

Christianity

Islam

Judaism

Sikhism   Jainism

Conservative

Roman Catholicism

Sunni

Kabbalah

Protestant

Shia

Liberal

Eastern Orthodox

Sufi

Orthodox

Pentecostal

Reform

Methodist

Secular

Baptist

Anglican

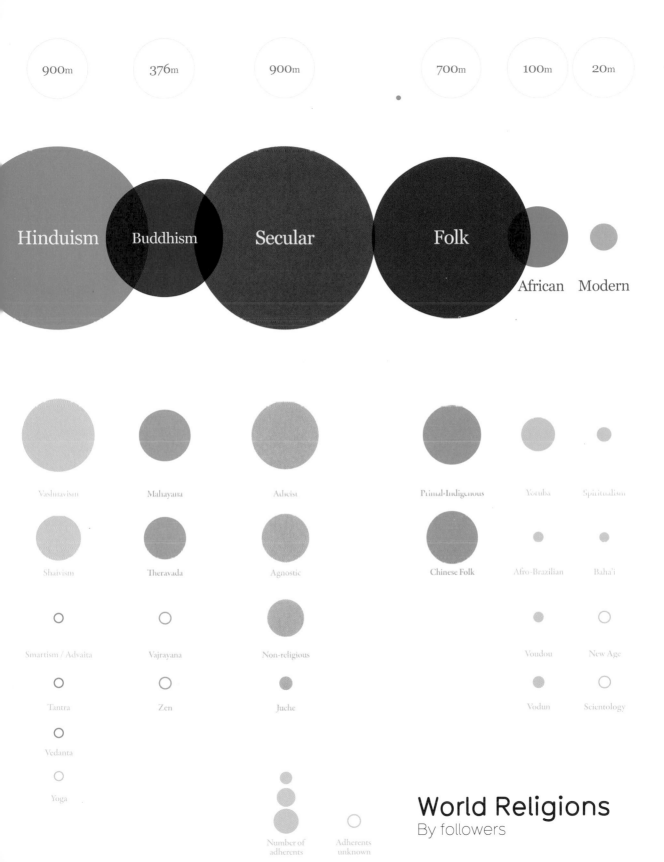

World Religions
By followers

source: Adherents.com

Moral Matrix

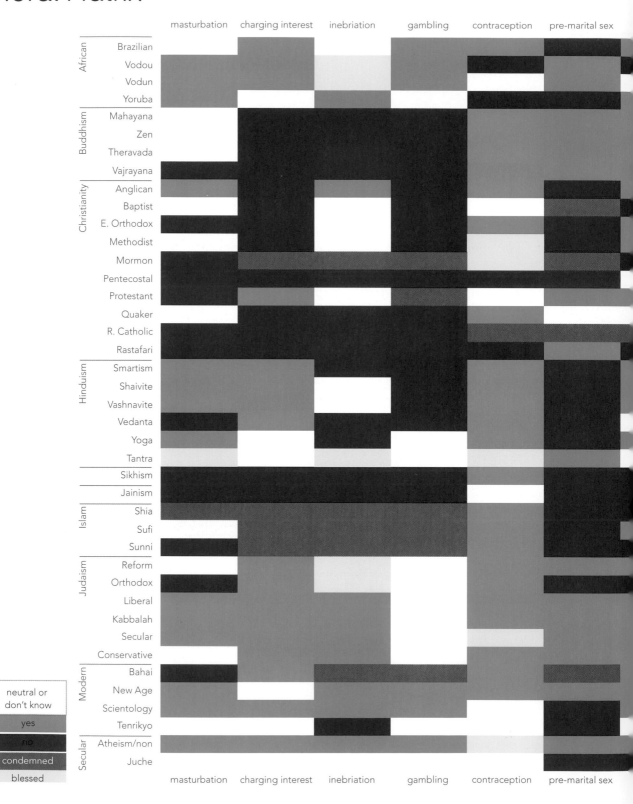

		masturbation	charging interest	inebriation	gambling	contraception	pre-marital sex
African	Brazilian						
	Vodou						
	Vodun						
	Yoruba						
Buddhism	Mahayana						
	Zen						
	Theravada						
	Vajrayana						
Christianity	Anglican						
	Baptist						
	E. Orthodox						
	Methodist						
	Mormon						
	Pentecostal						
	Protestant						
	Quaker						
	R. Catholic						
	Rastafari						
Hinduism	Smartism						
	Shaivite						
	Vashnavite						
	Vedanta						
	Yoga						
	Tantra						
	Sikhism						
	Jainism						
Islam	Shia						
	Sufi						
	Sunni						
Judaism	Reform						
	Orthodox						
	Liberal						
	Kabbalah						
	Secular						
	Conservative						
Modern	Bahai						
	New Age						
	Scientology						
	Tenrikyo						
Secular	Atheism/non						
	Juche						

Legend:
- neutral or don't know
- yes
- no
- condemned
- blessed

adultery married clergy female clergy being gay gay sex gay clergy gay marriage abortion

adultery married clergy female clergy being gay gay sex gay clergy gay marriage abortion

The Carbon Dioxide Cycle

Yearly man-made vs natural carbon emissions in gigatons (g)

emitted   absorbed

9g
a year

+

550g
already in the
atmosphere

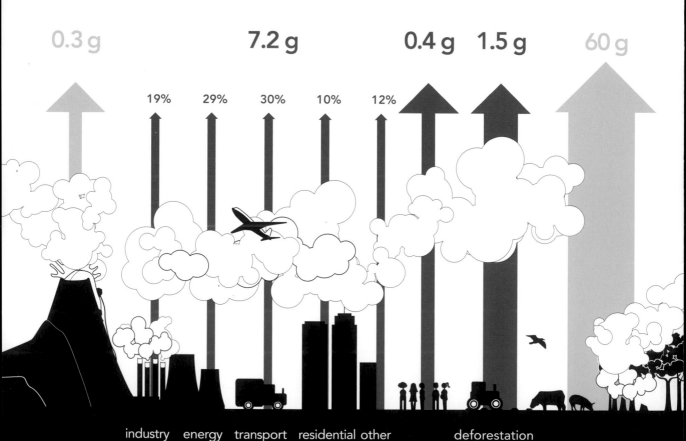

0.3 g   7.2 g   0.4 g   1.5 g   60 g

19%   29%   30%   10%   12%

industry energy transport residential other   deforestation

volcanoes   fossil fuels   people   animals forest fires

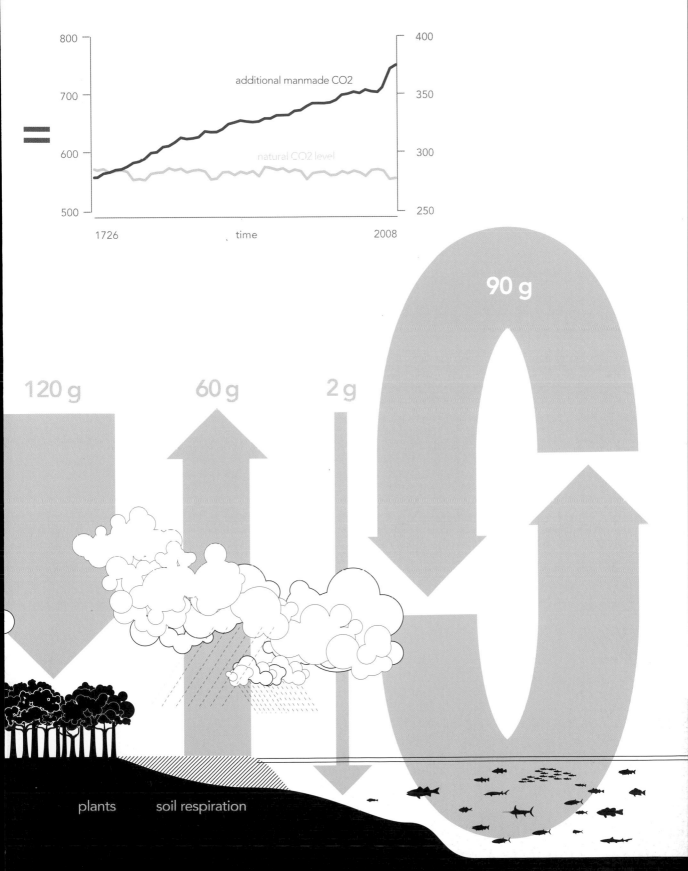

additional manmade CO2

natural CO2 level

800 — 400
700 — 350
600 — 300
500 — 250

1726   time   2008

90 g

120 g   60 g   2 g

plants   soil respiration

source: UNESCO Scope , IPCC 2007, Wikipedia, Realclimate.org

1250 MB/s

same bandwidth as a: computer network

125 MB/s

USB key

Low Resolution
Amount of sensory information reaching the brain per second

12.5 MB/s

hard-disk

Amount consciously perceived (0.045%) ──────

source: Tor Nørretranders, The User Illusion: Cutting Consciousness Down to Size

Taste Buds
Complementary tastes

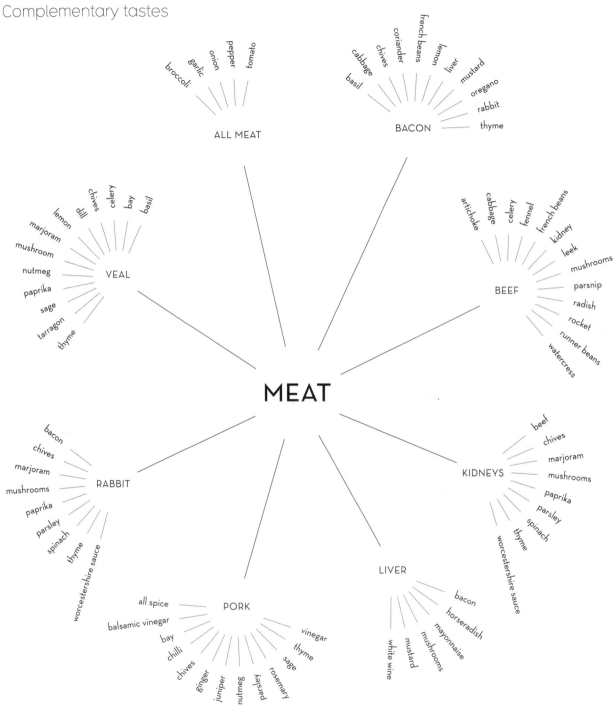

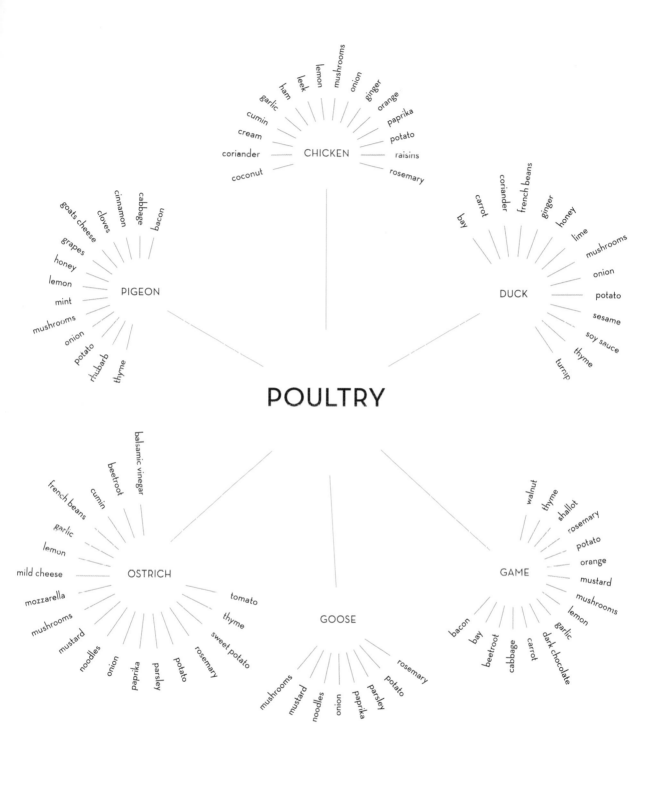

POULTRY

CHICKEN: garlic, ham, leek, lemon, mushrooms, onion, ginger, orange, paprika, potato, raisins, rosemary, coconut, coriander, cream, cumin

DUCK: bay, carrot, coriander, french beans, ginger, honey, lime, mushrooms, onion, potato, sesame, soy sauce, thyme, turnip

PIGEON: goats cheese, cloves, cinnamon, cabbage, bacon, grapes, honey, lemon, mint, mushrooms, onion, potato, rhubarb, thyme

GAME: walnut, thyme, shallot, rosemary, potato, orange, mustard, mushrooms, lemon, garlic, dark chocolate, carrot, cabbage, beetroot, bay, bacon

OSTRICH: french beans, cumin, beetroot, balsamic vinegar, garlic, lemon, mild cheese, mozzarella, mushrooms, mustard, noodles, onion, paprika, parsley, potato, rosemary, sweet potato, thyme, tomato

GOOSE: mushrooms, mustard, noodles, onion, paprika, parsley, potato, rosemary

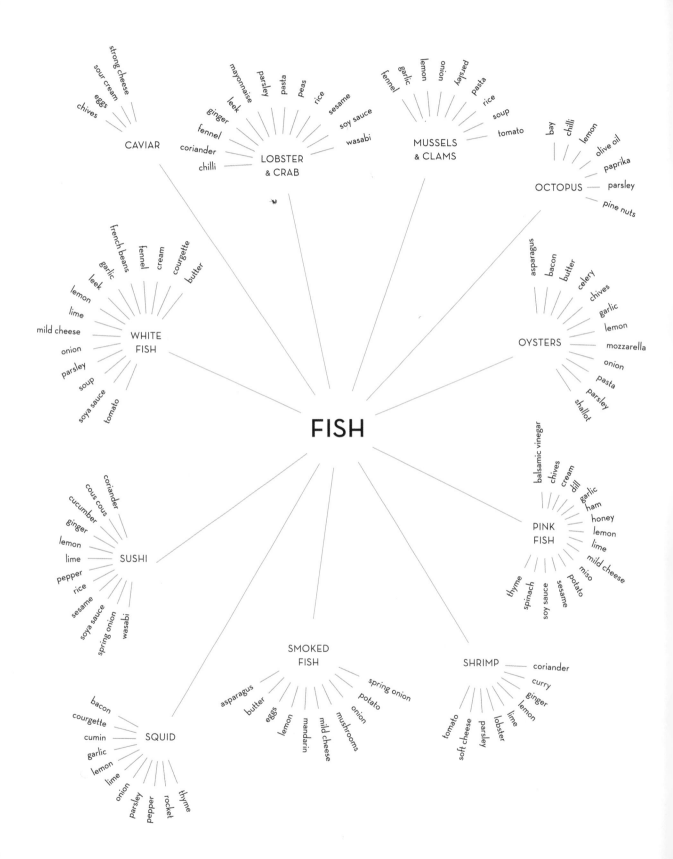

FISH

CAVIAR
strong cheese
sour cream
eggs
chives

LOBSTER & CRAB
mayonnaise
parsley
pasta
peas
rice
sesame
soy sauce
wasabi
leek
ginger
fennel
coriander
chilli

MUSSELS & CLAMS
fennel
garlic
lemon
onion
parsley
pasta
rice
soup
tomato

OCTOPUS
bay
chilli
lemon
olive oil
paprika
parsley
pine nuts

WHITE FISH
french beans
fennel
cream
courgette
butter
garlic
leek
lemon
lime
mild cheese
onion
parsley
soup
soya sauce
tomato

OYSTERS
asparagus
bacon
butter
celery
chives
garlic
lemon
mozzarella
onion
pasta
parsley
shallot

SUSHI
coriander
cous cous
cucumber
ginger
lemon
lime
pepper
rice
sesame
soya sauce
spring onion
wasabi

PINK FISH
balsamic vinegar
chives
cream
dill
garlic
ham
honey
lemon
lime
mild cheese
miso
potato
sesame
soy sauce
spinach
thyme

SMOKED FISH
spring onion
potato
onion
mushrooms
mild cheese
mandarin
lemon
eggs
butter
asparagus

SHRIMP
coriander
curry
ginger
lemon
lime
lobster
parsley
soft cheese
tomato

SQUID
bacon
courgette
cumin
garlic
lemon
lime
onion
parsley
pepper
rocket
thyme

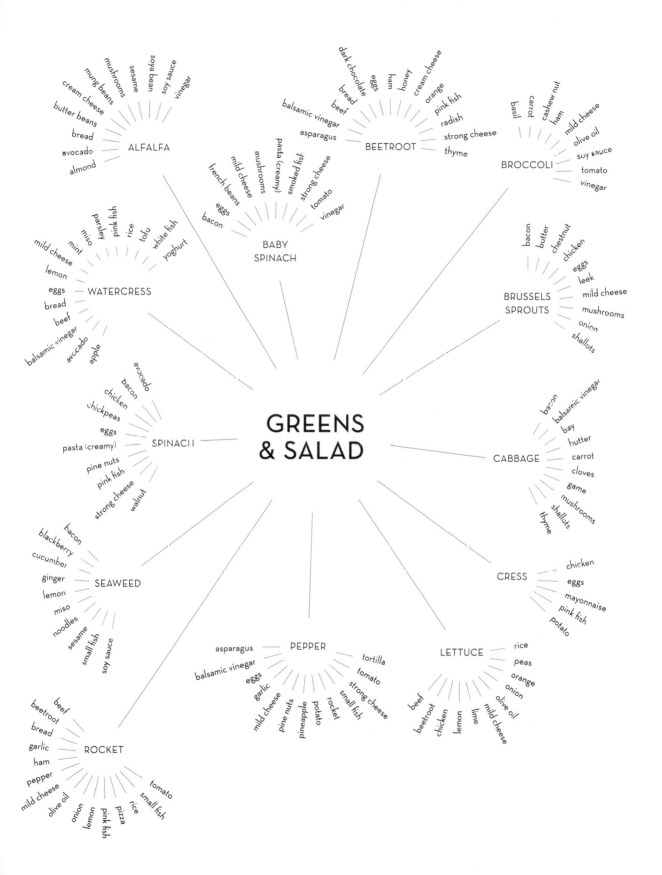

GREENS & SALAD

ALFALFA
soya bean, soy sauce, vinegar, sesame, mushrooms, mung beans, cream cheese, butter beans, bread, avocado, almond

BEETROOT
dark chocolate, ham, honey, cream cheese, eggs, orange, bread, pink fish, beef, radish, balsamic vinegar, strong cheese, asparagus, thyme

BROCCOLI
carrot, cashew nut, basil, ham, mild cheese, olive oil, soy sauce, tomato, vinegar

BABY SPINACH
pasta (creamy), smoked fish, mushrooms, strong cheese, mild cheese, tomato, french beans, vinegar, eggs, bacon

WATERCRESS
parsley, pink fish, mint, rice, miso, tofu, mild cheese, white fish, lemon, yoghurt, eggs, bread, beef, balsamic vinegar, avocado, apple

BRUSSELS SPROUTS
bacon, butter, chestnut, chicken, eggs, leek, mild cheese, mushrooms, onion, shallots

SPINACH
avocado, bacon, chicken, chickpeas, eggs, pasta (creamy), pine nuts, pink fish, strong cheese, walnut

CABBAGE
bacon, balsamic vinegar, bay, butter, carrot, cloves, game, mushrooms, shallots, thyme

SEAWEED
bacon, blackberry, cucumber, ginger, lemon, miso, noodles, sesame, small fish, soy sauce

CRESS
chicken, eggs, mayonnaise, pink fish, potato

PEPPER
asparagus, tortilla, balsamic vinegar, tomato, eggs, strong cheese, garlic, small fish, mild cheese, rocket, pine nuts, potato, pineapple

LETTUCE
rice, peas, orange, onion, olive oil, beef, mild cheese, beetroot, lime, chicken, lemon

ROCKET
beef, beetroot, bread, garlic, ham, pepper, mild cheese, olive oil, onion, lemon, pink fish, pizza, rice, small fish, tomato

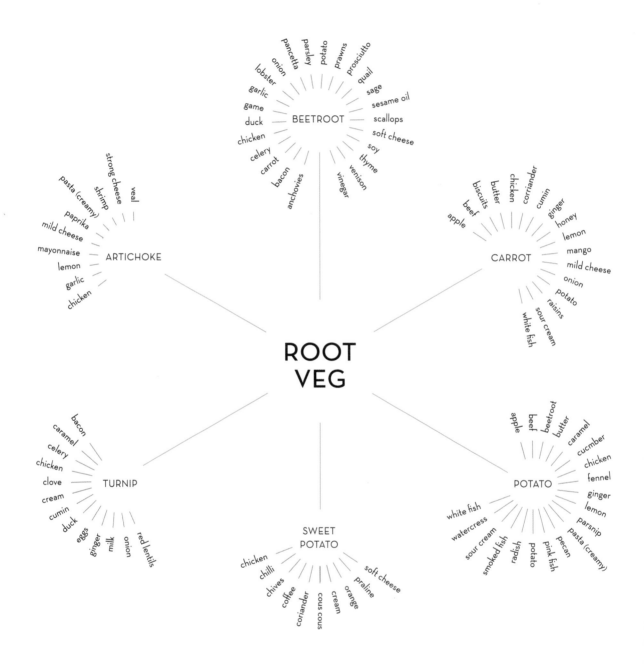

ROOT
VEG

BEETROOT

onion
pancetta
parsley
potato
prawns
prosciutto
quail
sage
sesame oil
scallops
soft cheese
soy
thyme
venison
vinegar
anchovies
bacon
carrot
celery
chicken
duck
game
garlic
lobster

ARTICHOKE

veal
strong cheese
shrimp
pasta (creamy)
paprika
mild cheese
mayonnaise
lemon
garlic
chicken

CARROT

chicken
coriander
cumin
ginger
honey
lemon
mango
mild cheese
onion
potato
raisins
sour cream
white fish
butter
biscuits
beef
apple

TURNIP

bacon
caramel
celery
chicken
clove
cream
cumin
duck
eggs
ginger
milk
onion
red lentils

SWEET
POTATO

chicken
chilli
chives
coffee
coriander
cous cous
cream
orange
praline
soft cheese

POTATO

apple
beef
beetroot
butter
caramel
cucmber
chicken
fennel
ginger
lemon
parsnip
pasta (creamy)
pecan
pink fish
potato
radish
smoked fish
sour cream
watercress
white fish

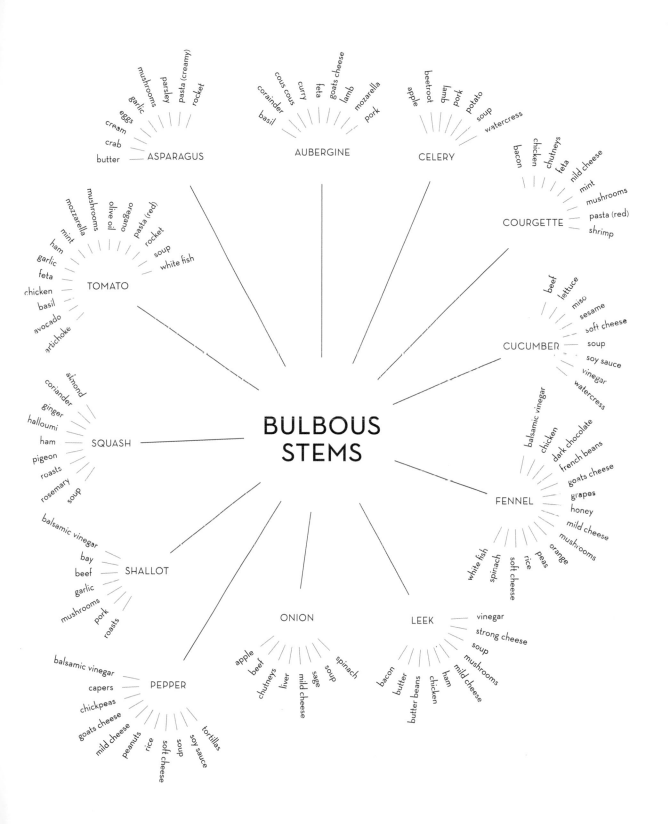

BULBOUS STEMS

ASPARAGUS: butter, crab, cream, eggs, garlic, mushrooms, parsley, pasta (creamy), rocket

AUBERGINE: basil, corainder, cous cous, curry, feta, goats cheese, lamb, mozarella, pork

CELERY: apple, beetroot, lamb, pork, potato, soup, watercress

COURGETTE: bacon, chicken, chutneys, feta, mild cheese, mint, mushrooms, pasta (red), shrimp

TOMATO: garlic, ham, mint, mozzarella, mushrooms, olive oil, oregano, pasta (red), rocket, soup, white fish, feta, chicken, basil, avocado, artichoke

CUCUMBER: beef, lettuce, miso, sesame, soft cheese, soup, soy sauce, vinegar, watercress

SQUASH: almond, coriander, ginger, halloumi, ham, pigeon, roasts, rosemary, soup

FENNEL: balsamic vinegar, chicken, dark chocolate, french beans, goats cheese, grapes, honey, mild cheese, mushrooms, orange, peas, soft cheese, spinach, white fish

SHALLOT: balsamic vinegar, bay, beef, garlic, mushrooms, pork, roasts

PEPPER: balsamic vinegar, capers, chickpeas, goats cheese, mild cheese, peanuts, rice, soft cheese, soup, soy sauce, tortillas

ONION: apple, beef, chutneys, liver, mild cheese, sage, soup, spinach

LEEK: bacon, butter, butter beans, chicken, ham, mild cheese, mushrooms, soup, strong cheese, vinegar

source: general internet and bbc.co.uk/food

Extinct
Most endangered species

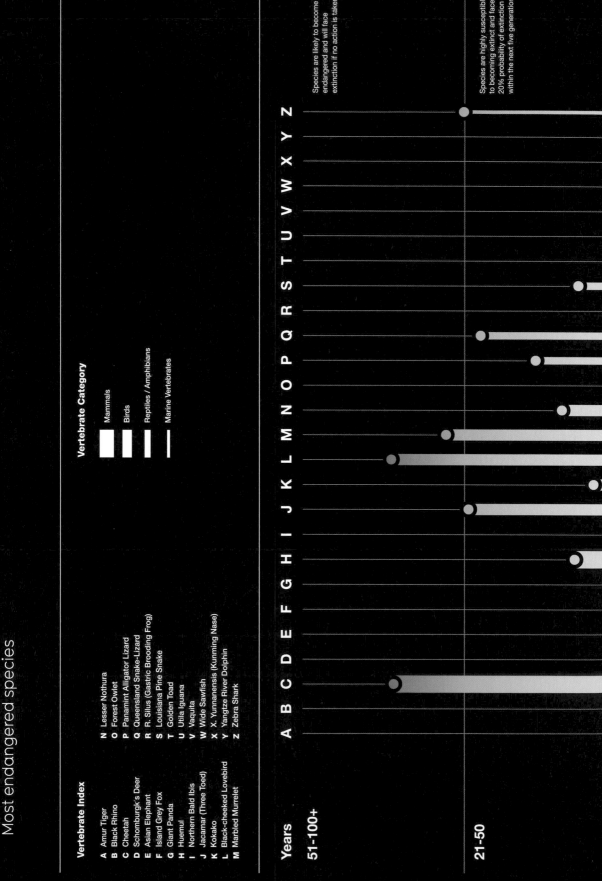

Vertebrate Index

A Amur Tiger
B Black Rhino
C Cheetah
D Schomburgk's Deer
E Asian Elephant
F Island Grey Fox
G Giant Panda
H Huemul
I Northern Bald Ibis
J Jacamar (Three Toed)
K Kokako
L Black-cheeked Lovebird
M Marbled Murrelet

N Lesser Nothura
O Forest Owlet
P Panamint Alligator Lizard
Q Queensland Snake-Lizard
R R. Silus (Gastric Brooding Frog)
S Louisiana Pine Snake
T Golden Toad
U Utila Iguana
V Vaquita
W Wide Sawfish
X X. Yunnanensis (Kunming Nase)
Y Yangtze River Dolphin
z Zebra Shark

Vertebrate Category

Mammals

Birds

Reptiles / Amphibians

Marine Vertebrates

Years

51-100+

Species are likely to become
endangered and will face
extinction if no action is taken

21-50

Species are highly susceptibl...
to becoming extinct and face
20% probability of extinction
within the next five generation...

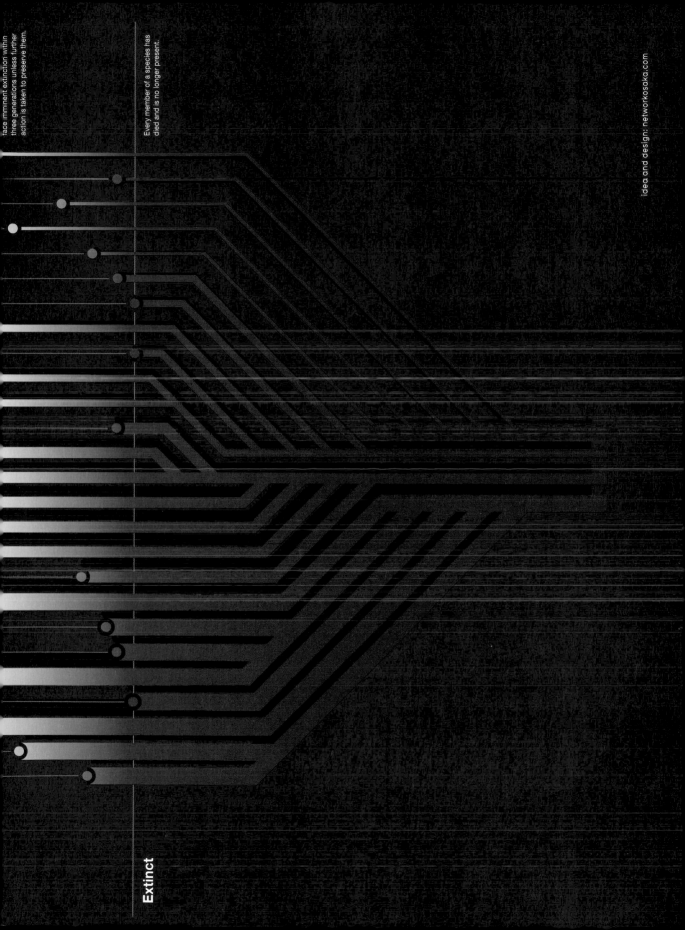

face imminent extinction within
three generations unless further
action is taken to preserve them.

Every member of a species has
died and is no longer present.

Extinct

International Number Ones

Because every country is the best at something

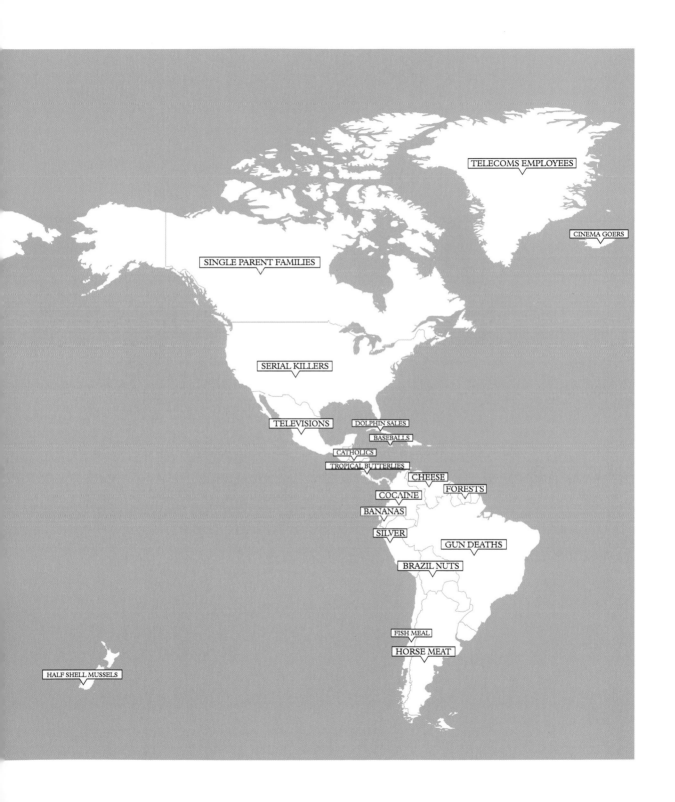

TELECOMS EMPLOYEES

CINEMA GOERS

SINGLE PARENT FAMILIES

SERIAL KILLERS

TELEVISIONS

DOLPHIN SALES

BASEBALLS

CATHOLICS

TROPICAL BUTTERLIES

CHEESE

FORESTS

COCAINE

BANANAS

SILVER

GUN DEATHS

BRAZIL NUTS

FISH MEAL

HORSE MEAT

HALF SHELL MUSSELS

The Poison

Margarita
- 1 Lime juice
- 1 Orange liqueur
- 1 Tequila

Martini
- 1 Vermouth
- 7 Gin

Manhattan
- Angoustura
- 1 Sweet Vermouth
- 4 Whisky

Mai Tai
- 8 White rum
- 1 Lime juice
- 1 Sugar syrup
- 1 Orange liqueur

Cosmopolitan
- Lime juice
- 1 Cranberry juice
- 1 Orange liqueur
- 1.5 Vodka

White Russian
- 12 Vodka
- 12 Kahlua
- 8 Single cream

Long Island Iced Tea
- 1 Sugar syrup
- 6 Lemon juice
- 6 Vodka
- 6 Gin
- 6 White rum

Mojito
- Mint leaves
- 12 White rum
- 2 Sugar
- 1 Lime juice
- 12 Club soda

Harvey Wallbanger
- 1 Galliano
- 2 Vodka
- 6 Orange juice

Whiskey Sour
- .75 Sugar syrup
- 1.5 Bourbon
- 1.5 Lemon juice

Daiquiri
- 2 Lime juice
- 1 Sugar syrup
- 8 White rum

Bloody Mary
- White pepper
- Worcester sauce
- Tabasco
- 1 Lemon juice
- 40 Tomato juice
- 12 Vodka

The Remedy
Hangover cures from around the world

pepper

egg yolk
-
1 lemon juice
1worcester s.

Traditional

egg yolk

1 worcester sauce

American

beer

Dutch

sour pickle juice

Polish

coffee

Italian

salt

strong coffee

French

water
1 salt
2 sugar

Isotonic

water
1 honey
1 cider vinegar

Icelandic

10 cow's stomach
5 root veg soup
2 cream
1 vinegar

Romanian

strong green tea

Chinese

baked beans
egg
bacon
sausage

British

diarrhoea medicine

water

Medical

mustard berries
juniper berries
pickled herring

Germanic

ginger ale
1 lime juice
6 brandy
6 gin

Hedonistic

source: Google

Salad Dressings
All in proportion

Vinaigrette

12 Oil
Vinegar
1 Mustard

Ranch

6 Buttermilk
8 Cottage cheese
2 Chives
1 Garlic
1 Parmesan

Honey

8 Oil
4 Honey
1 Garlic

Worcester sauce

Creamy Herb

8 Sour cream
16 Mayonnaise
8 Parsley
4 Basil
Chives
Vinegar
3 Onion
1 Garlic

Mayonnaise
Garlic
Mustard

Creamy Garlic

4 Oil
1 White wine vinegar

Lemon juice

Oil, Lemon & Garlic

6 Oil
Vinegar
1 Garlic

Worcester sauce
Garlic
Sugar

Thousand Island

16 Oil
White wine vinegar
2 Black olives
1 Egg

Lemon juice

Lemon, Herb & Yoghurt

16 Yoghurt
1 Mustard
Parsley, chives

Orange

2 Oil
8 Orange juice
1 Mustard
1 Root ginger

Oil & Lemon

6 Oil
2 Lemon juice

Lemon juice
Double cream

Caesar

8 Oil
2 Parmesan
1 Anchovy
1 Mustard
1 Garlic
1 Egg yolk

Lime juice
Soy sauce

Curry

4 Oil
1 Curry powder

Not Nice

Food colourings linked to unpleasant health effects

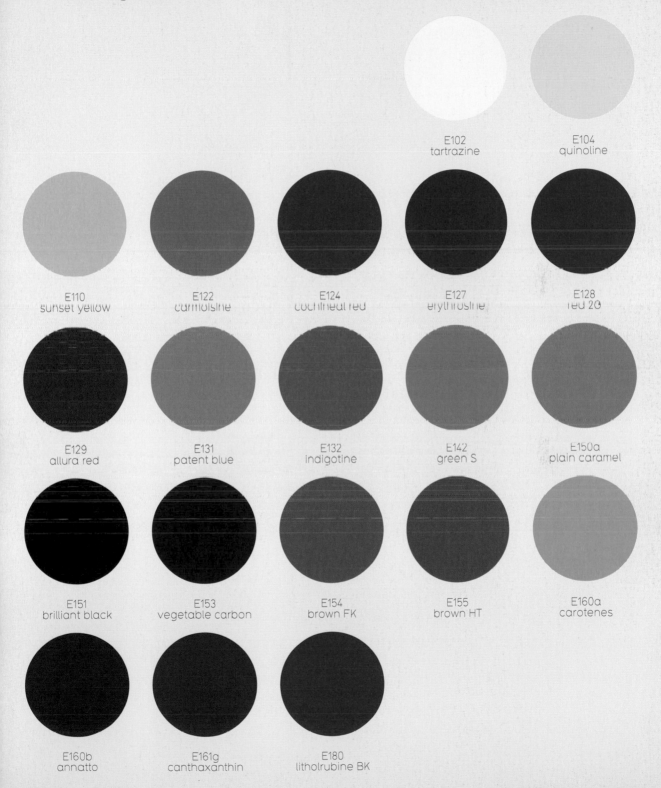

E102
tartrazine

E104
quinoline

E110
sunset yellow

E122
carmoisine

E124
cochineal red

E127
erythrosine

E128
red 2G

E129
allura red

E131
patent blue

E132
indigotine

E142
green S

E150a
plain caramel

E151
brilliant black

E153
vegetable carbon

E154
brown FK

E155
brown HT

E160a
carotenes

E160b
annatto

E161g
canthaxanthin

E180
litholrubine BK

source: Centre For Science In The Public Interest, Cspinet.org

20th Century Death

What's killed the most?

famine
111m

food
76m

 obesity 11m

diabetes 30m

heart disease 35m

disease
1390m

smallpox
500m

measles
200m

meningitis
190m

tuberculosis
150m

whooping cough
30m

influenza
30m

HIV
25m

ideology
16m

8.5m   7.1m   0.1m

war
124m

revolution
9.5m

5m   2m   1.6m   1m

nature
9.7m

tobacco
71m

suicide
70m

murder
20m

technology
0.2m

animals
4m

0.5m   90,000   29,000   5000   4000   100   100

source: Internet and wikipedia. Data very coarse. Some guesswork and extrapolation

THE GLOBAL WARMING SCEPTICS

We don't believe there is any credible evidence that mankind's activities are the cause of global warming if that's even happening at all. There's only circumstantial evidence of a link between carbon dioxide levels and rising global temperatures.

Rising CO_2 levels are not always linked with rising temperatures

Because of extreme weather, Arctic temperature is often a dramatic barometer of global climate. But the temperatures there match poorly with human CO_2 emissions.

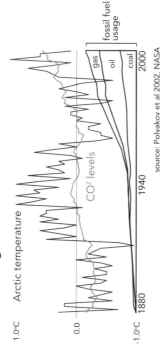

1.0°C   Arctic temperature

0.0

-1.0°C   1880   1940   2000

CO_2 levels

fossil fuel usage
gas
oil
coal

source: Polyakov et al 2002. NASA

In the past, CO_2 rises have occured after temperature rises

Recognise this from *The Inconvenient Truth?* Al Gore famously showed that temperature and CO_2 are clearly linked back over 400,000 years. But if you zoom in.....

...you see that CO_2 levels rise 800 years after the temperature does. This massive lag proves that CO_2 can't cause global warming!

THE SCIENTIFIC CONSENSUS

The earth's climate is rapidly warming. The cause is a thickening layer of carbon dioxide pollution, caused by humanity's activities. It traps heat in the atmosphere, creating a "greenhouse effect" which heats the earth. A rise in global temperatures of 3 to 9 degrees will cause devastation.

A single graph for a single small area is not enough evidence

You can't draw conclusions about the warming of the whole planet just by looking at a small area. It's like comparing apples and pears. It's impossible to tell what caused the warming of the Arctic in the 1930. Or whether it's the same mechanism that's causing global warming today.

We don't claim CO_2 caused temperature rises in the past

We say, because of its greenhouse effect, CO_2 makes natural temperature rises worse. Much worse in fact.

Historically, global warming cycles last 5000 years. The 800 year lag only shows that CO_2 did not cause the first 16% of warming. The other 4200 years were likely to have been caused by a CO_2 greenhouse effect.

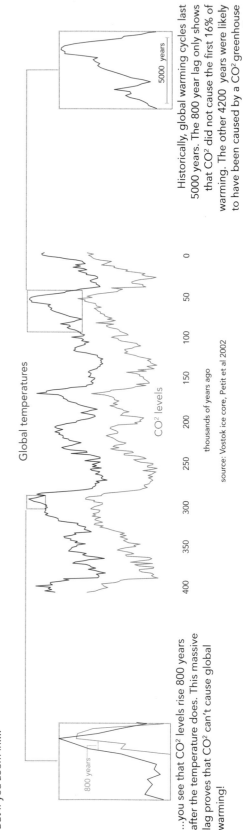

Global temperatures

CO_2 levels

400   350   300   250   200   150   100   50   0

thousands of years ago

source: Vostok ice core, Petit et al 2002

800 years

5000 years

We don't even have accurate temperature records

90% of temperature recording stations are on land. 70% of the world's surface is ocean. Cities and towns heat the atmosphere around land-based weather stations enough to distort the record of historical temperatures. It's called the urban heat island effect. And it's why we can't trust temperature records.

It was actually hotter in medieval times than today

Between AD 800 and 1300 was a Medieval Warm Period where temperatures were very high. Grapes were grown in England. The Vikings colonized Greenland. This occurred centuries before we began pumping CO_2 into the atmosphere.
More proof that CO_2 and temperature are not linked. Because of this - and to make 20th century warming look unique - UN scientists constantly play down this medieval period in their data.

The famous "hockey stick" temperature graph has been discredited

Made famous by Al Gore, the "hockey stick" graph shows that 20th century temperatures are showing an alarming rise. But the hockey stick appears or disappears depending on the statistical methods employed. So unreliable has it become that the UN's International Panel On Climate Change dropped it from their 2007 report.

We do have accurate temperature records

Distortion of temperature records is a very real phenomenon. But it's one climate scientists are well aware of. Detailed filters are used to remove the effect from the records.

Global weather recording stations

source: National Environmental Satellite Data and Information Service

It was hotter in some areas of the world and not in others

This was likely a local warming, rather than a global warming, equivalent to warming today. Ice cores show us that there were periods of both cold and warmth at the time. And there's no evidence it affected the southern hemisphere at all.
The records also show that the earth may have been slightly cooler (by 0.03 degrees Celsius) during the 'medieval warm period' than today.

Medieval Warm Period

Global temperatures

2.5°C

0°C

-2.5°C

800   1000   1200   1400   1600   1800   2000

source: NESDIS (smoothed data)

Reworked, enhanced versions still show the "hockey stick" shape

The hockey stick is 8 years old. There are dozens of other newer, more detailed temperature reconstructions. Each one is different due to different methods and data. But they all show similar striking patterns: the 20th century is the warmest of the entire record. And that warming is most dramatic after 1920 (when industrial activity starting releasing CO_2 into the atmosphere).

The Original "Hockey Stick"

A Modern 'Hockey Stick' Graph

0.5°C

0°C

-0.5°C

1880   1980   1400   1980

source: Author's composite Briffa Anmann & Wahl Mann 2003 Mann 1998

THE GLOBAL WARMING SCEPTICS

THE SCIENTIFIC CONSENSUS

Ice core data is unreliable

A lot of our temperature records come from measuring the gases trapped in ice cores. These are segments of deep ice unmelted for hundreds of thousands of years. The trapped air inside acts as "photographs" of the contents of the atmosphere going back millennia. But ice-cores are not "closed systems" that preserve ancient air perfectly. Air can get in and out. Water can also absorb the gases, changing the result. And deep ice is under huge amounts of pressure. Enough to squeeze gas out. All in all this adds up to make ice cores unreliable.

Ice records are reliable

Ice core data is taken from many different samples to reduce errors. Also, other evidence (temperature records, tree rings etc) back these readings up. All these results combined make the records very reliable.

The predictions of future global warming don't depend on ice cores. But ice cores do show that the climate is sensitive to changes in cycles and that CO_2 has a strong influence.

Overall, CO_2 levels from different ice cores are remarkably similar.

When the evidence doesn't fit, the scientists edit the evidence

Ice core data from Siple in the Arctic shows the concentrations of CO_2 in the atmosphere in 1890 to be 328 parts per million. However, according to the consensus, that level was not reached until 1973. So the rise in CO_2 levels happens 83 years too early.

To fix it, scientists moved the graph 83 years to the right to make the data exactly fit.

Scientists correct their results when new evidence comes to light

No other ice core data in the world shows CO_2 levels rising above 290 parts per million in the last 650,000 years. It's possible it might have happened for a year or a day. But consistently, no.

Some areas of ice are more porous than others. At Siple, the more recent shallow ice was quite porous. So new air was able to circulate quite far down. That affected the record.

We detected and compensated for this. That's why the data has been shifted.

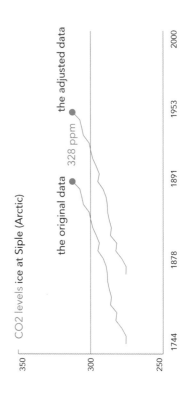

CO2 levels ice at Siple (Arctic)

the original data

328 ppm

the adjusted data

350

300

250

1744   1878   1891   1953   2000

Source: Neftel 1985, Friedli 1986

CO_2 only stays in the atmosphere for 5 to 10 years, not the 50–200 years stated by UN scientists

The ocean absorbs the CO_2 so it can't accumulate to dangerous levels in the atmosphere. In fact, the oceans are so vast they can absorb 50 times as much CO_2 as there is in the atmosphere - more than all the fossil fuels on the planet!

Conclusion: humans can't have been emitting CO_2 fast enough to account for all the extra CO_2 in the atmosphere.

CO_2 absorption by the oceans

CO_2
atmos

shallow
ocean
5-10 years

"fertilizer" for   dissolved as
plankton   carbonic acid

dead plankton   shells, bones

deep ocean
50-200 years

When you take the entire complex ocean-climate system into account 50–200 years is more accurate

CO_2 is absorbed in 5 to 10 years by the *shallow* ocean. Not the deep ocean. It takes 50-200 years for CO_2 to be mixed into the deep ocean where it stays. CO_2 in the shallow ocean however is prone to escaping back into the atmosphere. So CO_2 absorbed by the ocean often comes straight back out again.

Also the more carbon the ocean absorbs, the less it's able to absorb. It becomes saturated. It's a very complex process. But if you take the entire ocean-climate system, full absorption of atmospheric CO_2 takes around 50,000 years.

SCEPTICAL CONCLUSION

Man-made CO_2 cannot be driving climate change

Whatever affects global temperatures and causes global warming is not CO_2. Whatever the cause, it works like this. The cause affects the climate balance. Then the temperature changes accordingly. The oceans then adjust over a period of decades and centuries. Then the balance of CO_2 in the atmosphere increases.

So the global panic about CO_2 causing global warming is baseless and fear-mongering. The UN's reports on the matter are biased, unscientific and alarmist.

CONSENSUS CONCLUSION

Man-made CO_2 is driving climate change this time.

We don't claim that greenhouse gases are the major cause of the ice ages and warming cycles. What drives climate change has long been believed to be the variation in the earth's orbit around the sun over thousands of years.

In a normal warming cycle, the sun heats the earth, the earth gets hotter. The oceans warm up releasing huge amounts of CO_2. This creates a greenhouse effect that makes warming much, much more intense.

That's why humanity's release of CO_2 is so perilous. We're out of step with the natural cycle. And we haven't even got to the stage where the oceans warm up.

Behind Every Great Man...
Dictators' wives

	Nadezhda Alliluyeva	Eva Braun	Yang Kaihui	Imelda Marcos	Mirjana (Mira) Markovic
Wife					
Husband	Stalin	Hitler	Mao	Marcos	Milosevic
Pre-marital occupation	clerk	assistant and model	communist!	beauty queen	professor of sociology
How they met	her father sheltered Stalin in 1911 after he escaped from Siberian exile	she was assistant to his personal photographer	her father was Mao's teacher	whirlwind courtship during "holy week"	at school, she borrowed his card to rent *Antigone* from the library, Oh yeah?
Years of marriage	13	about 40 minutes	8	35	32
Children	2		3	4	2
Rumoured quality of marriage	strained and violent	changeable	troubled	good	very good
Political power rating	none	✊ (1)	none	✊✊✊✊✊ (5)	✊✊✊✊ (4)
Key governmental roles	none	none	prominent female member of party	Governor of Manila, Ambassador plenipotentiary	puppet-master, leader of "Yugoslav United Left"
Style rating	none	👠👠👠👠 (4)	👠👠👠👠 (4)	👠👠👠👠👠 (5)	👠👠👠👠👠 (5)
Nickname	none	The Rolleiflex Girl	none	The Steel Butterfly	The Red Witch
Notable talents	none - super dull	photography, athletics	very intelligent	none	politics
Trademark/idiosyncrasy	left-handed	nude sunbathing	feminist	very ostentatious and flamboyant	would berate her husband in front of state officials, wore only black Versace
Obsessions and pathologies	suicide	lots of make-up	good communists don't covet material things	shoes, clothes, paintings	media products, plastic surgeons, rich friends
Most salacious rumour	she was Stalin's daughter	she was pregnant when she died OR she didn't sleep in the same room as Hitler	said she would have killed herself when she and Mao divorced if she didn't have kids	sent a plane to pick up white sand from Australia for her beach resort	ordered the murder of Ivan Stambolic, a rival to her husband. Had at least four officials killed after they disagreed with her. Disappeared a journalist who criticised her.
Reason for death	officially "appendicitis" - really, shot	suicide - bit into a cyanide capsule	publicly executed by the Nationalists	still alive	still alive

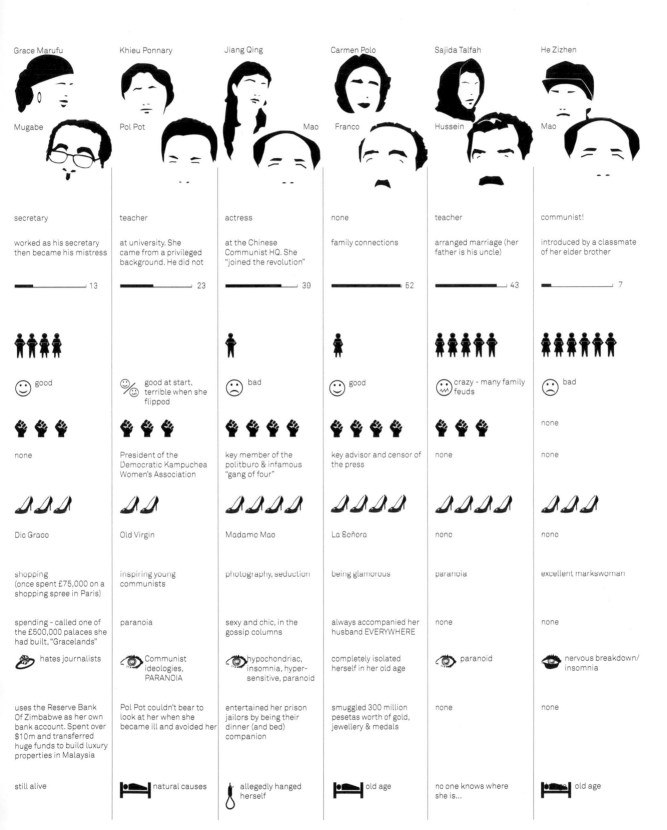

	Grace Marufu / Mugabe	Khieu Ponnary / Pol Pot	Jiang Qing / Mao	Carmen Polo / Franco	Sajida Talfah / Hussein	He Zizhen / Mao
profession	secretary	teacher	actress	none	teacher	communist!
how they met	worked as his secretary then became his mistress	at university. She came from a privileged background. He did not	at the Chinese Communist HQ. She "joined the revolution"	family connections	arranged marriage (her father is his uncle)	introduced by a classmate of her elder brother
age gap	13	23	39	52	43	7
children	4	1	1	1	5	6
relationship	good	good at start, terrible when she flipped	bad	good	crazy - many family feuds	bad
power	none	President of the Democratic Kampuchea Women's Association	key member of the politburo & infamous "gang of four"	key advisor and censor of the press	none	none
nickname	Die Grace	Old Virgin	Madame Mao	La Señora	none	none
known for	shopping (once spent £75,000 on a shopping spree in Paris)	inspiring young communists	photography, seduction	being glamorous	paranoia	excellent markswoman
	spending - called one of the £500,000 palaces she had built, "Gracelands"	paranoia	sexy and chic, in the gossip columns	always accompanied her husband EVERYWHERE	none	none
	hates journalists	Communist ideologies, PARANOIA	hypochondriac, insomnia, hyper-sensitive, paranoid	completely isolated herself in her old age	paranoid	nervous breakdown/ insomnia
	uses the Reserve Bank Of Zimbabwe as her own bank account. Spent over $10m and transferred huge funds to build luxury properties in Malaysia	Pol Pot couldn't bear to look at her when she became ill and avoided her	entertained her prison jailors by being their dinner (and bed) companion	smuggled 300 million pesetas worth of gold, jewellery & medals	none	none
death	still alive	natural causes	allegedly hanged herself	old age	no one knows where she is...	old age

source: Wikipedia

Bubble chart

Bubble comparison

Bubble race

Bubble race with strings

Bubble clusters

Bubble network

Bubble treemap

Bubble star ring

Infographic

Charticle

Word cloud

Matrix

Family tree

Mind map (tidy)

Mind map (organic)

Concept map

Bubbles (nested)

Polar grid (segmented)

Sun burst

Coxcomb

Polar grid

Icicle pie

Mandala (complex)

Mandala

Radar

Spiral

Concept fan

Fan

Synergy map

Bubble mind map

Ven bubbles

Semantic polar grid

Decision tree

Dunno what to call it

Conetree

Icicle tree

Treemap

Flowchart

Sankey

Periodic table

Types of Information Visualization

source: Edward Tufte, visual-literarcy.org

Pass the...
A table of condiments that periodically go bad

#	Symbol	Name	Shelf life
1	Tz	Tzatziki	2 days
2	Sa	Salsa	2 days
3	Gu	Guacamole	2 days
4	Ps	Peanut/Satay sauce	2 days
5	Be	Beef extract	3 days
6	L	Lemon Juice	3 days
7	Sc	Sour cream	3 days
8	Ss	Sweet and sour sauce	3 days
9	Ra	Raita	5 days
10	Mg	Meat gravy	5 days
11	Hu	Hummus	5 days
12	Ma	home-made mayonnaise	1 week
13	Wc	Whipped cream	1 week
14	Og	Onion gravy	1 week
15	O	Oyster sauce	2 weeks
16	Cu	Custard	3 weeks
17	Lc	Lime chutney	3 weeks
18	Pa	Parmesan cheese	3 weeks
19	B	Butter	3 weeks
20	M	Margarine	3 weeks
21	Gs	Granulated sweetener	3 weeks
22	J	Jam	1 month
23	Tr	Treacle	1 month
24	Mg	Mango chutney	1 month
25	T	Tomato chutney	1 month
26	Vg	Vegetable gravy	1 month
27	Bq	BBQ sauce	1 month
28	Ch	Chilli sauce	1 month
29	Pl	Plum sauce	1 month
30	Hs	Hoisin sauce	1 month
31	Fd	French dressing	1 month
32	Dm	Dijon mustard	1 month
33	Lc	Lemon curd	6 weeks
34	Bs	Brown sauce	6 weeks
35	H	Horseradish	6 weeks
36	K	Ketchup	6 weeks
37	Mi	Mint sauce	6 weeks
38	Ta	Tartar sauce	6 weeks
39	Pk	Pickle	6 weeks
40	Pi	Piccalilli	6 weeks
41	Sp	Sweet pickle	6 weeks
42	Id	Italian dressing	6 weeks
43	Td	Thousand island dressing	6 weeks
44	Ma	Mayonnaise	2 months
45	Sc	Salad cream	2 months
46	Fs	Flaxseed oil	2 months
47	Ca	Cayenne pepper	3 months
48	Ch	Chilli powder	3 months
49	Bm	Brown mustard	3 months
50	Wa	Wasabi	3 months
51	Ma	Marmalade	6 months
52	Pb	Peanut butter	6 months
53	Y	Yeast extract	6 months
54	Ta	Tahini	6 months
55	Ms	Maple syrup	1 year
56	Pa	Palm oil	1 year
57	P	Peanut oil	1 year
58	So	Soybean oil	1 year
59	Sf	Sunflower oil	1 year
60	C	Cocoa	1 year
61	Bb	Black pepper	1 year
62	Ym	Yellow mustard	18 months
63	Wv	White wine vinegar	2 years
64	Cv	Cider vinegar	2 years
65	W	Worcester sauce	2 years
66	Sy	Soy sauce	3 years
67	Ol	Olive oil	4 years
68	Bv	Balsamic vinegar	5 years
69	Mv	Malt vinegar	indefinite
70	H	Honey	indefinite
71	Sa	Salt	indefinite
72	Su	Sugar	indefinite

idea: Internet Apocryphal // source: Google

NATURE

vs.

NURTURE

Your genes control everything. Hair colour. Behaviour. Intelligence. Personality. Sure, environment has a role, but it's your genes that rule you.

You learn pretty much everything you do. From standing and walking to talking and socializing. Your environment and your choices make you who you are…

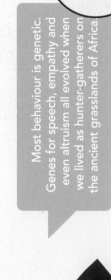

NATURE:

Most behaviour is genetic. Genes for speech, empathy and even altruism all evolved when we lived as hunter-gatherers on the ancient grasslands of Africa.

The proof is in the brain. It has evolved "modules" for all human abilities, even for religious experience!

Oh yeah? Animal breeders know it takes only a few generations of controlled mating to influence behaviours like fierceness or tameness in dogs.

Genes change the brain too. And at a more fundamental level, before your so-called "choices" come in. Try "deciding" to override a genetic expression. You can't! Hah!

Okay then, what about behavioural problems such as depression, mental illness and autism? They're all highly inheritable.

NURTURE:

The evidence for that ancient lifestyle is complete guesswork.

Nah. Those "structures" could simply be projections of human interpretation on the brain. Behaviour isn't genetically evolved. We learn it.

Dogs, maybe. But complex human behaviour like musical ability or humour? C'mon. These are learnt. In fact, learning, we now know, changes the physical structure of the brain! So much for genes.

Most genetic expression, from traits to behaviours, are triggered by your environment. Nurture comes first!

Yeah it's fashionable to say that yes. But, even after years of study, researchers have failed to turn up a

Ahhhh but behavioural disorders like autism are highly inheritable. In identical twins, if one twin is autistic, the other has a 60% chance of being autistic. In non-identical twins the chance is only 5%. That goes for intelligence too.

In autism, maybe. But you can't then stretch it to all behaviour and certainly not intelligence. Intelligent parents *teach* their kids to be intelligent.

But don't intelligent parents also provide the genes for high IQ? Twins separated at birth are often remarkably similar in IQ and personality, even when they haven't met. This proves there are genetic influences for everything. Even taste in music!

Yeah but if it was all genes, you'd expect identical twins to be 100% the same. Figures for IQ may be high. But it's way less to non-existent for other traits like personality.

But identical twins reared apart become more alike, even when they haven't met. That means that genes must shape our personalities.

Frnnnnnnnn Many studies of twins are flawed and biased. Often they just compare identical twins reared apart after birth. They don't use "controls" of unrelated people with the same background as the twins to check that age, gender, ethnicity and cultural environment are not also influencing personality. The whole field is biased.

Pfff.

Grrrr!

CONCLUSION
50-50

Both nature and nurture each contribute
(in arguable proportions) to who we are.
They also "speak the same language".
That is, they both change the structure of the brain.
In summary, humans are dynamic creative organisms.
Learning and experience amplify the effect of genes on behaviour.

source: Skeptic.com

Postmodernism

Postmodernism is pretty much a buzz word now. Anything – and everything – can be described as postmodern now. The design of a building. The samples used in a record. The layout of a page. The collective mood of a generation. Cultural or political fragmentation. The rise of blogging and crowd-wisdom. Anything that starts with the word "meta". But what does it mean?

In art, where it all began, it's a style of sorts. Ironic and parodying. Very playful and very knowing. Knowing of history, culture, and often knowing of itself. Postmodern art and entertainment is often self-conscious. It calls attention to itself as a piece of art, or a production, or something constructed. A character who knows they are a character in a novel, for example. Or even the appearance of an author in their own book. (Like me, David, writing this. Hello.)

Overall, postmodern art says there's no difference between refined and popular culture, "high" or "low" brow. It rejects genres and hierarchies. Instead, it embraces complexity, contradiction, ambiguity, diversity, interconnectedness, and criss-crossing referentiality.

The idea is: let's not pretend that art can make meaning or is even meaningful. Let's just play with nonsense.

All of this springs from the discovery of a new relationship to truth. In a postmodern perspective, truth is a not single thing "out there" to be discovered. Instead truth must be assembled or constructed. Sometimes, it's constructed visibly, from many different components (i.e. scientists gathering results of multiple studies). Other times, it happens invisibly by society, or by cultural mechanisms and other processes that can't be easily seen by the individual.

So when somone "speaks the truth", what they are saying is actually an assemblage of their schooling, their cultural background, and the thoughts and opinions they've absorbed from their environment. In a way, you could say that their culture is speaking through them.

For that reason, it becomes more accurate and safer, in postmodern times, to assemble truth with the help of other people, rather than just decide it independently.

A clear example of this is the scientific method. Any scientist can do an experiment and declare a discovery about the world. But teams of other scientists must verify or "peer-review" that truth before it's safe to accept it. The truth here has been assembled by many people.

All the time, though, there is an understanding that even this final "truth" may well just be temporary or convenient, a place-holder to be changed or binned later on. (Well, that *should* be the case. Even scientific discoveries have a tendency to harden into dogma.)

If you accept this key postmodern insight, then immediately it becomes impossible for any individual to have a superior belief. There's no such thing as "absolute truth". No one "knows" the truth. Or can have a better truth than someone else. If an individual – or a group, organization or government – does claims to have truth and declares that truth to you, they are likely to be attempting to overpower and control you.

Confusingly, these kinds of entities are known as "Modernist". Modernity is all about order and rationality. The more ordered a society is, Modernists believe, the better it functions. If "order" is superior, then anything that promotes "disorder" has to be wrong. Taken to an extreme, that means anything different from the norm – ideas, beliefs, people – must be excluded. Or even destroyed. In the history of Western culture this has usually meant anyone non-white, non-male, non-heterosexual and non-rational.

This is one reason why tension still erupts between holders of "absolute truth" (say the Church) and postmodern secular societies. Or between an entity like an undemocratic government which seeks to control its populace and the internet, a truly postmodern piece of technology. This is because postmodernity has a powerful weapon that can very easily and very quickly corrode Modernist structures built on "old-fashioned" absolute truth: *deconstruction*.

If all truth is constructed, then deconstruction becomes useful. Really useful. If you deconstruct something, its meanings, intentions and agendas separate and rise to the surface very quickly – and everything quickly unravels.

Take a novel for example. You can deconstruct the structure of the text, and the personality of the characters. Then you can deconstruct the author's life story, their psychological background, and their culture and see how that influenced the text. If you keep going, you can start on the structure of human language and thought. Beyond that, a vast layer of human symbols. Beyond that ... well, you can just keep going...

Belief systems and modernist structures protect themselves from threats like deconstruction with "grand narratives". These are compelling stories to explain and justify why a certain belief system exists. They work to gloss over and mask the contradictions, instabilities and general "scariness" inherent in nature and human life.

Liberate the entire working class. Peace on Earth. There is one true God. Hollywood is one big happy family. History is progress. One day we will know everything. These are all grand narratives.

All modern societies – even those based on science – depend on these myths. Postmodernism rejects them on principle. Instead it goes for "mini-narratives", stories that explain small local events – all with an awareness that any situation, no matter how small, reflects in some way the global pattern of things. Think global, act local, basically.

So a postmodern society, unglossed-over by a grand narrative, must embrace the values of postmodernity as its key values. That means that complexity, diversity, contradiction, ambiguity, and interconnectedness all become central. In social terms that means a lack of obvious hierarchies (equal rights for all), embracing diversity (multi-culturalism), and that all voices should be heard (consensus). Interconnectedness is reflected in our technology and communications. In the 21st century anything that cannot be stored by a computer ceases to be knowledge.

That's the goal anyway. There are pitfalls. Runaway postmodernism creates a grey goo of no-meaning. Infinite consensus creates paralysis. Over-connection leads to saturation. Too much diversity leads to disconnection. Complexity to confusion.

So in the midst of all this confusion and noise and diversity, without a grand narrative, who are you? Postmodern personal values are not moral but instead values of participation, self-expression, creativity. The focus of spirituality shifts from security in absolute given truth to a search for significance in a chaotic world. The idea that there is anything stable or permanent disappears. The floor drops away. And you are left there, playing with nonsense.

source: constructed from Wikipedia, an essay by Mary Klages, University of Colorado, Wisegeek.com

Dangers of Death
You're going to go one way. Which way?

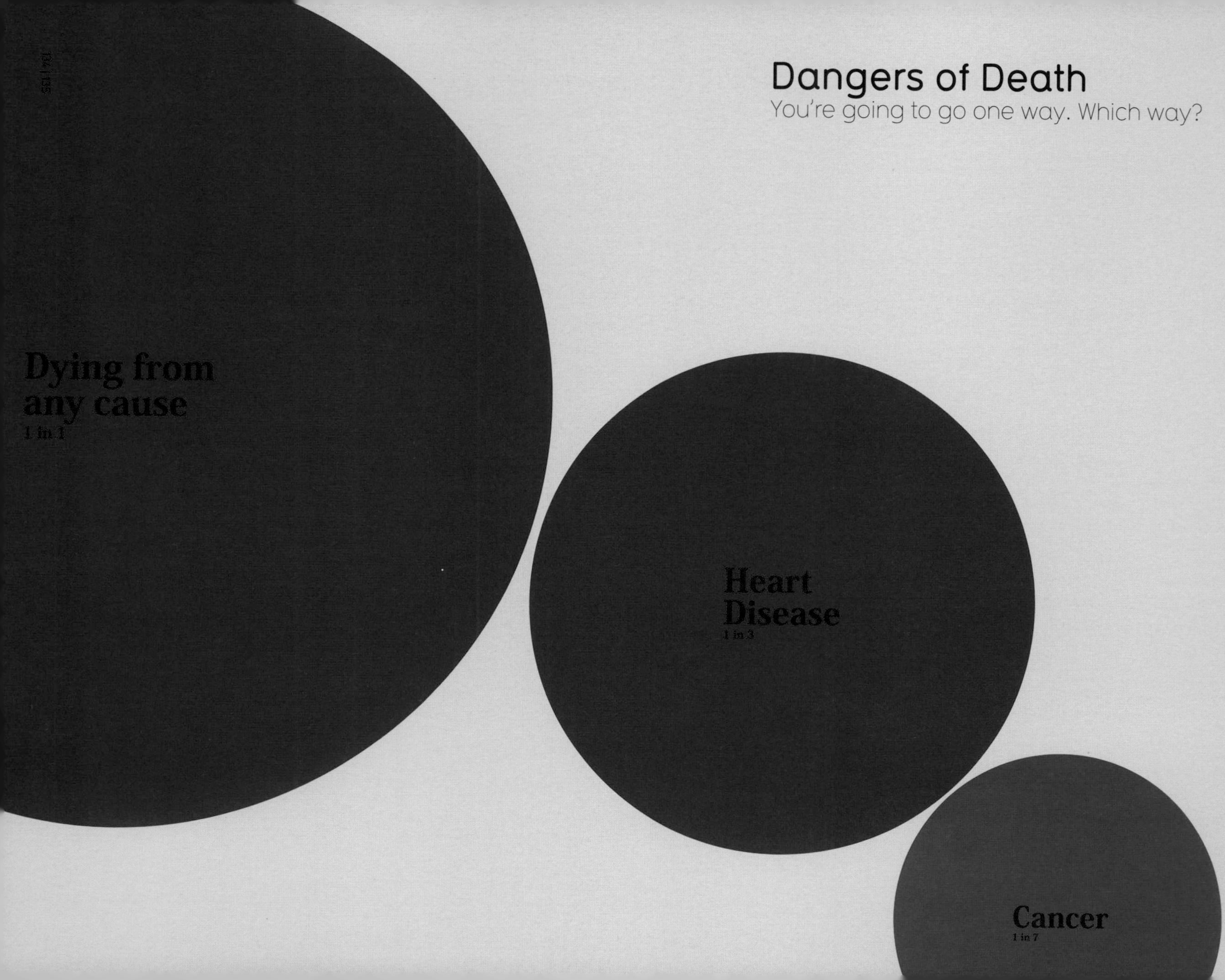

Cancer
1 in 7

Heart Disease
1 in 3

Dying from any cause
1 in 1

Stroke
1 in 23

Bus /train accident
1 in 77

Ageing sun engulfs Earth

Medical error (hospital)
1 in 300

Assault by firearm
1 in 325

House fire
1 in 1431

Diabetes
1 in 4996

Freak lawnmower accident
1 in 5300

Passive smoking
1 in 7895

Electrocution (home)
1 in 9308

Suicide
1 in 9380

Assault
1 in 16,421

Hernia
1 in 16,742

Murder
1 in 18,000

Drug overdose
1 in 18,125

Car accident
1 in 18,585

Flu
1 in 19,415

Falling down
1 in 20,666

Skin cancer
1 in 29,500

Power-line accident
1 in 40,103

Super volcano
Destroys climate

Tsunami (coastal dweller)
1 in 50,000

Walking down the street
1 in 52,000

Food poisoning
1 in 55,600

Avalanche
1 in 78,535

Accidental drowning
1 in 79,065

Fire
1 in 81,524

Choking
1 in 97,000

Explosion
1 in 107,787

Dog attack
1 in 147,717

Act of nature
1 in 225,107

Runaway climate change
Earth cooked

Magnetic Field Reversal
Earth fried by cosmic radiation

Freezing
1 in 400,900

Falling off a boat

Asteroid impact
1 in 469,000

Bicycle accident
1 in 578,000

Terrorist attack (overseas)
1 in 650,000

Drowning in the bath
1 in 685,000

Choking on your own vomit
1 in 740,000

Heat stroke
1 in 950,000

Fireworks accident
1 in 1,000,000

Asteroid collision
Seismic shock wave destroys us

Falling out of bed
1 in 72,000,000

Falling off a ladder
1 in 2,300,000

Lightning
1 in 2,320,000

Flood
We all drown

Legal execution
1 in 3,441,325

UV radiation kills all life
Ozone layer destruction

Nuclear accident
1 in 10,000,000

Global nuclear war
That was our planet you maniac

Plane crash
1 in 11,000,000

Bee sting
1 in 15,000,000

Bubonic plague
1 in 30,000,000

Super virus

Ignition of nitrogen
1 in 30,589,556

Crushing magnetic black hole
Tears planet apart

Mountain lion attack
1 in 32,000,000

Catastrophic cloud collapses

Freak solar flare
Fries us all

Grey goo
Runaway nanotech eats us

Blogging
1 in 35,000,000

Mad Cow Disease
1 in 40,000,000

Amusement park accident
1 in 72,300,000

SARS
1 in 100,000,000

Gamma ray burst
Nearby dying star irradiates us

Cybernetic revolution
All hail our new robotic overlords

Hadron Collider accident
Oops! Scientists create a black hole

Alien invasion
All hail our new extraterrestrial overlords

Falling coconut
1 in 250,000,000

Omega Point
Storage capacity of Universe hit

New Ice Age
Planet freezes

Shark attack
1 in 578,000,000

Meteor landing on your house
1 in 182, 139,00,000

Biblical apocalypse
Jesus returns for Judgement Day

personal threats – planetary threats

source: Guardian.co.uk, Time, Google

Google Insights

The intensity of certain search terms compared

Beer vs. Wine

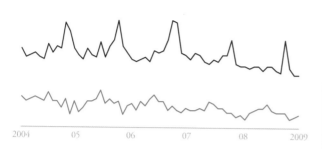

| 2004 | 05 | 06 | 07 | 08 | 2009 |

Tea vs. Coffee

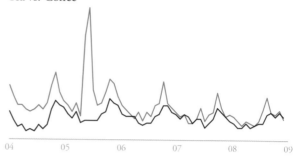

| 04 | 05 | 06 | 07 | 08 | 09 |

Lipstick vs. Recession

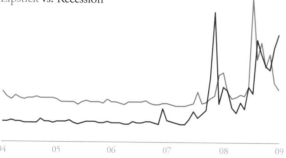

| 04 | 05 | 06 | 07 | 08 | 09 |

Marriage vs. Divorce

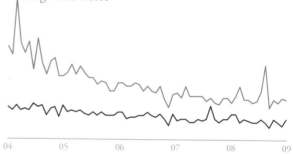

| 04 | 05 | 06 | 07 | 08 | 09 |

Microsoft vs. Apple

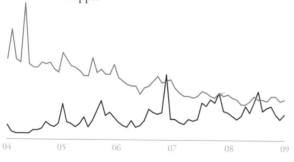

| 04 | 05 | 06 | 07 | 08 | 09 |

MySpace vs. Facebook

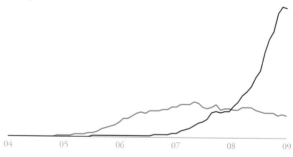

| 04 | 05 | 06 | 07 | 08 | 09 |

Cornflakes vs. Muesli vs. Porridge

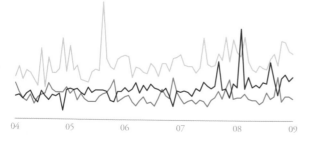

| 04 | 05 | 06 | 07 | 08 | 09 |

Cornflakes vs. Muesli vs. Porridge vs. Toast

| 04 | 05 | 06 | 07 | 08 | 09 |

What's Better Than Sex?
PTO for the answer

Britney Spears **vs.** Paris Hilton

04   05   06   07   08   09

Lap Band **vs.** Gastric Bypass

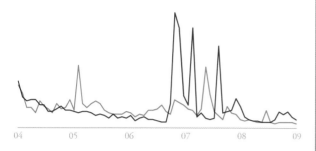

04   05   06   07   08   09

Facebook **vs.** Twitter

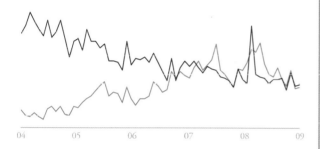

04   05   06   07   08   09

Chocolate Ice Cream **vs.** Vanilla Ice Cream

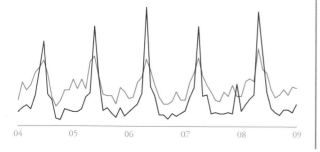

04   05   06   07   08   09

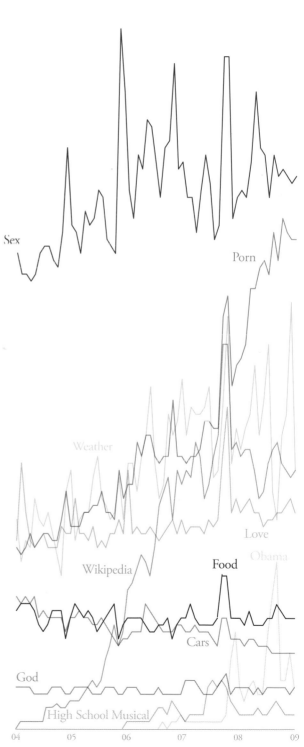

Sex

Porn

Weather

Love

Wikipedia

Food

Obama

Cars

God

High School Musical

04   05   06   07   08   09

source: Google Insights

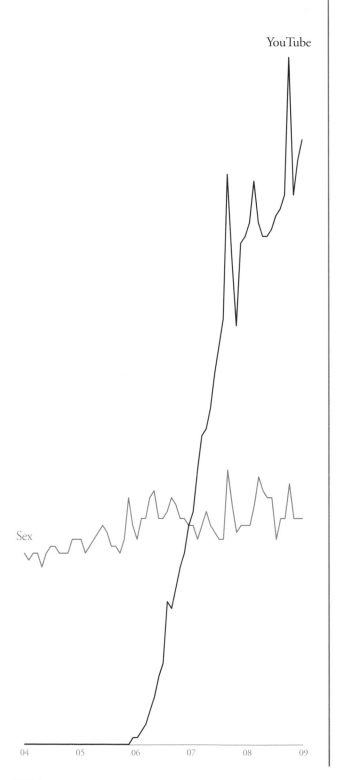

YouTube

Sex

04   05   06   07   08   09

Kyoto Targets

 target % on target % off target % on target (with "extras")

Bullseye!

Greece   Germany   Sweden   England

On target

these countries look like they're doing very well due of a lack of pre-1997 records to compare against

Bulgaria   Czech Republic   Hungary   Poland   Romania   Slovak Republic

Dependent on "extras"

Belgium   Croatia   Portugal   Slovenia   France   Netherlands

Off target

Austria   Finland   Ireland   Luxembourg   Japan   Norway

Fail

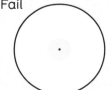   

Canada   Denmark   Italy   Scotland   Spain   Switzerland

Despite Kyoto, the EU's carbon emmissions will increase by 1% by 2012

source: European Environment Agency

The Varieties of Romantic Relationship

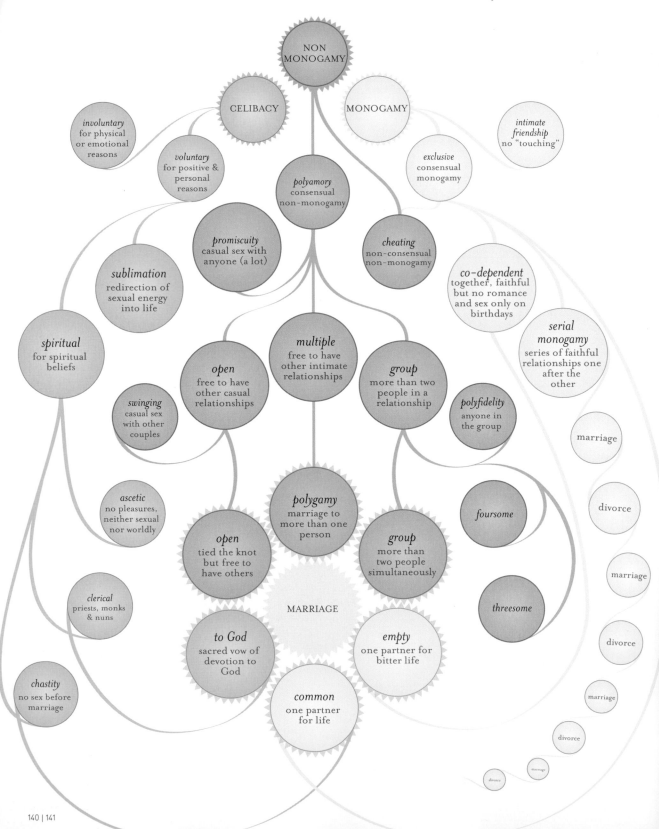

NON MONOGAMY

CELIBACY

MONOGAMY

involuntary
for physical or emotional reasons

voluntary
for positive & personal reasons

polyamory
consensual non-monogamy

intimate friendship
no "touching"

exclusive
consensual monogamy

promiscuity
casual sex with anyone (a lot)

cheating
non-consensual non-monogamy

sublimation
redirection of sexual energy into life

co-dependent
together, faithful but no romance and sex only on birthdays

spiritual
for spiritual beliefs

multiple
free to have other intimate relationships

group
more than two people in a relationship

serial monogamy
series of faithful relationships one after the other

open
free to have other casual relationships

swinging
casual sex with other couples

polyfidelity
anyone in the group

ascetic
no pleasures, neither sexual nor worldly

open
tied the knot but free to have others

polygamy
marriage to more than one person

group
more than two people simultaneously

foursome

marriage

divorce

clerical
priests, monks & nuns

MARRIAGE

threesome

marriage

chastity
no sex before marriage

to God
sacred vow of devotion to God

empty
one partner for bitter life

divorce

common
one partner for life

marriage

divorce

marriage

divorce

The Evolution of Marriage in the West

Courtly love
PRE-17TH CENTURY

MARRIAGE

passionate love

Marriage an economic & political contract negotiated by families. Love, a divine madness, always found outside of marriage.

By arrangement
17TH-19TH CENTURY

MARRIAGE

romance

love

Marriages arranged but expected to lead to romance and, ultimately, love.

The romantics
19TH CENTURY ON

romance

MARRIAGE

love

Romance, the essential spark that leads first to marriage and then to enduring love.

The sexual revolution
1960+

sex

romance

love

MARRIAGE

Sexual gratification and pleasure necessary for romance. That may, in turn, lead to love and *only* then to marriage.

source: Wikipedia

30 Years Makes A Difference II

LAKE CHAD

THE ARAL SEA

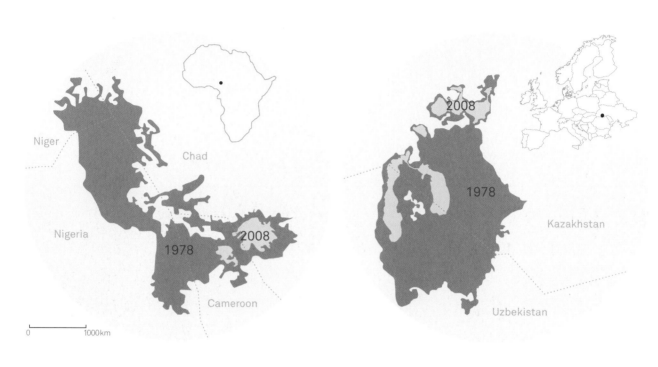

OZONE HOLE

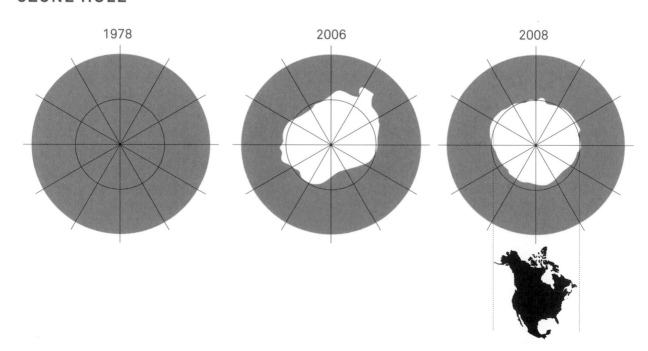

NORTH POLAR ICE CAP

+50°

−40°

−130°

1978   2008

source: NASA

"buddha stretches a thous and hands" / "censorship jail" / "chinese central propaganda department" / "chinese democracy moven..."

"brutal torture" / "brain wash" / "usan..."

"blocking"

"anti-communist" / "anti-society"

"gedhun choekyi nyima" / "genocide" / "zhongnanhai" / "human rights" / "june 4th" / "lun gong" / "mein kam pf" / "newsblackout" / "no-limit browser" / "oppression" / "perse..." / "political dissident" / "red terror" / "

The Great Firewall of China
Blocked sites. Banned search terms.

source: Wikipedia, ConceptDoppler.org

Better Than Bacon
The real centre of the Hollywood universe

A study of over 1 million films and actors at oracleofbacon.org
has revealed a series of actors who are way better connectors
for the game Six Degrees Of Kevin Bacon than Mr Bacon himself.

John Geilgud

Robert Mitchum
16th

Sean Connery
13th

Brion James

James Caan

Kirk Douglas

Robert De Niro

Jack Lemmon

Malcolm McDowell

Gene Hackman
12th

Donald Sutherland
4th

Martin Landau

Omar Sharif

Anthony Quinn
19th

Burt Reynolds

Mickey Rooney

Eli Wallach

John Hurt

Clint Eastwood

Robert Wagner

Michael Caine
8th

Ernest Borgnine
20th

Karen Black
21st

Tony Curtis

Peter Ustinov

Shelley Winters

Vanessa Redgrave

Charlton Heston
11th

Peter Falk

James Earl Jones

Robert Mitchum
16th

George Segal

William Smith

Donald Pleasance
6th

Jack Palance

Jeanne Moreau

Charles Bronson

John Carradine

Robert Duvall

James Mason

Max Von Sydow
7th

Martin Sheen
9th

Faye Dunaway

Burgess Meredith

Orson Welles
15th

Christopher Walken

Roddy McDowall

F. Murray Abraham

Harvey Keitel
19th

Teri Garr

M. Emmet Walsh

Gerard Depardieu

Harrison Ford

Shirley MacLaine

Robert Vaughn

Jacqueline Bisset

Jeff Goldblum

Rod Steiger
1st

Burt Lancaster

Rip Torn

Paul Newman

Dennis Hopper
3rd

Christopher Lee
2nd

Kevin Bacon
1094th

source: OracleOfBacon.org

What Are the Chances?
Cancer survival rates compared with the US

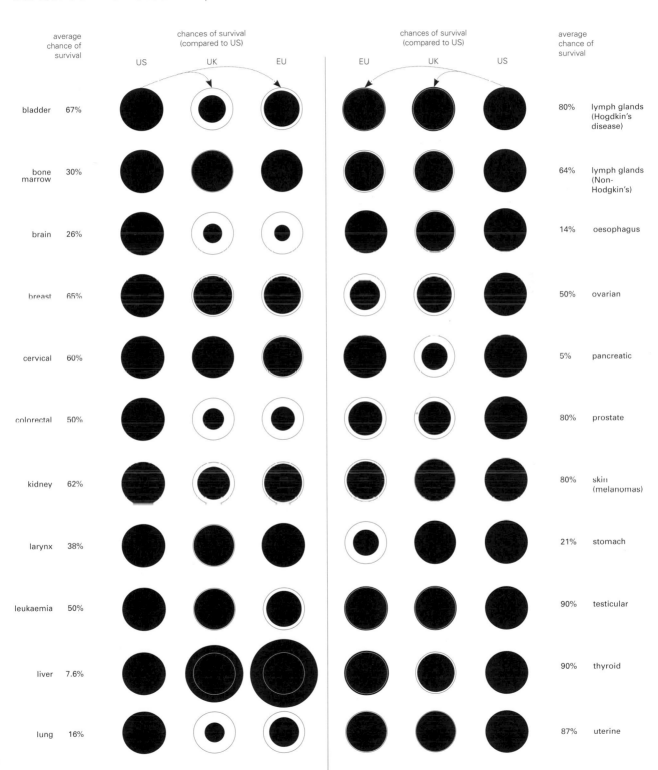

average chance of survival		chances of survival (compared to US)			chances of survival (compared to US)			average chance of survival	
		US	UK	EU	EU	UK	US		
bladder	67%							80%	lymph glands (Hogdkin's disease)
bone marrow	30%							64%	lymph glands (Non-Hodgkin's)
brain	26%							14%	oesophagus
breast	65%							50%	ovarian
cervical	60%							5%	pancreatic
colorectal	50%							80%	prostate
kidney	62%							80%	skin (melanomas)
larynx	38%							21%	stomach
leukaemia	50%							90%	testicular
liver	7.6%							90%	thyroid
lung	16%							87%	uterine

source: The Lancet, Office For National Statistics, Cancer Research

Some Things You Can't Avoid

Characteristics and behaviours that increase the likelihood of certain ailments

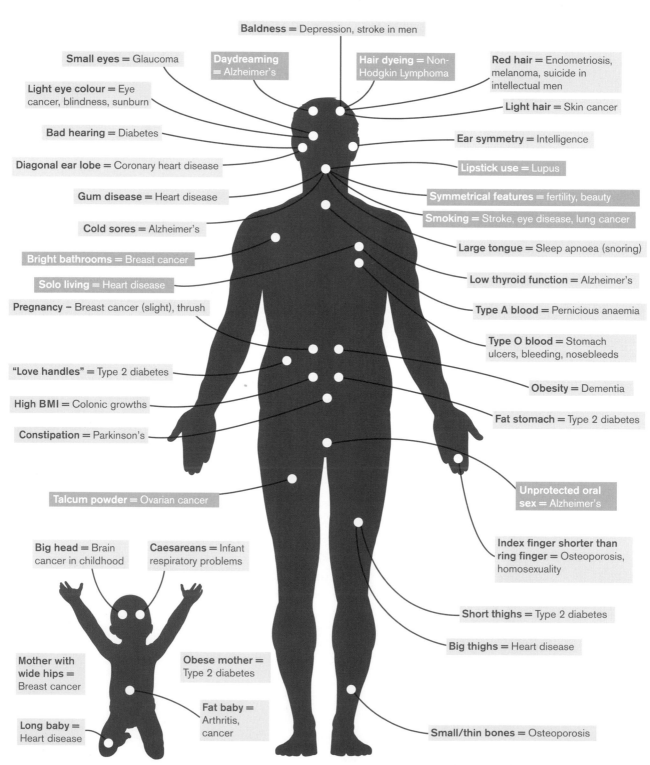

Baldness = Depression, stroke in men

Small eyes = Glaucoma

Daydreaming = Alzheimer's

Hair dyeing = Non-Hodgkin Lymphoma

Red hair = Endometriosis, melanoma, suicide in intellectual men

Light eye colour = Eye cancer, blindness, sunburn

Light hair = Skin cancer

Bad hearing = Diabetes

Ear symmetry = Intelligence

Diagonal ear lobe = Coronary heart disease

Lipstick use = Lupus

Gum disease = Heart disease

Symmetrical features = fertility, beauty

Smoking = Stroke, eye disease, lung cancer

Cold sores = Alzheimer's

Large tongue = Sleep apnoea (snoring)

Bright bathrooms = Breast cancer

Solo living = Heart disease

Low thyroid function = Alzheimer's

Pregnancy – Breast cancer (slight), thrush

Type A blood = Pernicious anaemia

Type O blood = Stomach ulcers, bleeding, nosebleeds

"Love handles" = Type 2 diabetes

High BMI = Colonic growths

Obesity = Dementia

Constipation = Parkinson's

Fat stomach = Type 2 diabetes

Talcum powder = Ovarian cancer

Unprotected oral sex = Alzheimer's

Big head = Brain cancer in childhood

Caesareans = Infant respiratory problems

Index finger shorter than ring finger = Osteoporosis, homosexuality

Short thighs = Type 2 diabetes

Big thighs = Heart disease

Mother with wide hips = Breast cancer

Obese mother = Type 2 diabetes

Fat baby = Arthritis, cancer

Long baby = Heart disease

Small/thin bones = Osteoporosis

Or decrease the likelihood

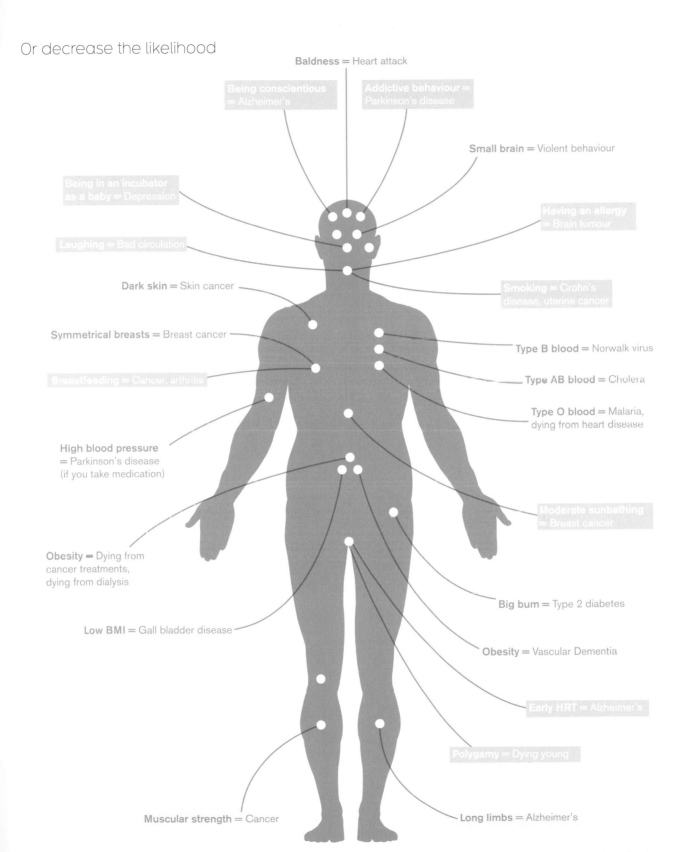

Baldness = Heart attack

Being conscientious = Alzheimer's

Addictive behaviour = Parkinson's disease

Small brain = Violent behaviour

Being in an incubator as a baby = Depression

Having an allergy = Brain tumour

Laughing = Bad circulation

Dark skin = Skin cancer

Smoking = Crohn's disease, uterine cancer

Symmetrical breasts = Breast cancer

Type B blood = Norwalk virus

Breastfeeding = Cancer, arthritis

Type AB blood = Cholera

Type O blood = Malaria, dying from heart disease

High blood pressure = Parkinson's disease (if you take medication)

Moderate sunbathing = Breast cancer

Obesity = Dying from cancer treatments, dying from dialysis

Big bum = Type 2 diabetes

Low BMI = Gall bladder disease

Obesity = Vascular Dementia

Early HRT = Alzheimer's

Polygamy = Dying young

Muscular strength = Cancer

Long limbs = Alzheimer's

source: PubMed, Medscape.com, HealthDay, biomedicine.org, eupedia.com, Reuters, yale.edu, NHSdirect.nhs.uk

By Descent
Decreased risk – increased risk

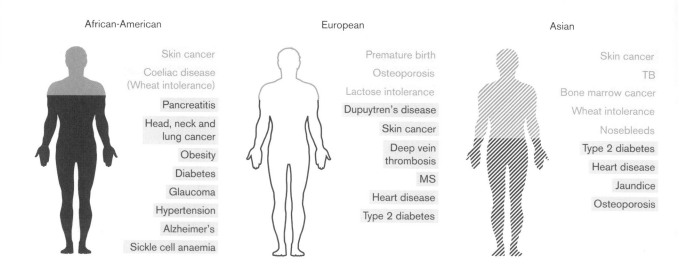

African-American
Skin cancer
Coeliac disease
(Wheat intolerance)
Pancreatitis
Head, neck and
lung cancer
Obesity
Diabetes
Glaucoma
Hypertension
Alzheimer's
Sickle cell anaemia

European
Premature birth
Osteoporosis
Lactose intolerance
Dupuytren's disease
Skin cancer
Deep vein
thrombosis
MS
Heart disease
Type 2 diabetes

Asian
Skin cancer
TB
Bone marrow cancer
Wheat intolerance
Nosebleeds
Type 2 diabetes
Heart disease
Jaundice
Osteoporosis

By Gender
Decreased risk – increased risk

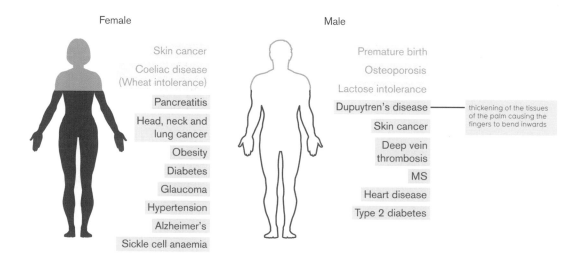

Female
Skin cancer
Coeliac disease
(Wheat intolerance)
Pancreatitis
Head, neck and
lung cancer
Obesity
Diabetes
Glaucoma
Hypertension
Alzheimer's
Sickle cell anaemia

Male
Premature birth
Osteoporosis
Lactose intolerance
Dupuytren's disease — thickening of the tissues
of the palm causing the
fingers to bend inwards
Skin cancer
Deep vein
thrombosis
MS
Heart disease
Type 2 diabetes

source: PubMed, Medscape.com, HealthDay, biomedicine.org, eupedia.com, Reuters, yale.edu, NHSdirect.nhs.uk

Body By

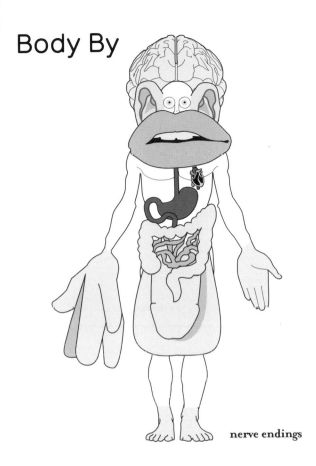

nerve endings

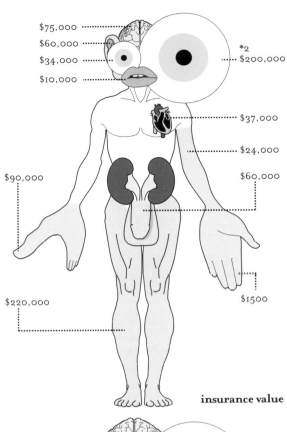

$75,000
$60,000
$34,000
$10,000

*2
$200,000

$37,000

$24,000

$90,000

$60,000

$220,000

$1500

insurance value

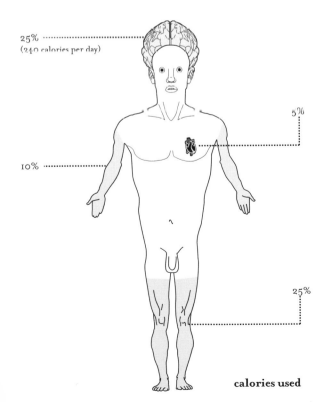

25%
(340 calories per day)

5%

10%

25%

calories used

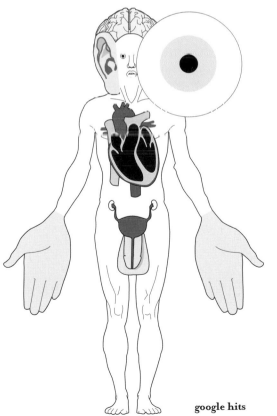

google hits

source: Google, Wikipedia

Microbes Most Dangerous
By survival time outside the body

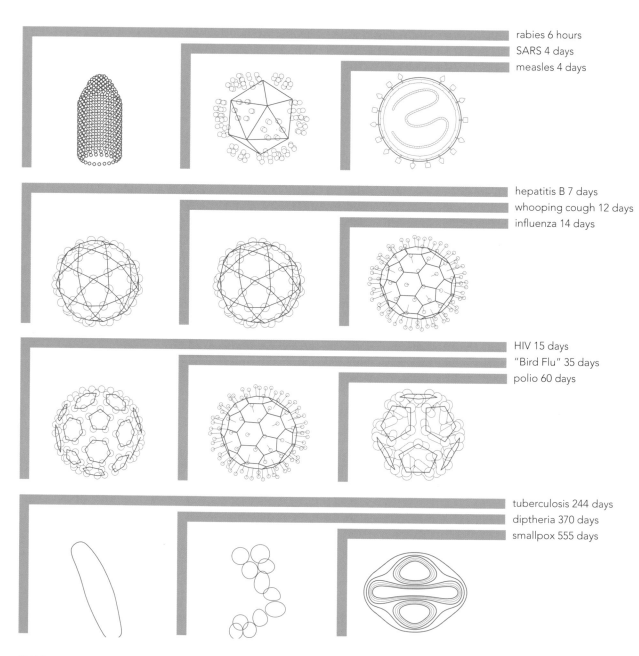

rabies 6 hours
SARS 4 days
measles 4 days

hepatitis B 7 days
whooping cough 12 days
influenza 14 days

HIV 15 days
"Bird Flu" 35 days
polio 60 days

tuberculosis 244 days
diptheria 370 days
smallpox 555 days

source: Centre For Disease Control & Prevention, NewScientist.com. Design inspired by Geigy.

Cosmetic Ingredients
Shampoo. Suntan lotion. Soap. Cleanser. Lipstick.

CHLORHEXIDINE DIGLUCONATE, 1,4-DIOXANE, ACETATE, ACETONE, ACETYLATED LANOLIN ALCOHOL, ACRYLATES COPOLYMER, ACRYLATES / OCTYLPROPENAMIDE COPOLYMOR, ALCOHOL DENAT, ALCOHOL SD-40, ALGAE/SEAWEED EXTRACT, ALLANTOIN, ALPHA HYDROXY ACID, ALPHA LIPOIC ACID, ALPHA-ISOMETHYL IONONE, AMMONIUM LAURETH SULFATE, AMMONIUM LAURYL SULPHATE, ANIGOZANTHOS FLAVIDUS (BLOODWORT), ARACHIDYL PROPIONATE, ASCORBIC ACID, ASCORBYL PALMITATE, BEESWAX, BENZALKONIUM CHLORIDE, BENZOIC ACID, BENZOYL PEROXIDE, BENZYL SALICYLATE, BETA HYDROXY ACID (SALICYLIC ACID), BORIC ACID, BUTYL METHOXYDIBENZOYLMETHANE, BUTYLATED HYDROXYANISOLE, BUTYLENE GLYCOL DICAPRYLATE/DICRAPATE, BUTYLPARABEN, BUTYLPHENYL METHYLPROPIONAL, C12-15 ALKYL BENZOATE, CAFFEINE, CAMPHOR, CARBOMERS (934, 940, 941, 980, 981), CARICA PAPAYA (PAPAYA), CARMINE, CARNAUBA WAX, CAVIAR (ROE EXTRACT), CELLULOSE, CERAMIDES, CETALKONIUM CHLORIDE, CETEARETH, CETEARYL ALCOHOL, CHAMOMILLA RECUTITA (CHAMOMILE), CL 14700 (E125), CL 191140 (YELLOW 5 ALUMINIUM LAKE), CITRONELLOL, COCAMIDE MEA, COCAMIDOPROPYL BETAINE, COLLAGEN, COUMARIN, CYCLIC (HYDROXY) ACID, CYCLOMETHICONE, D&C RED NO. 6 BARIUM LAKE, DIETHANOLAMINE (DEA), DIETHYLHEXYL BUTAMIDO TRIAZONE, DIEMETHICONE, DIOCTYL SODIUM SULFOSUCCINATE, DISODIUM COCOAMPHODIACETATE, DISODIUM LAURYL PHENYL ETHER DISULFONATE, DMDM HYDANTOIN, EDTA, ELASTIN, ELLAGIC ACID, ETHYL ALCOHOL (ETHANOL), ETHYLPARABEN, EUGENOL, FD&C YELLOW NO. 5 ALUMINUM LAKE, GLYCERIN, GLYCERYL STEARATE SE, GLYCINE, GLYCOGEN, GLYCOL STEARATE, GLYCOLIC ACID, GRAPE SEED EXTRACT, GREEN TEA EXTRACT (CAMELLIA SINENSIS), HEXYL CINNAMAL, HYALURONIC ACID, HYDROGEN PEROXIDE, HYDROLYZED COLLAGEN, HYDROQUINONE, HYDROXYLSOHEXYL 3-CYCLOHEXENE CARBOXALDEHYDE, ISOPROPYL ALCOHOL, ISOPROPYL ISOSTEARATE, ISOPROPYL IANOLATE, ISOPROPYL MYRISTATE, ISOPROPYL PALMITATE, ISOSTEARAMIDOPROPYL ETHYLDIMONIUM ETHOSULFATE, ISOSTEARIC ACID KAOLINE (CHINA CLAY), KOJIC ACID, L-ERGOTHIONEINE, LACTIC ACID, LAMINARIA DIGITATA (HORSEHAIR KELP), LANOLIN, LECITHIN, LICORICE EXTRACT (BHT), LIGHT MINERAL OIL, LIMONENE, LINALOOL, LINOLEAMIDOPROPYL, LINOLEIC ACID, LYSINE, METHYLISOTHIAZOLINONE, METHYLPARABEN, MINERAL OIL, MYRISTYL MYRISTATE, MYRTRIMONIUM BROMIDE, OCTOCRYLENE, OCTYL METHOXYCINNAMATE, OCTYL PALMITATE, OCTYLDODECANOL, OLEYL ALCOHOL, OXYBENZONE (BENZOPHENONE-3), PABA (PARAA-AMINOBENZOIC ACID), PADIMATE O, PANTHENOL, PARABEN, PARAFFIN, PARFUM, PC-DIMONIUM CHLORIDE PHOSPHATE, PEG-40 CASTOR OIL, PETROLATUM, PHENOXYETHANOL, PHENYL TRIMETHICONE, PHENYLBENZIMIDAZOLE SULFONIC ACID, PHTHALATES, POLY HYDROXY ACID, POLYBUTENE, PROLINE, PROPYLENE GLYCOL, PROPYLPARABEN, QUATERNIUM-15, RESVERATROL, RETINOL (ALSO VITAMIN A), RETINYL PALMITATE, RETINAL PALMITATE POLYPEPTIDE, ROSE HIPS, SALYCYLIC ACID, SILICONE (DIMETHYL SILICONE), SILICA, SILK POWDER, SILK PROTEINS, SODIUM ACRYLATES/C10-30 ALKYL ACRYLATE CROSSPOLYMER, SODIUM BICARBONATE, SODIUM BORATE, SODIUM CETEARYL SULFATE, SODIUM CHLORIDE, SODIUM FLUORIDE, SODIUM HYALURONATE, SODIUM LAUREL SULFATE, SODIUM LAURETH SULFATE, SODIUM LAURYL SULFATE, SODIUM METHACRYLATE, SORBIC ACID, SORBITOL (MINERAL OIL), STEARIC ACID, SULFUR, TALC, TAPIOCA STARCH, TARTARIC ACID, TITANIUM DIOXIDE, TOCOPHERYL ACETATE, TRICLOSAN, TRIDECETH-12, TRIMETHOXYCAPRYLYLSILANE, TRISODIUM EDTA, TYROSINE, VITAMIN A (RETINOL), VITAMIN B, VITAMIN C (CITRIC ACID), VITAMIN D, VITAMIN E (TOCOPHEROL), WATER, WHITE PETROLATUM, WHITE WAX, XANTHAN GUM

GOOD   FINE   OKAY   NASTY   TOXIC   DEADLY

source: CosmeticDatabase.com, Environmental Working Group

Things That'll Give You Cancer
Source: the media

abortion

acrylamide

agent orange

Nut mould. Nasty.

alcohol aldrin alfatoxin

asphalt fumes atrazine

meat benzene benzidine

High doses in smokers linked to lung cancer

betacarotene betel nuts birth

bread breasts bus stations cadmium

Fungicide

captan carbon tetrachloride careers

Vinyl acetate in gum

foods chewing gum Chinesefood Chinese herbal

chlordane chlorinated camphene

chloroform cholesterol chromium coaltar

curry cyclamates dairyproducts DDT deodorants depleted

diesel exhaust diet soda dimethylsulphate

Safe

epichlorhydrin ethilenedibromide ethnic beliefs

Lack of real contact alters our biology apparently

facebook fat fibre fluoridation flying formaldehyde

gingerbread global warming gluteraldehyde granite grilled

supplements heliobacter pylori hepatitis B

In poorly ventilated spaces

bone mass HRT hydrazine hydrogen peroxide incense

Higher risk of breast cancer

laxatives lead left handedness Lindane Listerine low

Minimal risk

mammograms manganese menopause methylbromide

No link. Now proven.

mixed spices mobile phones moisturizers mould MTBE

breast feeding not having a twin nuclear power

Contains carcinogens

juice oxygenated gasoline oyster sauce ozone

When mouldy

PCBs peanuts pesticides pet birds plastic

It's the creosote. Don't lick.

PVC radio masts radon railway sleepers

sausage dye selenium semi conductor plants

soy sauce statins stress strontium styrene

sunscreen talc testosterone tetrachloroethylene

toothfillings toothpaste toothwhitening

Probably okay

under-armshaving unvented stoves

vegetables vinyl bromide

vitamins vitreous fibres wallpaper

water wifi wine winter

x - r a y s

a c r y l o n i t r i l

air   pollution   alar

Pesticide & fruit spray

arsenic   **asbestos**

AZT   babyfood   **barbecued**

benzopyrene   **beryllium**

control pills bottled water bracken

Only if contaminated

calcium channel blockers   cannabis

Aggressive form of testicular cancer but also anti-tumour

for women car fumes casual sex celery **charred**

supplements chinese medicine chips chloramphenicol

Antibiotic

chlorinated   water   **chlorodiphenyl**

coffee **coke ovens** cooked foods crackers creosote

May help combat cancer

uranium depression **dichloryacetylene dieldrin**

dinitrotouluene dioxane dioxin dogs

unproven links to breast cancer

ethyleacrilate ethylene **ethylenedichloride** Ex-Lax

free radicals french fries fruit frying **gasoline** genes

meat **Gulf war hair dye** hamburgers health

Linked to many cancers

virus hexachlorbutadiene hexachlorethane high

infertility jewellery **Kepone kissing** lack of exercise

Kissing disease (infectious mononucleosis)

cholesterol low fibre diet magnetic fields **malonaldehyde**

methylenechloride microwave ovens milk hormones

nickel night lighting **nightshifts nitrates not**

Probable cause of cancer

plants Nutrasweet **oestrogen** olestra olive oil orange

ozone depletion papaya **passive smoking**

IV bags polio vaccine power lines proteins Prozac

redmeat Roundup saccharin salmon salt sausage

Most red meat linked to bowel cancer

shaving shellfish sick buildings smoked fish

Air quality

sulphuricacid sunbeds sunlight

tight bras toast toasters **tobacco**

train stations **trichloroethylene** tritium

uranium   **UVradiation**

vinyl chloride vinyl toys

weight gain welding fumes **well**

wood dust work

source: UK and US media reports [via numberwatch.co.uk], Wikipedia

Types of Coffee

Espresso
[ess-press-oh]

Espresso Macchiato
[ess-press-oh mock-e-ah-toe]

Espresso con Panna
[ess-press-oh kon pawn-nah]

Caffé Latte
[caf-ay lah-tey]

Flat White
[Fla-te-why-te]

Caffé Breve
[caf-ay brev-ay]

Cappuccino
[kap-oo-chee-noh]

Caffé Mocha
[caf-ay moh-kuh]

Americano
[uh-mer-i-kan-oh]

Caffeine content

Large coffee-house coffee
240 milligrammes

Regular coffee house coffee
200

Brewed coffee
200

Large cappuccino
150

Pain reliever
130

Energy drink
120

Coffee ice cream
90

Freddo
[fred-oh]

COLD MILK FOAM
ICE
ESPRESSO

Marocchino
[mar-oh-cheen-oh]

MILK FOAM
CHOCOLATE POWDER
ESPRESSO

Stretto
[stret-toh]

ESPRESSO

Ristretto
[wrist-tret-oh]

CONCENTRATED
ESPRESSO

Irish
[eye-rish]

WHIPPED CREAM
WHISKEY
WATER
ESPRESSO

Granita con Panna
[gran-ee-ta-kon-pan-na]

WHIPPED CREAM
FROZEN ESPRESSO

Corretto
[kor-ret-oh]

BRANDY
ESPRESSO

Con Leche
[kon-letch-eh]

STEAMED MILK
ESPRESSO

Crappa
[krap-aaahhh!]

WATER
INSTANT COFFEE

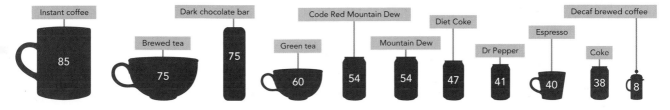

Instant coffee 85
Brewed tea 75
Dark chocolate bar 75
Green tea 60
Code Red Mountain Dew 54
Mountain Dew 54
Diet Coke 47
Dr Pepper 41
Espresso 40
Coke 38
Decaf brewed coffee 8

idea: Lokesh Dhakar @ lokeshdhakar.com

Tons Of Carbon II

2.1

average meat-
based diet
per year

1.2

average
vegetarian diet

0.1

vegan diet

100 m² of forest
per year

1,653

163

David Beckham
per year

Madonna Tour 2008

5,336,600

global wine
industry per year

6,100,000

aircraft industry per year

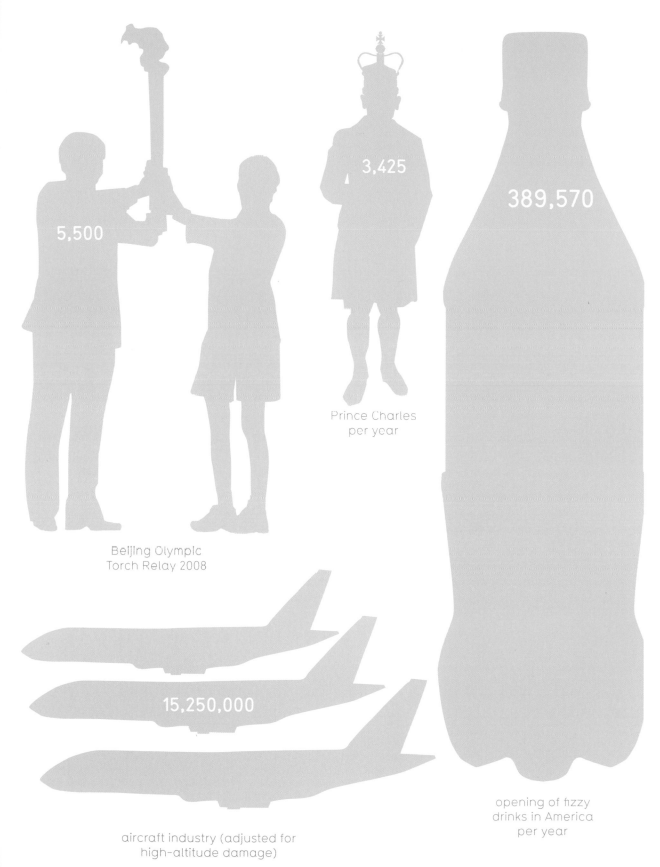

5,500

Beijing Olympic
Torch Relay 2008

3,425

Prince Charles
per year

389,570

opening of fizzy
drinks in America
per year

15,250,000

aircraft industry (adjusted for
high-altitude damage)

source: New York Times, Environmental Protection Agency, IPCC, Energy Information Administration. UNESCO

Articles of War
Most edited Wikipedia pages

Lamest / key argument (Approximate number of edits)

Death Star
120km or 160km in diameter?

J.K. Rowling
Is her name pronounced like "rolling" or does it rhyme with "howling"? (1943)

The Beatles
Should they be listed in the "traditional" order or in alphabetical order? Is it "The Beatles" or "the Beatles" (1073)

Hummus
Should it be in Israeli cuisine? Or is it a purely Arab food that the Zionists have illegally occupied?

Wii
"Wii" or "Nintendo Wii"? "Wii" or "the Wii"? Or maybe "Nintendo Wii"? Does it rhyme with "We" or "Wee"? Is "Wee" slang or a euphemism for urine? Is it a British or International slang word for urine? etc. (12,465)

Avril Lavigne
"I'm With You" or "I'm with You"? (3398)

Freddie Mercury
Ancestry. Iranian? Indian? Parsi? Azeri? (1731)

Cute
Is it NPOV (Neutral Point Of View) to say an animal is "cute"?

Kiev, capital of Ukraine
Kiev (Russian)? Or Kyiv (Ukrainian)? Battle involved both Russian and Ukrainian governments. (1323)

2006 FIFA World Cup
So should the German name use "Fußball" or "Fussball"? Unresolved. (2199)

Arachnophobia
Appropriate to use a huge pic of a tarantula on a page about fear of spiders?

Cow tipping
Appropriate to use a picture of a cow with the caption: "An unsuspecting victim"?

Anus
Should article use an image of a human anus? If so, male or female? Hairless or "Moderately" hairy?

Grey or Gray Squirrel
Slow and remorseless edit war over this spelling.

Sulfur or Sulphur?
(3100)

Christianity
Use of the word "orthodoxy" before "heresy" in the following sentence: "...Church authorities condemned some theologians as heretics, defining orthodoxy in contrast to heresy, the most notable being Christian Gnosticism." (9539)

Jesus
Very long running dispute over whether to use BC or AD. (15,386)

Alumin(i)um
MASSIVE (1609)

Grand Theft Auto IV
Is the main character Serbian, Slovak, Bosnian, or from some other Eastern European country? (1485)

Palin
Is a political candidate more famous than a Monty Python member?

Nicolaus Copernicus
Polish, German or Prussian? Don't ask. (2612)

Brazil or Brasil?

Tiger
Should it be described as the "most powerful living cat"?

United States presidential election 08
Was American comedian Stephen Colbert a serious candidate? If so, is the candidate Stephen Colbert (comedian) or Stephen Colbert (character)?

Jennifer Aniston
American or American-born? Greek-American? English-American (1306)

Fossil fuel for reciprocating piston engines equipped with spark plugs
Should this substance be called "gasoline" or "petrol"? (1599)

Wrestlemania III
Was the attendance of the event in question 78,000 or 93,178 – or is it really 75,500? (3100)

John Kerry
His first Purple Heart award in Vietnam. Was it just a wound or a "minor wound"? Was the injury "bandaged", or simply wrapped with "gauze"? (9718)

Yoghurt or Yogurt?

Clover (creature)
Cloverfield. Clover. The Cloverfield creature. Clover (creature). WHICH?

Gdanzig
What is the exact name of this Polish German Prussian Eastern Central Northern European Baltic Baltijas city? LEGENDARY (500)

Faeces
Should this page include this picture of a large human turd? (3972)

Potato Chip
Flavoured or flavored? Compromise reached: "seasoned".

Money
What exactly is the time signature of this Pink Floyd song? The band, who have no musical training, say 7/8. Most people say 7/4. Experts will go as far as to say 21/8. (4446)

Grace Kelly & Cher
Are they gay icons?

Iron Maiden
Should this direct to the band or the torture device? (2785)

Nikola Tesla
Born of Serbian parents in Austrian Empire, a part of the Hungarian half of Austria-Hungary and is now in Croatia. Category nightmare! (1260)

Cat
What describes the correct relationship? "Owner", "caregiver", or "human companion". LEGENDARY (500+)

Wikipedia
Is Jimmy Wales the founder or a co-founder with Larry Sanger. (21,748)

"Heather" of Silent Hill 3
The protagonist from Konami's survival horror video game. What is her last name? (1598)

Ann Coulter
Was the American political commentator born in 1961 or 1963? (7696)

Mayonnaise
Does traditional Mayonnaise contain lemon juice or not?

U2
Is it relevant that Bono plays the harmonica? (2988)

Angels & Airwaves
Angels & Airwaves IS a band or ARE a band? (British English requires "are" as the band comprises multiple people, while American English requires "is", as the band is a singular entity.) FIGHT! (2463)

2000
As there was no year zero, the millennium we are currently in started in 2001 (2835)

Street Fighter Characters
Drawn-out revert wars over the correct heights and weights of fictional characters like Ken Masters and Balrog. (1048)

Star Wars
Are Anakin Skywalker and Darth Vader considered one character or two separate ones? Do they deserve separate listings in the "credits" section? Should *Star Wars Episode III* should be listed as the "preceding film" in the infobox. (8610)

2006 Atlantic Hurricane Season
Should a tropical cyclone that formed on December 30, 2005 and lasted until January 6, 2006 be placed in the 2006 Atlantic hurricane season article or the 2005? (2477)

source: Wikipedia: Lamest_edit_wars

Water Towers

Daily total use
per person
4645 bottles

Direct use   Indirect use

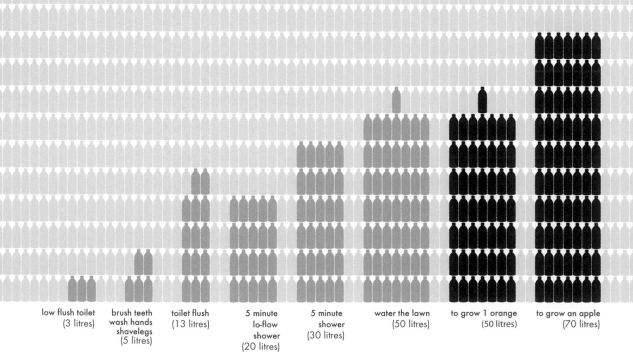

low flush toilet
(3 litres)

brush teeth
wash hands
shavelegs
(5 litres)

toilet flush
(13 litres)

5 minute
lo-flow
shower
(20 litres)

5 minute
shower
(30 litres)

water the lawn
(50 litres)

to grow 1 orange
(50 litres)

to grow an apple
(70 litres)

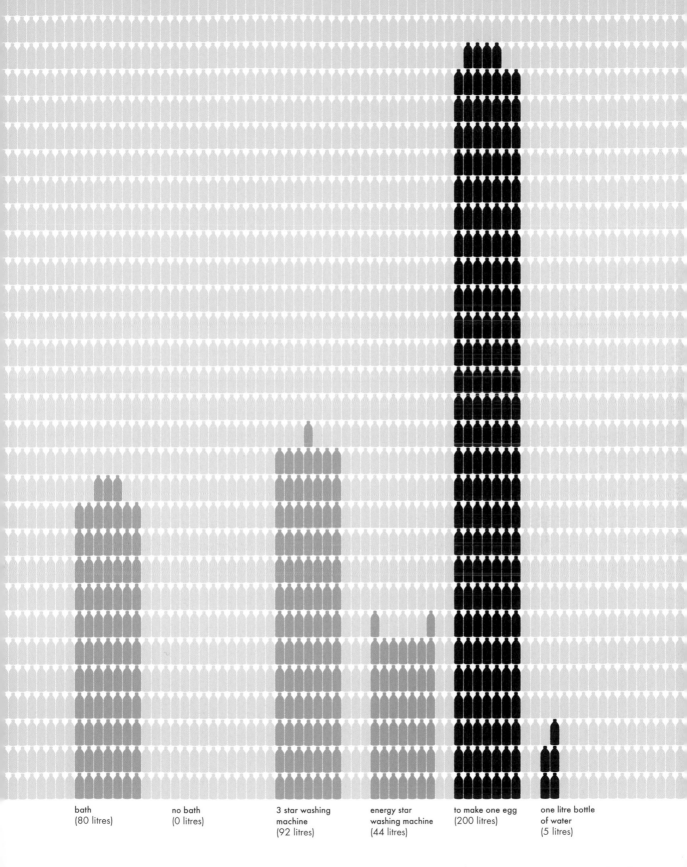

bath
(80 litres)

no bath
(0 litres)

3 star washing
machine
(92 litres)

energy star
washing machine
(44 litres)

to make one egg
(200 litres)

one litre bottle
of water
(5 litres)

source: Wikipedia, Good Magazine

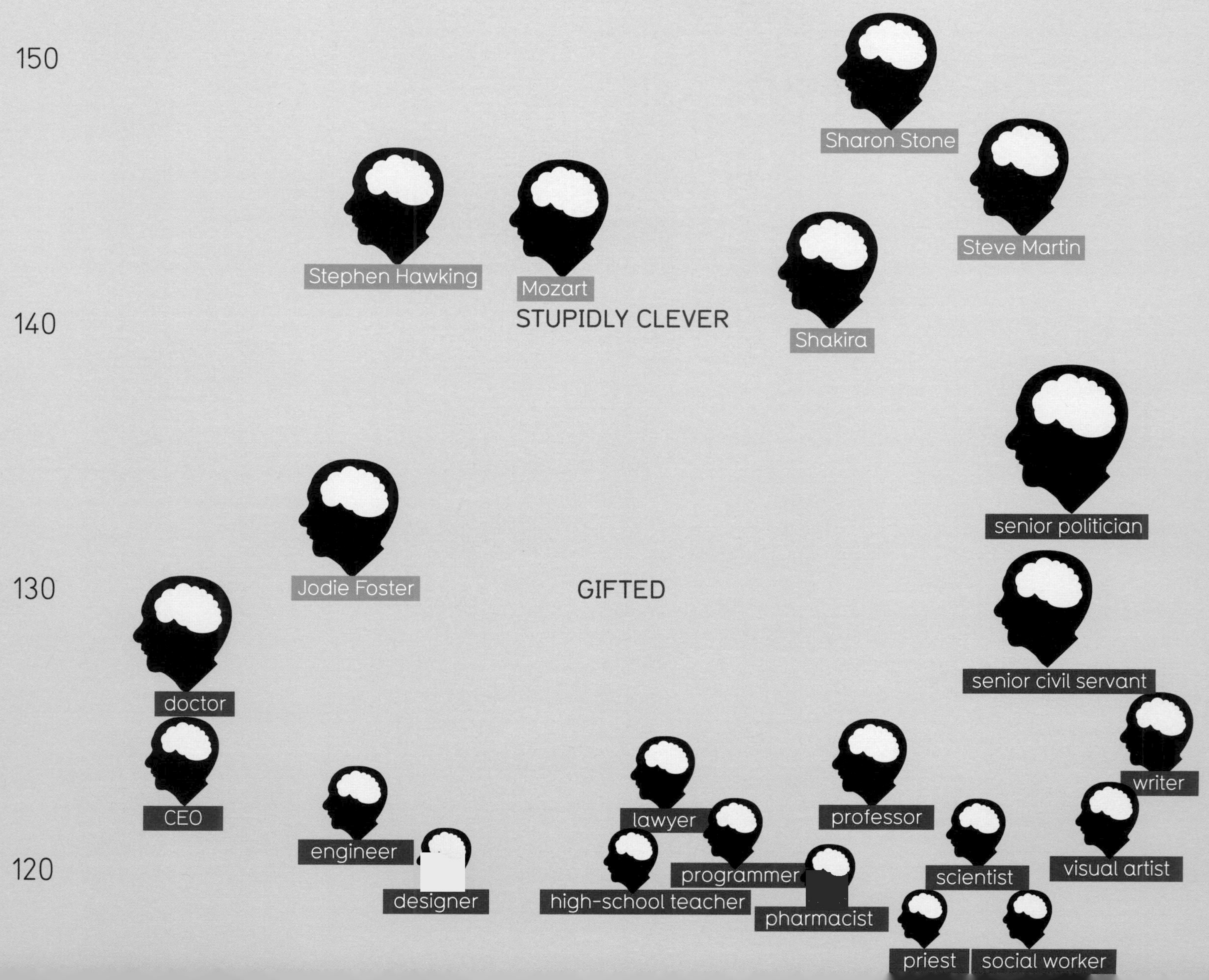

150

140

STUPIDLY CLEVER

Stephen Hawking

Mozart

Sharon Stone

Steve Martin

Shakira

130

GIFTED

senior politician

senior civil servant

writer

visual artist

scientist

professor

social worker

priest

pharmacist

programmer

high-school teacher

lawyer

Jodie Foster

120

engineer

designer

doctor

CEO

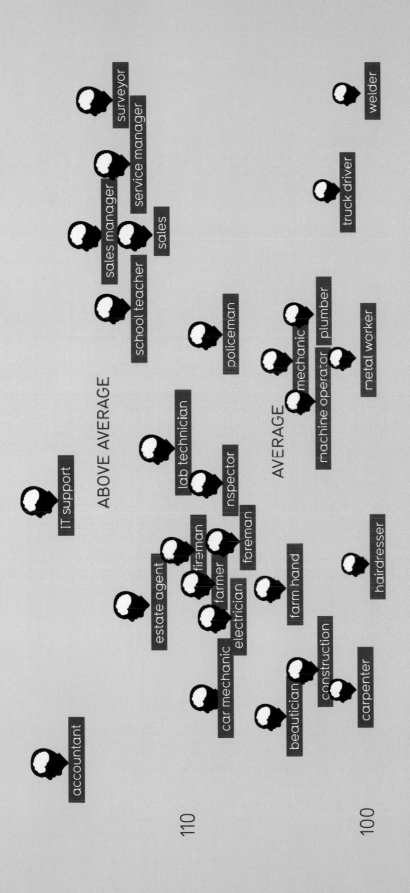

Who Clever Are You?
Average IQs of different callings

source: University Of Wisconsin Henmon–Nelson IQ Distributions 1992–94 (via Hauser, Robert M 2002)

The Media Jungle

Selected international magazines, newspapers and tv channels

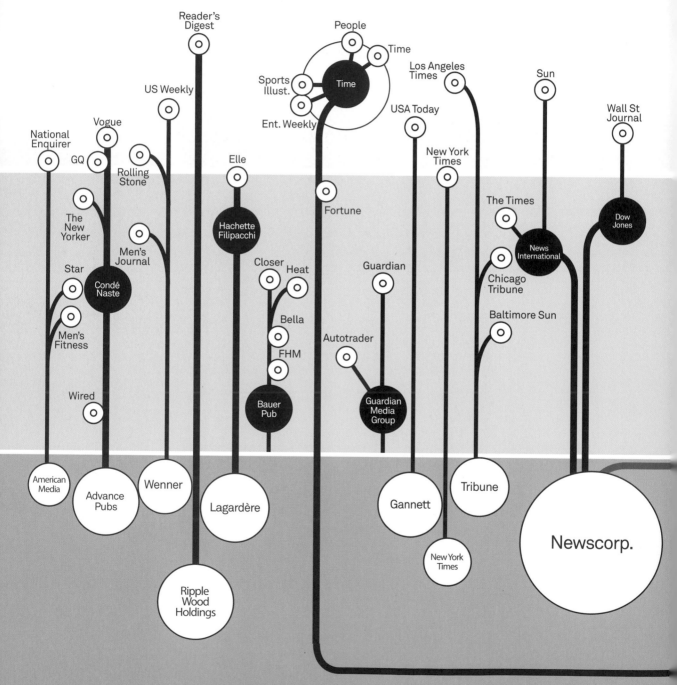

Heavy weights $2bn+

Middle weights <$2bn

Reader's Digest

People

Time

Los Angeles Times

Sun

Wall St Journal

US Weekly

Sports Illust.

USA Today

Vogue

Ent. Weekly

Time

National Enquirer

GQ

Rolling Stone

Elle

New York Times

The Times

Dow Jones

The New Yorker

Men's Journal

Fortune

News International

Star

Condé Naste

Closer

Heat

Guardian

Chicago Tribune

Men's Fitness

Bella

Baltimore Sun

FHM

Autotrader

Wired

Hachette Filipacchi

Bauer Pub

Guardian Media Group

American Media

Advance Pubs

Wenner

Lagardère

Gannett

Tribune

Newscorp.

Ripple Wood Holdings

New York Times

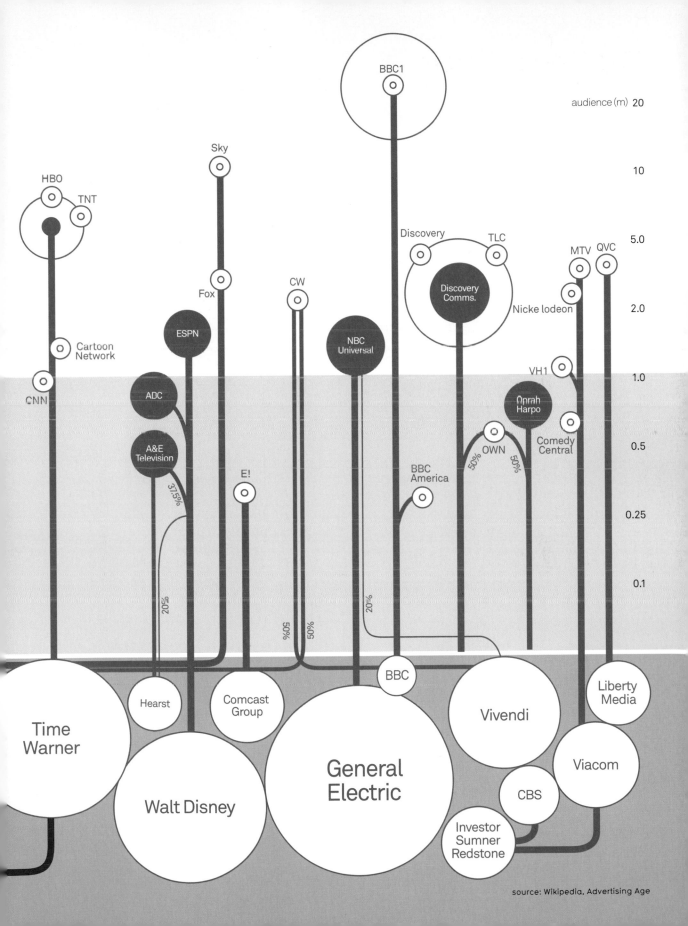

BBC1

audience (m) 20

Sky

HBO

TNT

10

Discovery TLC

MTV QVC

5.0

Cartoon Network

CW

Fox

ESPN

NBC Universal

Discovery Comms.

Nicke lodeon

2.0

CNN

ABC

A&E Television

37.5%

VH1

Oprah Harpo

1.0

Comedy Central

0.5

E!

BBC America

50% OWN 50%

0.25

20% 50% 50% 50%

20%

0.1

BBC

Hearst

Comcast Group

Vivendi

Liberty Media

Time Warner

General Electric

Viacom

Walt Disney

CBS

Investor Sumner Redstone

source: Wikipedia, Advertising Age

	MORNING				AFTERNOON			
ATKINS	omelette			tomato	salmon			salad
LOW G.I.	porridge		skim milk	oj	carrot & barley soup			
WEIGHT WATCHERS	porridge & raisins			brown sugar	small burger		salad	apple
ZONE	grapes	rye toast	fruit	peanut butter				
CABBAGE SOUP	fruit				cabbage soup			
DETOX	oats		yoghurt	fruit	tzatziki		veg crudités	
JUICE DIET	carrot & apple				carrot & veg juice			
CALORIE COUNTING	4 tbs branflakes		skim milk	apple	mozzarella, tomato & avocado salad			french bread
MEDITERRANEAN	toast	yoghurt	blueberries	almonds	chickpea salad			
WEIGHT GAIN	6 x cream cheese bagels		yoghurt	oj	pitta bread	tuna	lentil soup	apple juice
SUNLIGHT	sunlight				sunlight			
SCARSDALE	grapefruit		toast	black coffee	assorted cold cuts		stewed tomatoes	

EVENING				SNACKAGE		WATER
grilled chicken		veg		chocolate shake	granola bar	x 8
whole wheat pasta bake				yoghurt	raspberries	x 8
tuna steak	olive sauce	assorted veg	french bread	fat free yoghurt		x 8
grapes	rye bread	olive oil	peanut butter			x 8
cabbage soup				fruit		x 8
potato & bean casserole				yoghurt	fruit	x 8
veg juice						x 8
roast pork				hummus	crudités	x 8
spinach frittata				hummus	crisp bread	x 8
spaghetti	salami	bread	milk	bread & jam	ice cream	x 8
vitamin D				oxygen		x 8
shellfish	salad	veg		hummus		x 8

Calories In
Average load

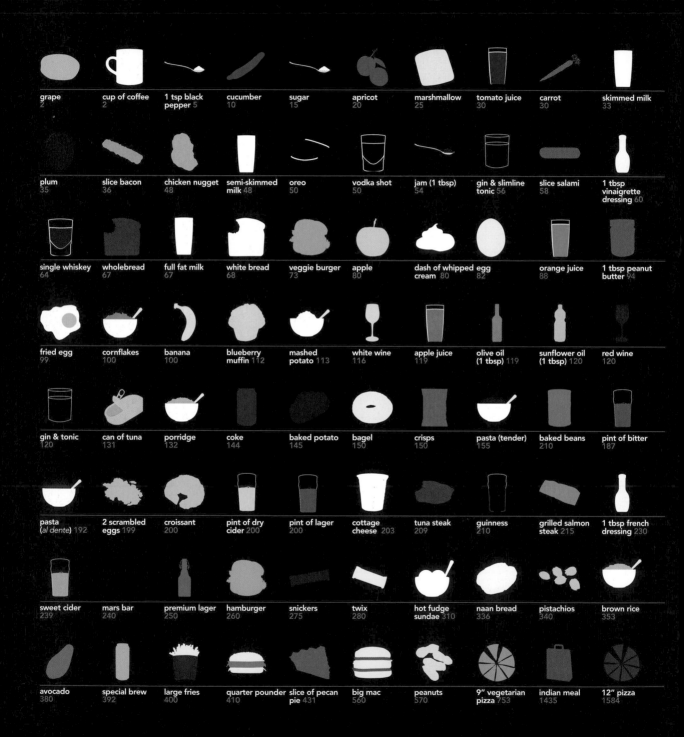

grape
2

cup of coffee
2

1 tsp black
pepper 5

cucumber
10

sugar
15

apricot
20

marshmallow
25

tomato juice
30

carrot
30

skimmed milk
33

plum
35

slice bacon
36

chicken nugget
48

semi-skimmed
milk 48

oreo
50

vodka shot
50

jam (1 tbsp)
54

gin & slimline
tonic 56

slice salami
58

1 tbsp
vinaigrette
dressing 60

single whiskey
64

wholebread
67

full fat milk
67

white bread
68

veggie burger
73

apple
80

dash of whipped
cream 80

egg
82

orange juice
88

1 tbsp peanut
butter 94

fried egg
99

cornflakes
100

banana
100

blueberry
muffin 112

mashed
potato 113

white wine
116

apple juice
119

olive oil
(1 tbsp) 119

sunflower oil
(1 tbsp) 120

red wine
120

gin & tonic
120

can of tuna
131

porridge
132

coke
144

baked potato
145

bagel
150

crisps
150

pasta (tender)
155

baked beans
210

pint of bitter
187

pasta
(al dente) 192

2 scrambled
eggs 199

croissant
200

pint of dry
cider 200

pint of lager
200

cottage
cheese 203

tuna steak
209

guinness
210

grilled salmon
steak 215

1 tbsp french
dressing 230

sweet cider
239

mars bar
240

premium lager
250

hamburger
260

snickers
275

twix
280

hot fudge
sundae 310

naan bread
336

pistachios
340

brown rice
353

avocado
380

special brew
392

large fries
400

quarter pounder
410

slice of pecan
pie 431

big mac
560

peanuts
570

9" vegetarian
pizza 753

indian meal
1435

12" pizza
1584

Calories Out
Average burn for 30 minutes of...

praying 36	lying down 36	meditating 36	sex (light) 36	queueing 40	knitting 43	toilet 44	reading 48	sex (moderate) 48	socializing 55
sex (vigorous) 57	desk work 66	pallbearing 68	brushing teeth 71	milking a cow 88	camping 92	baseball 93	darts 93	decorating 103	sailing 110
walking 110	frisbee 110	surfing 110	bowling 140	fishing 110	curling 118	juggling 148	horseriding 148	cricket 166	gardening 166
tai chi 166	golf 166	dancing 166	badminton 166	hopscotch 185	skateboarding 195	punching a bag 222	wheelchair 240	swimming laps 258	rowing 258
cycling 208	aerobics 258	tennis 258	skiing 258	football 265	running 295	push ups sit ups 295	climbing 295	circuit training 295	basketball 295
american football 310	yoga 310	martial arts 369	rugby 443	squash 443	roller-blading 443	boxing 443			

source: cross-referenced from various dieting websites

Types of Facial Hair
A little hair says a lot about a man

Major
Al Assad, Hafez
Sudan (reigned 1971-2000)
Killed: 25,000

Traditional
Al-Bashir, Omar
Sudan (1989-)
Killed: 400,000

Painter's Brush
Kai-Shek, Chiang
China (1928-31)
Killed: 30,000

Pyramid
Franco, Francisco
Spain (1939-75)
Killed: 30,000

Freestyle
King Abdulla
Saudi Arabia (2005-)
Killed: -

Chevron
Lenin, Vladimir Illyich
Russia (1917-24)
Killed: 30,000

Handlebar
Stalin, Joseph
Soviet Union (1924-53)
Killed: 23,000,000

Natural Full
Castro, Fidel
Cuba (1976-2008)
Killed: 30,000

Horseshoe
Habre, Hissene
Chad (1982-90)
Killed: 40,000

Toothbrush
Hitler, Adolf
Germany (1933-45)
Killed: 58,000,000

Walrus
Hussein, Saddam
Iraq (1979-2003)
Killed: 6,000,000

Zappa
Mengitsu, Haile Maiam
Ethiopa (1987-91)
Killed: 150,000

Fu Manchu
Temujin, Genghis Khan
Mongolia (1205-27)
Killed: millions

Nu Geek
McCandless
UK (1971)
Killed: 0

source: Wikipedia and general web

Vintage Years White Wine

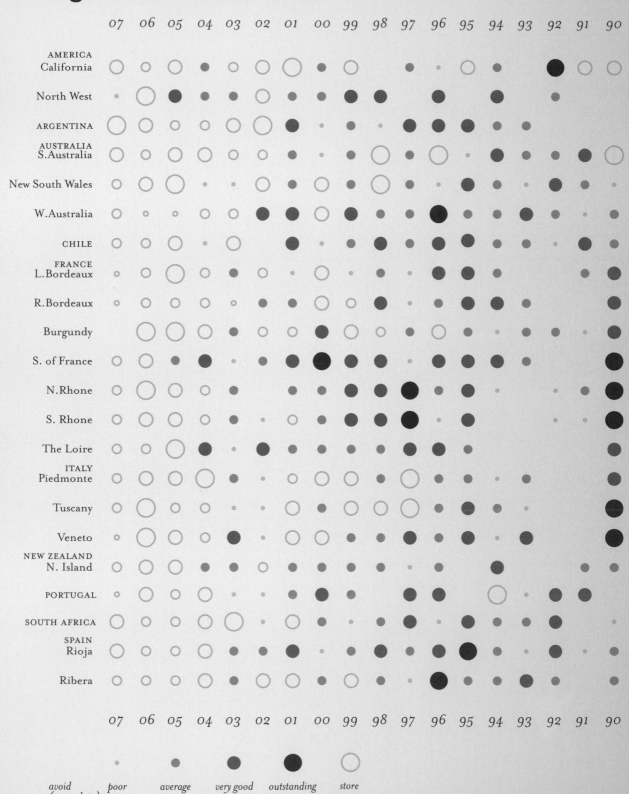

	07	06	05	04	03	02	01	00	99	98	97	96	95	94	93	92	91	90
AMERICA California																		
North West																		
ARGENTINA																		
AUSTRALIA S.Australia																		
New South Wales																		
W.Australia																		
CHILE																		
FRANCE L.Bordeaux																		
R.Bordeaux																		
Burgundy																		
S. of France																		
N.Rhone																		
S. Rhone																		
The Loire																		
ITALY Piedmonte																		
Tuscany																		
Veneto																		
NEW ZEALAND N. Island																		
PORTUGAL																		
SOUTH AFRICA																		
SPAIN Rioja																		
Ribera																		

	07	06	05	04	03	02	01	00	99	98	97	96	95	94	93	92	91	90

avoid (or no data)   *poor*   *average*   *very good*   *outstanding*   *store*

Vintage Years Red Wine

	07	06	05	04	03	02	01	00	99	98	97	96	95	94	93	92	91	90

AMERICA
California

ARGENTINA

AUSTRALIA
S.Australia

W.Australia

Hunter Valley

Victoria

AUSTRIA
Riesling

FRANCE
Alsace

Bordeaux

Burgundy

Chablis

Champagne

Loire Valley Sweet

Loire Valley Blanc

North Rhone

GERMANY
Mosel

Rheingau

ITALY
North Italy

NEW ZEALAND
Marlborough

SOUTH AFRICA

CHILE

SPAIN
Rioja

07	06	05	04	03	02	01	00	99	98	97	96	95	94	93	92	91	90

store   outstanding   very good   average   poor   avoid
(or no data)

Amphibian Extinction Rates
Canaries in a coal mine?

Normal rate
1x

Chrytid fungus   Habitat Loss   UV-Radiation   Insecticides

In the 1930s, the
African clawed frog,
an immune carrier of
this deadly fungus,
was popular for
pregnancy tests.
Doctors injected a
pregnant frog with a
woman's urine. If it
gave birth, the
woman was
pregnant. Escaped
frogs gradually
spread the fungus
among their
non-immune peers.

Even a tiny amount
of Malathion, the
most common
insecticide in the
US, can lead to a
devastating chain
reaction that
destroys bottom-
dwelling algae, the
primary food of
tadpoles. It, and
another pesticide,
Atrazine, are
considered key
factors in the loss of
entire populations.

Today
25,400x

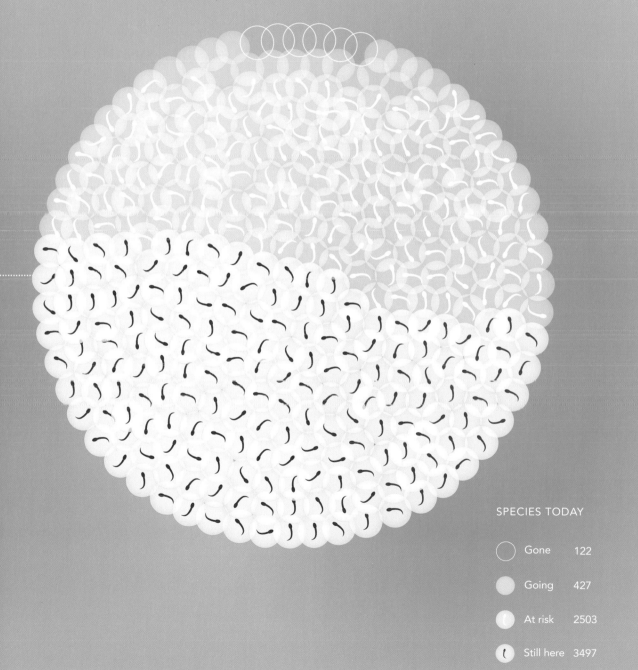

SPECIES TODAY

○ Gone   122

● Going   427

● At risk   2503

● Still here   3497

source: National Academy Of Sciences, Discovery.com

Motive

Searches for the phrase "we broke up because…"

he couldn't keep his hands to himself • "we're at different stages in our lives" • she was cheating with women • he wanted to experience the whole college thing • he said he needed space • he's a complete idiot • I was guy I **I don't clip my toenails enough** cheating on him so he made-out with the was cheating on him with • of Drugs • of Def Jam • of her partying ways • his parents don't like me • his girlfriend got suspicious • her husband needs oral sex • I didn't love her • i too much control him • of all of the time he spent on his attempts to break into film-making • we had different life goals • of religious reasons – he refused to worship me • of my drinking – I binge drink • he has a small pee-pee and wouldn't buy me any jewellery • I smothered her • we didn't have anything in common and everything was completely physical • of parental disapproval • he pressured me into having sex • I have a high-pitched voice! • **she just realized I'm a better friend** I wasn't comfortable telling her who I really am • we fell out of love • he couldn't keep his hands to himself • he is traumatized by his former relationship and can't reach his feelings for anything or anyone. • We, well, my family has money • i moved. i want him back more than i can say • I basically caught him in bed with one of his co-workers • he liked another guy. Yes, a guy • he was short and kind of looked like a giant mole that stood upright • of one of those arguments • she was way too hurt by my lack of effort to call her • I "bug" him • I was overprotective? • he lied too much & went crazy & punched a hole in the wall • he made out with my friend • i realized me being insecure due to the hurtful past experiences, was not going to enable us to **he doesn't have "love" for me** take our relationship to the next level • he said i wasnt treating him right. and i wasnt • of time and dist. • I was a complete arsehole to her • of this election • i asked "are we ok?" caused she seemed a little weird lately and she said next time you ask that again we are thru • we fought a lot and several red flags kept showing up • I felt that he deserved better than me. • I needed help. I have abandonment, insecurity, and anxiety issues • she wants to find herself as an individual • she likes to deal with her problems alone and not to really share them • he thinks his career won't match up to mine • I realized that I had been gradually developing strong feelings for one of her close friends • He belonged to a different religion and wanted me to convert • not because I got somebody pregnant • she hurt me on Valentines night • we love each other? • we had never been with anyone else and we felt it was too serious for our age **of artistic differences** • We Were On A Break And I Started To Treat Him Bad • i lied about my age • I can't make him stay with me • He's in love with his mother • I'm "immature" & like to party too much...... ummm hello I'm twenty-one!!!! • I couldn't have a tree • she didn't want to change her FB status • of the stock market • I'm passive • I wouldn't submit to his views on what a wife should be • we couldn't agree on a sex position together • he only saw me as a weekend fling • he has a fatal flaw, as caring, romantic, and intuitive as he is, he has a horrid temper... • I felt that he wasn't present in the relationship. I felt alone while seeing him • he was gay • I feel that I hurt her too much and I feel she deserves better • i told simple lies (small lies that i didnt have to tell) • im too "clingy" • he cheated on me twice **he told people I was crazy** and it was a year ago • I was jealous that he swiped her ass with her credit card, and not mine • she was too flirty • she just realized I'm a better friend. • he always ignored me and got mad over any little thing. He was extremely jealous • he messed around with my worse enemy • the sex was bad • his fear of commitment?!? • he is not financially stable • I am dangerous • no reason

source: searches for "we broke up because…" on Facebook, Twitter & Google. Apologies for heterosexual bias.

Timing

Most common break-up times, according to Facebook status updates

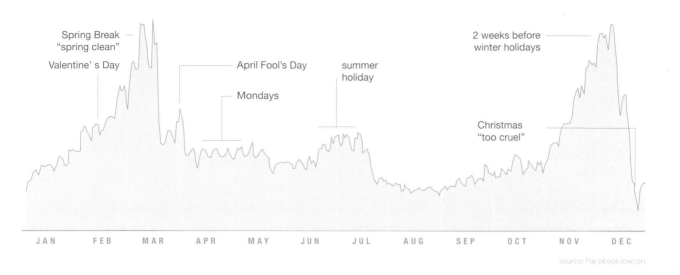

Spring Break
"spring clean"

Valentine's Day

April Fool's Day

Mondays

summer
holiday

2 weeks before
winter holidays

Christmas
"too cruel"

JAN   FEB   MAR   APR   MAY   JUN   JUL   AUG   SEP   OCT   NOV   DEC

source: Facebook lexicon

Delivery

Most common methods of break-up

Those born before 1975

74%   16%   4%   4%   3%

IN PERSON   PHONE   EMAIL   FACEBOOK   IM

47%   30%   4%   5%   14%

Those born after 1984

source: survey of 10,000 Twitter users

Good News
It's all we could find. Sorry.

Booming trees & plants

6.2%

Thanks to climate change. source: NASA

National smoking bans

source: Wikipedia

Smokers quitting

4%

source: Cancer Council Victoria

Russian health spending

+ 200%

source: WHO

The Good of Bush
Stuff that improved under Dubya

Artificial limb research funds

$7.2m

source: *Christian Science Monitor*

Violent crime

8%

source: US Dept. Justice

Painkiller sales

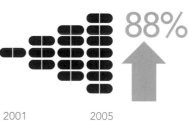

88%

2001   2005

source: *Pharmatimes*

Roads in Afghanistan

2793 km
1999

Mobile phones & cancer

SAFE

source: 20-year 420,000 person Danish study

CFC usage

96%

1986   2006

source: NASA

Gender pay gap

20%

2001

16%

2007

source: OECD

Shark Attacks

2000

79

2007

62

source: University Of Florida

Leaded fuel

2001

1%   2006

source: UN

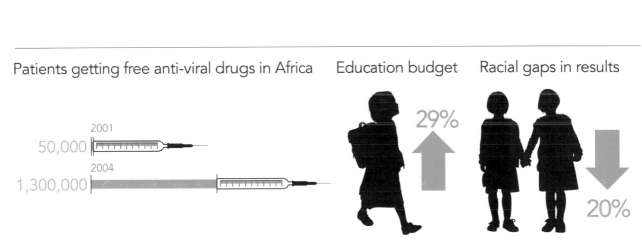

Patients getting free anti-viral drugs in Africa

2001
50,000

2004
1,300,000

source: *The Independent*

Education budget

29%

Racial gaps in results

20%

source: US Dept. of Education

12350 km
2008

source: USAID

Feeding Frenzy
The organic food market

● corporation size
● mega corporation size

Other brands
Bisquick
Cheerios
Green Giant
Häagen-Dazs

General Mills

 Heinz

THE HAIN CELESTIAL GROUP

WEST SOY

MUIR GLEN

Cascadian Farm

RICE DREAM

CELESTIAL SEASONINGS

Casbah

SOY DREAM

Banquet
Jiffy

ConAgra Foods

ALL NATURAL
Arrowhead Mills

ALEXIA

DAGOBA

Reese **HERSHEY'S**

odwalla

BEAR NAKED

Naked
JUICE

Coca-Cola

Kellogg's

PEPSI

INDEPENDENTS
Amy's Kitchen
Applegate Farms
Cedarlane
Clif Bar
Eden Foods
Golden Temple
Lundberg Family Farm
Nature's Path
Newman's Own Organics
Pacific Natural Foods

Lay
Tropicana
Gatorade
Doritos

PHILIP MORRIS

Jacobs
Oreo
Kenco

KRAFT

Mars

COMMUNITY

OrgraN

Dr Ritter
Zonnateur

SEEDS of CHANGE

BACK to NATURE
est.1960

SANCHI

CRAZY JACK

(Wessanen)

NATURE VALLEY

Boca

whole earth

HOLLAND & BARRETT —

NBTY
(was Nature's Bounty)

MORNINGSTAR FARMS®

Organix

PJ's   Rachel's

Snapple

GREEN &BLACK'S

Hero

HORIZON

Cadbury Schweppes

Dean
FOODS

INDEPENDENTS
Clearspring
Groovy Foods
Hipp Organic
Meridian
Marigold
Riverford
RDA
Suma
The Health Store
YeoValley

source: Dr Philip Howard, Michigan State University

Virtual Kingdoms
Massively multiplayer online worlds

Nordheim

Vanaheim Asgard Hyperborea ○Sythia *Pathe*

○Korvela *Cimmeria* *Brythunia*

○Venarium **Hyrkania**○**W**

Border Kingdom Nemedia ○Yezud ○Rhamdam

Aquilonia ○Belverus ○Yaralet

Tanasub ○Galparan Numalia ○Shadizar *Vilayet* *Kus*

○Tarantia ○Khorosun *Sea*

Shanor ○Sultanapur ○Onagrul

○Lanthe Polopponi ○Aghrapur ○Khoraf

Kordava *Argos* *Koth* **Turan** ○Akhlat ○Secunderam

○Zingara ○Eruk ○Kuthchemes Samara Meru

Barachan ○Messantta Asgalun *Shem* Shangara *Ghulist*

Isles ○Khemi *River Styx* ○Set ○Ayodhya

Isle Of The Sukhmet *Stygia* ○Luxur ○Petion *Iranistan* Kosala ○Peshkhauri

Black Ones *Kush* ○Xuchot *Keshan* ○Yanaidor Anshan ○Khorala

Eastern Xuthal ○Gazal Alkmeenon Keshai ○Kassali **Yola Pong** **Vendh**

Plaguelands Tomalku Black Kingdoms ○Denizkenar *Isles Of* *Misty*

Western *Pearl* *Isles*

Tirisfal Glades *Plaguelands* ○Kulalo ○Abombi **The Forbidden City**

●**Undercity** *Southern*

Lordamere Lake *Isles* **HYBORIA**

Alterac Mountains *The Hinterlands* **Age Of Conan**

○Iarren Mill ○Hammerfall *Western Minir*

○Southshore *Zone*

Iverpine Aerie Peak *Aralhi Highlands* ○Dwarven Vill

Forest ○Frozen Vall

Wetlands *Valley Of* *Plunderous Plain*

Menethil *The Lords* **Schuttgart** Archaic Fort

Harbour ○Orc Village *Pavel Ruins*

●**Ironforge** *Valley Of Heroes* ○Monastic

Loch Modan *Fortress*

Dun Morogh *Valley Ut*

○Kargath Swamp *Saints*

Searing Gorge *Badlands* **Rune**○ Fortress ○**G**

Swamp of Screams

○Blackrock Spire ○Western F

Burning Steppes Fortress of *Blazing S*

●**Stormwind** Primeval Isle the Dead *Forest Of Evil*

Elwynn Forest **ADEN** Dark Elven Village Ivory Fortress

Redridge Mountains **Lineage II** **Aden**

Swamp of Sorrows Elven Village *Enchanted* Bay

○Darkshire ○Stonard *Swampland* *Valley* *Narsell L*

Deadwind Kamael Village Elven Fortress ●**Oren**

Pass ○Nethergarde Keep *Iris* *Forsa*

The Blasted Lands *Hills Of Gold* *Neutral Zone* *Lake*

Grom'Gol *Evil Hunting Grounds* *Death Marsh* *Hunters Fortres*

Base Camp Gludio ●**Cruma Tower** *Dragon Valley*

Stranglehorn *Cruma Marshlands* ●**Giran**

Vale ●Dion

○Booty Bay **Gludin** ● *Plains Of Dion* Alligator *Isle C*

Floran *Island* *Praye*

Wasteland ○Hive Fortress Aaru Fortress

ELEVATION (in magic metres) *Devil's*

Langk Lizardmen *Isle*

Dwellings ○Heine

Southern Fortress

Talking 2000 +1000 +500 +250 +50 +0 50 +200 +500 +1000 +2000

Island

●Undercity

Sentinel Hill○

Westfall

Stormwind

Darkshire

Avatars
Most common online character names

source: Obijan.com, World Of Warcraft forums

Immortality

Biographies of the famously long-lived examined for clues to longevity

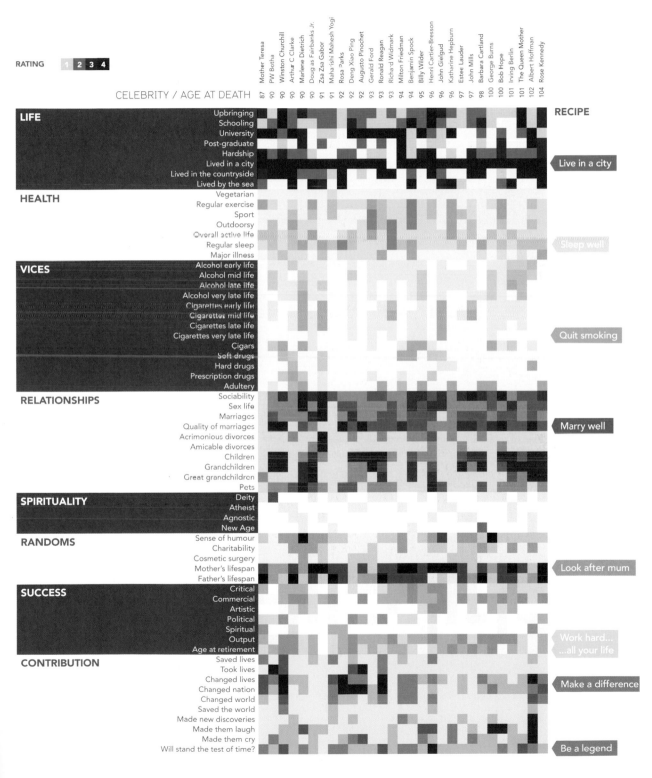

RATING 1 2 3 4

CELEBRITY / AGE AT DEATH

Columns: Mother Teresa (87), PW Botha (90), Winston Churchill (90), Arthur C Clarke (90), Marlene Dietrich (90), Doug as Fairbanks Jr. (90), Zsa Zsa Gabor (91), Maharishi Mahesh Yogi (91), Rosa Parks (92), Deng Xiao Ping (92), Augusto Pinochet (92), Gerald Ford (93), Ronald Reagan (93), Richard Widmark (93), Milton Friedman (94), Benjamin Spock (94), Billy Wilder (95), Henri Cartier-Bresson (96), John Gielgud (96), Katharine Hepburn (96), Estée Lauder (97), John Mills (97), Barbara Cartland (98), George Burns (100), Bob Hope (100), Irving Berlin (101), The Queen Mother (101), Albert Hoffman (102), Rose Kennedy (104)

LIFE
- Upbringing
- Schooling
- University
- Post-graduate
- Hardship
- Lived in a city
- Lived in the countryside
- Lived by the sea

HEALTH
- Vegetarian
- Regular exercise
- Sport
- Outdoorsy
- Overall active life
- Regular sleep
- Major illness

VICES
- Alcohol early life
- Alcohol mid life
- Alcohol late life
- Alcohol very late life
- Cigarettes early life
- Cigarettes mid life
- Cigarettes late life
- Cigarettes very late life
- Cigars
- Soft drugs
- Hard drugs
- Prescription drugs
- Adultery

RELATIONSHIPS
- Sociability
- Sex life
- Marriages
- Quality of marriages
- Acrimonious divorces
- Amicable divorces
- Children
- Grandchildren
- Great grandchildren
- Pets

SPIRITUALITY
- Deity
- Atheist
- Agnostic
- New Age

RANDOMS
- Sense of humour
- Charitability
- Cosmetic surgery
- Mother's lifespan
- Father's lifespan

SUCCESS
- Critical
- Commercial
- Artistic
- Political
- Spiritual
- Output
- Age at retirement

CONTRIBUTION
- Saved lives
- Took lives
- Changed lives
- Changed nation
- Changed world
- Saved the world
- Made new discoveries
- Made them laugh
- Made them cry
- Will stand the test of time?

RECIPE
- Live in a city
- Sleep well
- Quit smoking
- Marry well
- Look after mum
- Work hard... ...all your life
- Make a difference
- Be a legend

source: Wikipedia

Red Vs. Blue

Scientists have discovered that when two evenly matched teams compete,
the team wearing red wins most often

American Football
San Francisco 49'ers / Denver Broncos

American Football
Kansas City Chiefs / Tennessee Titans/ Houston Oilers

Football
Arsenal / Chelsea

Football
Manchester United / Manchester City

Handball
Norway / France

Baseball
LA Anaheim Angels / Toronto Blue Jays

Ice Hockey
Detroit Red Wings / Columbus Blue Jackets

Rugby League
Wigan Warriors / Leeds Rhinos

Rugby Union
Gloucester / Bristol

Ten Pin Bowling
U.S.A. / Europe

Politics
Republican / Democrats

Politics
Labour / Conservative

Red
Vs.
Blue

win 8
draw 2
win 2

source: Hill & Barton, University Of Durham, Journal Of Sports Sciences [via Nature], Wikipedia

Man's Humanity to Man
Ah, that's better

Live Aid
$283m

9/11 Concert
$35m

Wikipedia
$6.2m

over 18m prescriptions worth $3.3 billion free thanks to Patient Assistant Programs

● Free full education (inc. university)

● Free universal healthcare

● Both

MOST GENEROUS CELEBRITIES % of income given to charity

11%

Oprah Winfrey · Nicolas Cage · Michael Jordan · Jerry Seinfeld · Sandra Bullock · Rush Limbaugh · Celine Dion · Paul McCartney · Steven Spielberg

MOST GENEROUS COUNTRIES % of national income given as overseas aid

 1%

Norway · Sweden · Luxembourg · Denmark · Netherlands · Ireland · Austria · Belgium · Spain

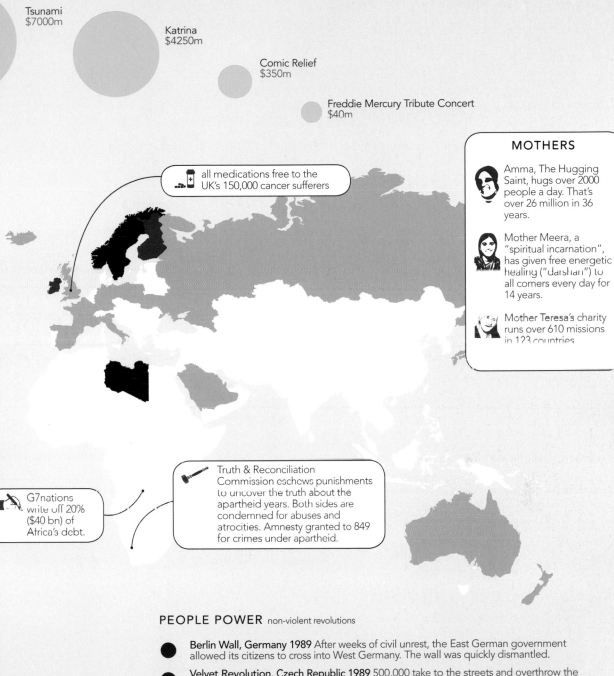

Tsunami
$7000m

Katrina
$4250m

Comic Relief
$350m

Freddie Mercury Tribute Concert
$40m

all medications free to the UK's 150,000 cancer sufferers

MOTHERS

Amma, The Hugging Saint, hugs over 2000 people a day. That's over 26 million in 36 years.

Mother Meera, a "spiritual incarnation", has given free energetic healing ("darshan") to all comers every day for 14 years.

Mother Teresa's charity runs over 610 missions in 123 countries.

G7 nations write off 20% ($40 bn) of Africa's debt.

Truth & Reconciliation Commission eschews punishments to uncover the truth about the apartheid years. Both sides are condemned for abuses and atrocities. Amnesty granted to 849 for crimes under apartheid.

PEOPLE POWER non-violent revolutions

● **Berlin Wall, Germany 1989** After weeks of civil unrest, the East German government allowed its citizens to cross into West Germany. The wall was quickly dismantled.

● **Velvet Revolution, Czech Republic 1989** 500,000 take to the streets and overthrow the communist government without a shot being fired.

● **Bulldozer Revolution, Serbia 2000** Slobodan Milosevic usurped. Named after a bulldozer operator who charged the HQ of Serbian State Television.

● **Rose Revolution, Georgia 2003** A disputed election led to the peaceful overthrow of president-elect Eduard Shevardnadze.

● **Orange Revolution, Ukraine 2004** Thousands protest a presidential election marred by fraud and corruption. Election annulled.

● **Blue Revolution, Kuwait 2005** Kuwaitis protest in support of giving women the vote. The government gives in and women vote in 2007.

source: Wikipedia, Unicef.org, Forbes.com, Un.org

Fast Internet
Most Popular Search Terms 2006

Most Popular Search Terms 2008

idea: Christian Lange coccu.de source: Google Zeigeist

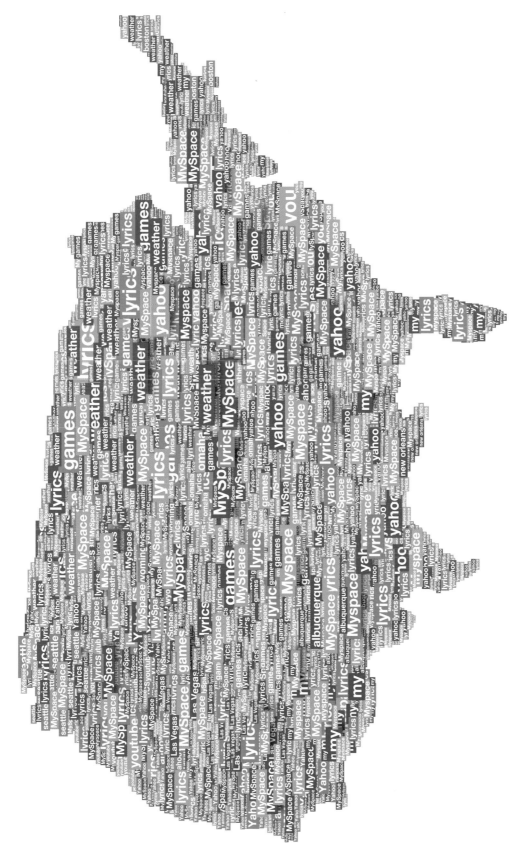

Most Popular Search Terms 2008

idea: Christian Lange coccu.de source: Google Zeigeist

Simple Part II

Time to Get Away
Legally required paid annual leave in days per year

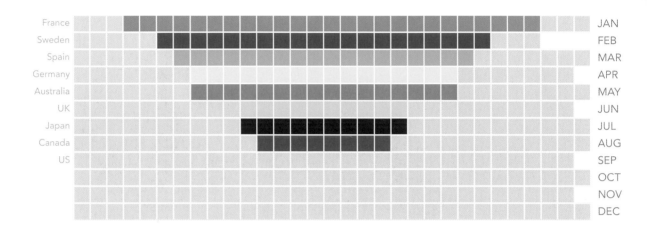

source: Center for Economic & Policy Research, 2007

Lack of Conviction
Rape in England and Wales

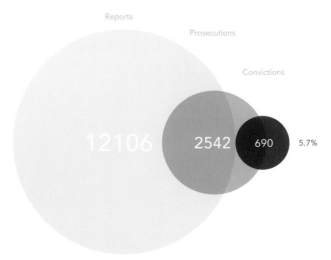

Reports
Prosecutions
Convictions

12106   2542   690   5.7%

source: UK Home Office. Figures for 2007.

Trafficking
World internet bandwidth usage

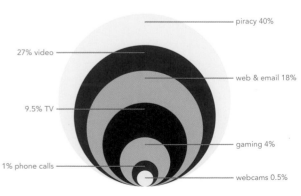

piracy 40%
27% video
web & email 18%
9.5% TV
gaming 4%
1% phone calls
webcams 0.5%

source: Cisco visual networking index

Fat Chance
Who has the most influence on your weight?

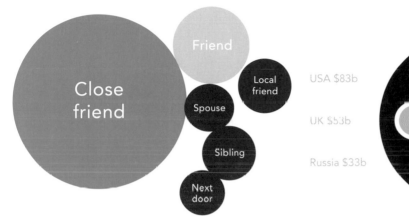

source: N.Fowler, J.Christakis, *N. England Journal Of Medicine*
[via *New Scientist*]

Shooting Stars
Worldwide yearly arms sales

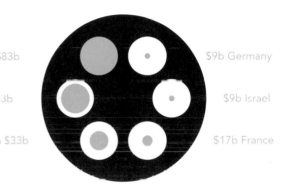

USA $83b $9b Germany

UK $53b $9b Israel

Russia $33b $17b France

source: Guardian.co.uk

Caused by Global Warming
according to media reports

CLIMATE CHANGE Alaska reshaping, oak deaths, ozone repair slowing, El Nino intensification, Gulf Stream failure, new islands, sinking islands, melting alps, mud slides, volcanic eruptions, subsidence, wildfires, earthquakes, tsunamis RANDOMS witchcraft executions, violin decline, killer cornflakes, tabasco tragedy, truffle shortage, tomato rot, fashion disasters, gingerbread house collapse, mammoth dung melt, UFO sightings, mango harvest failure ANIMALS cannibal polar bears, brain-eating amoebas, aggressive elephants, cougar attacks, stronger salmon, rampant robins, shark attacks, confused birds THE EARTH! light dimming, slowing down, spins faster, wobbling, exploding SOCIAL PROBLEMS floods of migrants, suicides, drop in brothel profits, civil unrest, increased taxes, teenage drinking, early marriages, crumbling roads, deformed railways, traffic jams FOOD soaring prices, sour grapes, shop closures, haggis threat, maple syrup shortage, rice shortage, beer shortage! THE TREES! growth increase, growth decline, more colourful, less colourful HEALTH PROBLEMS dog disease, cholera, bubonic plague, airport malaria, asthma, cataracts, smaller brains, HIV, heart disease, depression LESS moose, geese, ducks, puffins, koalas EVEN LESS krill, fish, glaciers, antarctic ice, ice sheets, avalanches, coral reef MOUNTAINS shrinking, taller, flowering, breaking up INVASIONS cat, crabgrass, wasp, beatle, midge, cockroach, stingrays, walrus, giant pythons, giant oysters, giant squid MORE HEALTH PROBLEMS salmonella, kidney stones, anxiety, childhood insomnia, frostbite, fainting, dermatitis, fever, encephalitis, declining circumcision, diarrhoea, fever, dengue, yellow, west nile, hay DISASTER! boredom, next ice age, cannibalism, societal collapse, release of ancient frozen viruses, rioting and nuclear war, computer models, terrorism, accelerated evolution, conflict with Russia. billions of deaths, the end of the world as we know it

source: UK and US media reports [via numberswatch.co.uk]

Life Times

How will you spend your 77.8 years?

sleeping	working	watching TV	doing house wor
28 years	24.5 years	8.5 years	5 years

Visible Spectrum

Current best guess for the composition of the universe

// Dark matter // Intergalactic gas // Normal ma

Invisible

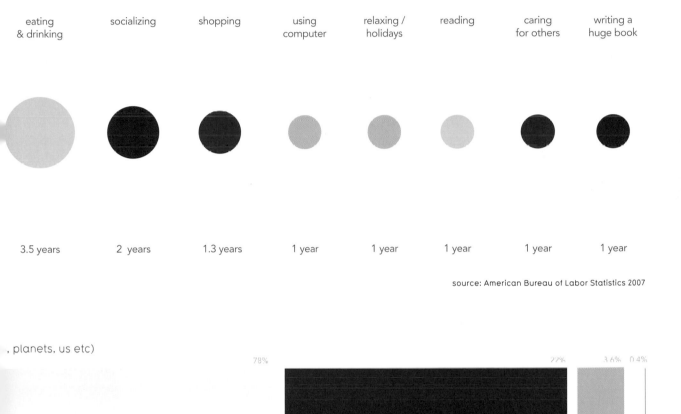

eating & drinking	socializing	shopping	using computer	relaxing / holidays	reading	caring for others	writing a huge book
3.5 years	2 years	1.3 years	1 year	1 year	1 year	1 year	1 year

source: American Bureau of Labor Statistics 2007

, planets, us etc)

78%   22%   3.6%   0.4%

Visible

source: Wikipedia

Mainstream-O-Meter

Average listener counts on Last.fm

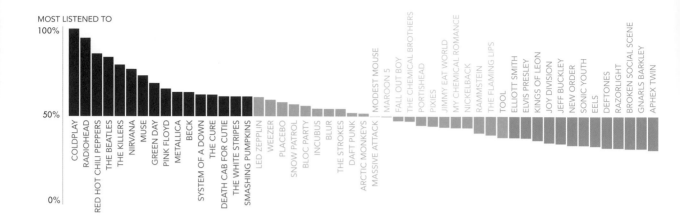

MOST LISTENED TO
100%

50%

0%

COLDPLAY
RADIOHEAD
RED HOT CHILI PEPPERS
THE BEATLES
THE KILLERS
NIRVANA
MUSE
GREEN DAY
PINK FLOYD
METALLICA
BECK
SYSTEM OF A DOWN
THE CURE
DEATH CAB FOR CUTIE
THE WHITE STRIPES
SMASHING PUMPKINS
LED ZEPPLIN
WEEZER
PLACEBO
SNOW PATROL
BLOC PARTY
INCUBUS
BLUR
THE STROKES
DAFT PUNK
ARCTIC MONKEYS
MASSIVE ATTACK
MODEST MOUSE
MAROON 5
FALL OUT BOY
THE CHEMICAL BROTHERS
PORTISHEAD
PIXIES
JIMMY EAT WORLD
MY CHEMICAL ROMANCE
NICKELBACK
RAMMSTEIN
THE FLAMING LIPS
TOOL
ELLIOTT SMITH
ELVIS PRESLEY
KINGS OF LEON
JOY DIVISION
JEFF BUCKLEY
NEW ORDER
SONIC YOUTH
EELS
DEFTONES
RAZORLIGHT
BROKEN SOCIAL SCENE
GNARLS BARKLEY
APHEX TWIN

Who's a Clever Boy?

Brain mass proportional to body mass

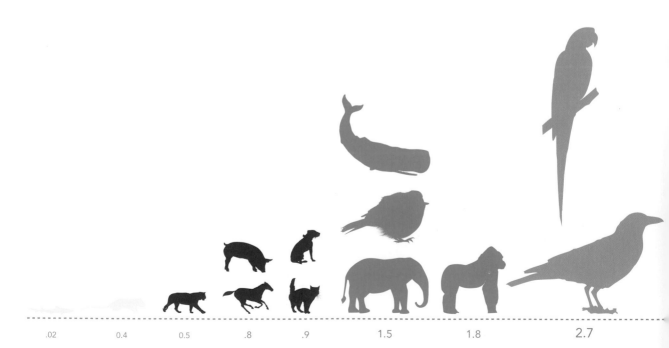

.02   0.4   0.5   .8   .9   1.5   1.8   2.7

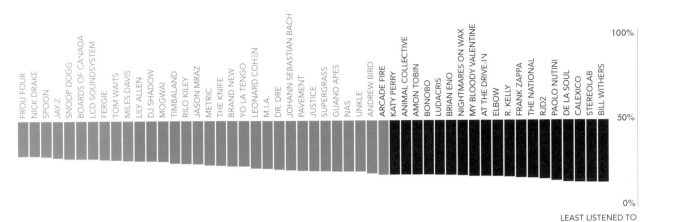

FROU FOUR · NICK DRAKE · SPOON · JAY-Z · SNOOP DOGG · BOARDS OF CANADA · LCD SOUNDSYSTEM · FERGIE · TOM WAITS · MILES DAVIS · LILY ALLEN · DJ SHADOW · MOGWAI · TIMBALAND · RILO KILEY · JASON MRAZ · METRIC · THE KNIFE · BRAND NEW · YO LA TENGO · LEONARD COHEN · M.I.A. · DR. DRE · JOHANN SEBASTIAN BACH · PAVEMENT · JUSTICE · SUPERGRASS · GUANO APES · NAS · UNKLE · ANDREW BIRD · ARCADE FIRE · KATY PERRY · ANIMAL COLLECTIVE · AMON TOBIN · BONOBO · LUDACRIS · BRIAN ENO · NIGHTMARES ON WAX · MY BLOODY VALENTINE · AT THE DRIVE-IN · ELBOW · R. KELLY · FRANK ZAPPA · THE NATIONAL · RJD2 · PAOLO NUTINI · DE LA SOUL · CALEXICO · STEREOLAB · BILL WITHERS

100%

50%

0%

LEAST LISTENED TO

source: mainstream.vincentahrend.com

2.8   5.8   6.8   8   9

times bigger than expected

source: figures use Encephalization Quotient from Martin (1984), Stanyon, Consigliere, Moreschalchi (1993) and Jerison (1973)

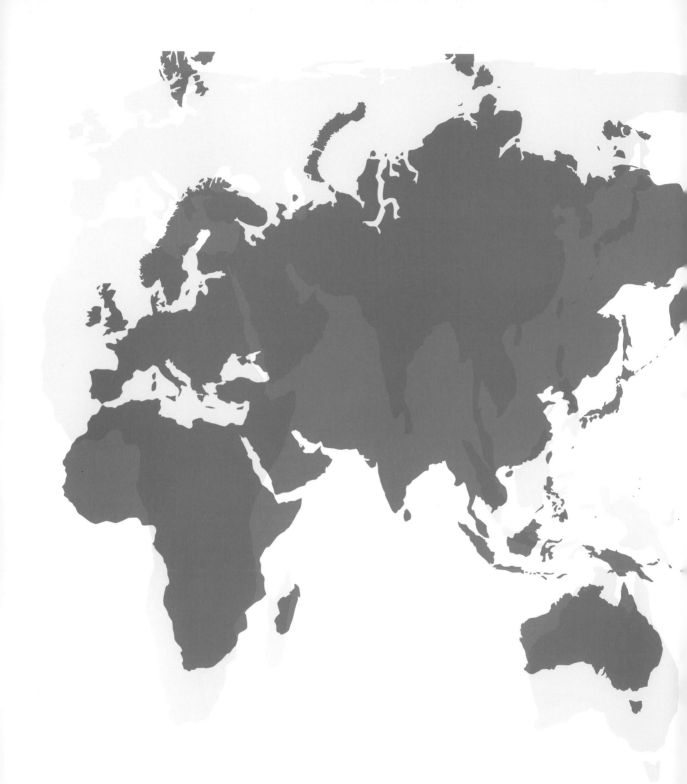

Peter's Projection
The true size of the continents

The standard "Mercator" world map inflates the size of nations depending to their distance from the equator. This means that many developing countries end up much smaller than they are in reality (i.e. most of Africa). The Peter's Projection corrects this.

Alternative Medicine

Scientific evidence for complementary therapies

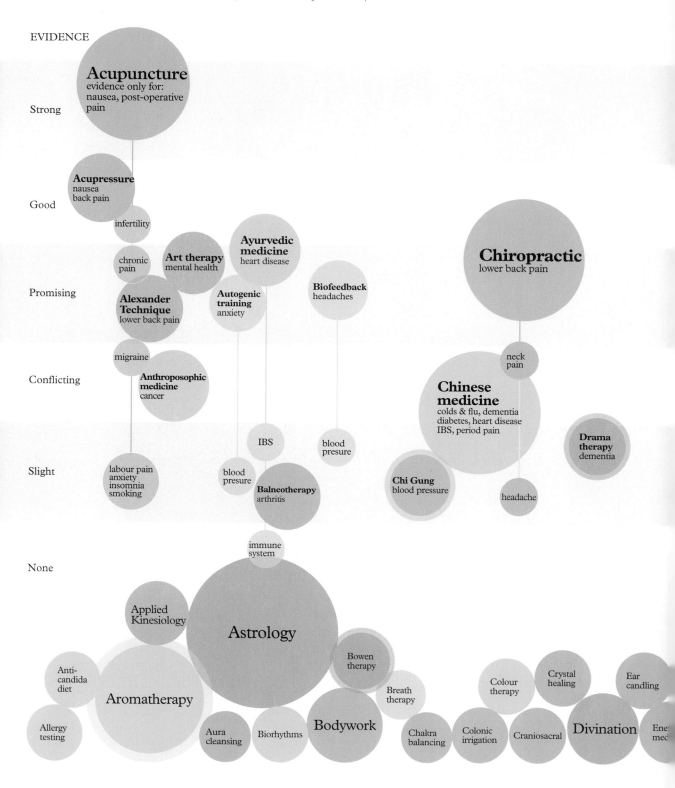

EVIDENCE

Strong

Acupuncture
evidence only for:
nausea, post-operative
pain

Good

Acupressure
nausea
back pain

infertility

chronic
pain

Art therapy
mental health

**Ayurvedic
medicine**
heart disease

Chiropractic
lower back pain

Promising

**Alexander
Technique**
lower back pain

**Autogenic
training**
anxiety

Biofeedback
headaches

migraine

Conflicting

**Anthroposophic
medicine**
cancer

neck
pain

**Chinese
medicine**
colds & flu, dementia
diabetes, heart disease
IBS, period pain

**Drama
therapy**
dementia

IBS

blood
presure

Slight

labour pain
anxiety
insomnia
smoking

blood
presure

Balneotherapy
arthritis

Chi Gung
blood pressure

headache

immune
system

None

Applied
Kinesiology

Astrology

Bowen
therapy

Anti-
candida
diet

Breath
therapy

Colour
therapy

Crystal
healing

Ear
candling

Aromatherapy

Allergy
testing

Aura
cleansing

Biorhythms

Bodywork

Chakra
balancing

Colonic
irrigation

Craniosacral

Divination

Ene
med

body • energy • expressive • psyche • mystical • multiple • natural substances

Popularity   Promising

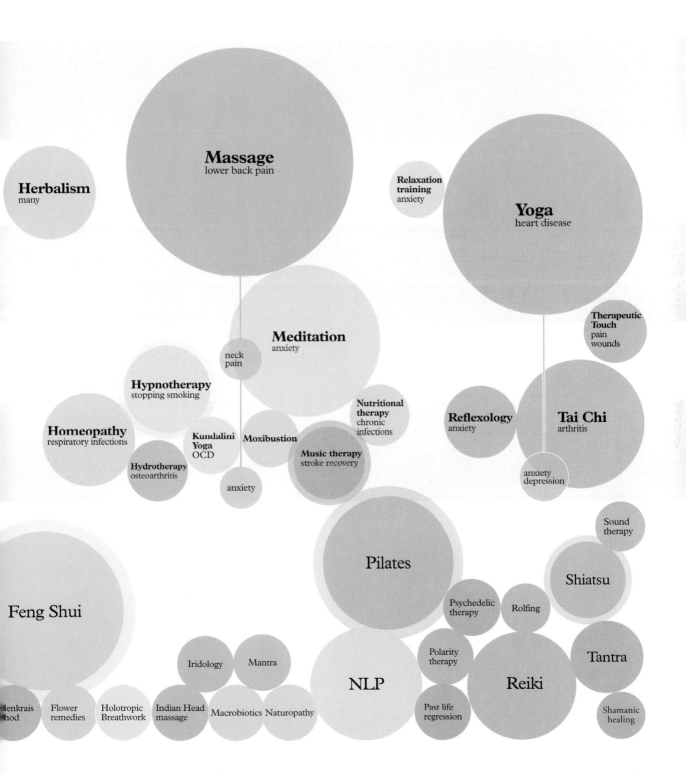

Herbalism
many

Massage
lower back pain

Relaxation training
anxiety

Yoga
heart disease

Meditation
anxiety

neck pain

Therapeutic Touch
pain wounds

Hypnotherapy
stopping smoking

Homeopathy
respiratory infections

Kundalini Yoga
OCD

Moxibustion

Nutritional therapy
chronic infections

Reflexology
anxiety

Tai Chi
arthritis

Hydrotherapy
osteoarthritis

Music therapy
stroke recovery

anxiety

anxiety depression

Sound therapy

Pilates

Shiatsu

Feng Shui

Psychedelic therapy

Rolfing

Iridology   Mantra

Polarity therapy

Tantra

NLP

Reiki

Flenkrais
thod

Flower remedies

Holotropic Breathwork

Indian Head massage

Macrobiotics Naturopathy

Past life regression

Shamanic healing

source: Cochrane.org and other English language meta-studies (via Pubmed.org)

The Cloud
Who owns the top 100 websites?

Size of corporate owner
Most influential

BBC

Disney
ABCNews

Amazon
Alexa
amazon.com
A9
IMDb

Adobe

Tripod

Orange

Go

ESPN

Nokia

NY Times
The New York Times Company

About

Friendster

Brides

Newsweek

Wikipedia

IBM

Ning
Miniclip

Wikia
Target

IStockPhoto

Livejournal

BoingBoing

gettyimages
JupiterImages

Napster

Reuters

Expedia

Last.fm
Cnet
Metacritic
Download
MySimon
GameFAQs

Ultimate Guitar

BEST BUY

Channel4

TV

CBS

Skyrock

Wordpress

TechRepublic
VersionTracker

Game Spot
GameRankings
ZDNet
Mp3

ArsTechnia

Reddit
Style

CondeNet

Bestbuy

Walmart

Telegraph

Perfspot

The Huffington Post

Wired

Neopets
Pandora

Washington Post

Scribd

Delicious

Atom
Game Trailers

FT

LinkedIn

Wowhead

FoxyTunes
Flickr
YAHOO!

VIACOM

Playstation

Yell

Tumblr

Military

Upcoming.org
MyBlogLog

MTV

Argos
Sourceforge

Tesco

Yahoo!
Geocities

Metafilter

Xfire

Netflix

Monster
monster
ProNurses

Fasteweb

NBA

Weather
iVillage

TheRoot

HMForces
Rhapsody

Xanga

Real

Perezhilton

NBC UNIVERSAL

Hulu

Netlogs

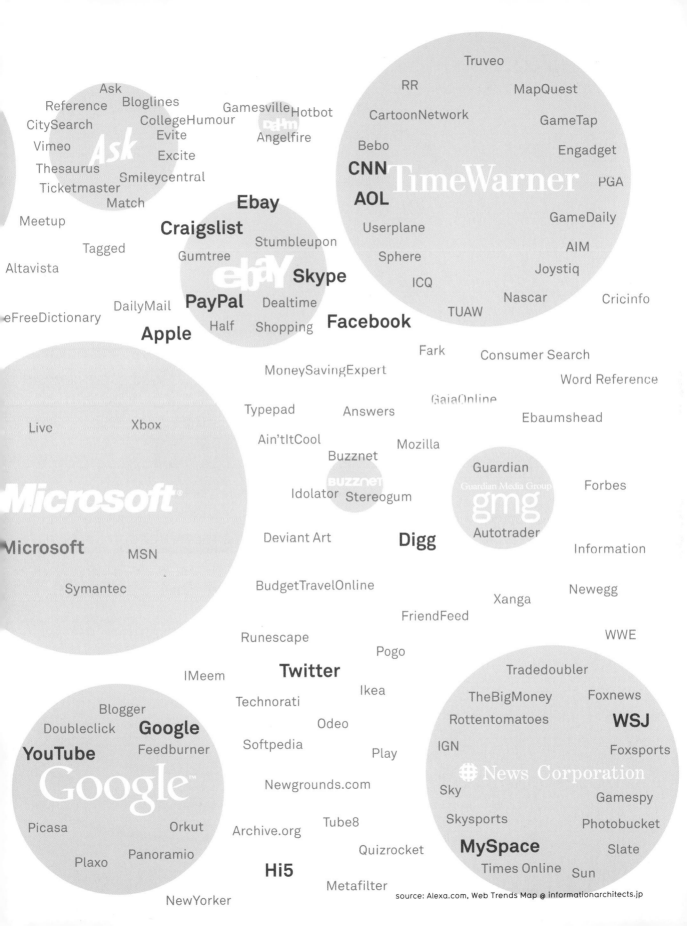

source: Alexa.com, Web Trends Map @ informationarchitects.jp

Being Defensive
How psychotherapy sees you

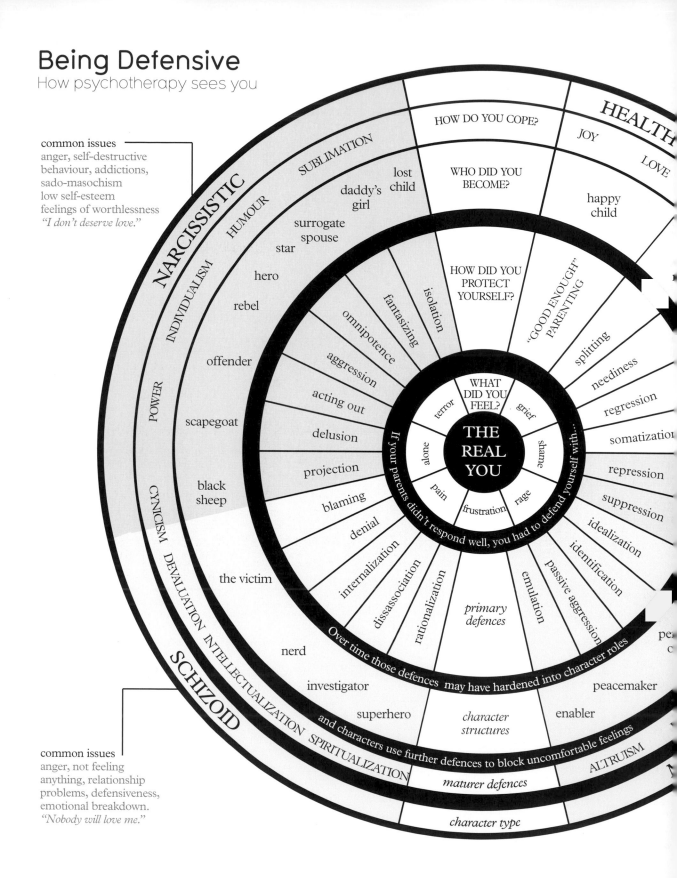

common issues
anger, self-destructive
behaviour, addictions,
sado-masochism
low self-esteem
feelings of worthlessness
"I don't deserve love."

NARCISSISTIC

HUMOUR

SUBLIMATION

INDIVIDUALISM

POWER

CYNICISM   DEVALUATION   INTELLECTUALIZATION

SCHIZOID   SPIRITUALIZATION

common issues
anger, not feeling
anything, relationship
problems, defensiveness,
emotional breakdown.
"Nobody will love me."

daddy's
girl

lost
child

surrogate
spouse

star

hero

rebel

offender

scapegoat

black
sheep

the victim

nerd

investigator

superhero

HOW DO YOU COPE?

HEALTH

JOY

LOVE

WHO DID YOU
BECOME?

happy
child

HOW DID YOU
PROTECT
YOURSELF?

"GOOD ENOUGH"
PARENTING

WHAT
DID YOU
FEEL?

THE
REAL
YOU

terror

grief

alone

shame

pain

rage

frustration

If your parents didn't respond well, you had to defend yourself with...

isolation

fantasizing

omnipotence

aggression

acting out

delusion

projection

blaming

denial

internalization

dissassociation

rationalization

*primary
defences*

emulation

passive aggression

identification

idealization

suppression

repression

somatization

regression

neediness

splitting

Over time those defences may have hardened into character roles

and characters use further defences to block uncomfortable feelings

*character
structures*

peacemaker

enabler

ALTRUISM

maturer defences

character type

pe

c

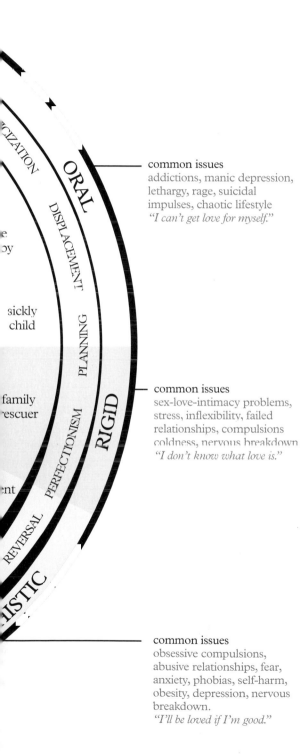

common issues
addictions, manic depression, lethargy, rage, suicidal impulses, chaotic lifestyle
"I can't get love for myself."

common issues
sex-love-intimacy problems, stress, inflexibility, failed relationships, compulsions coldness, nervous breakdown
"I don't know what love is."

common issues
obsessive compulsions, abusive relationships, fear, anxiety, phobias, self-harm, obesity, depression, nervous breakdown.
"I'll be loved if I'm good."

PRIMARY DEFENCES

acting out
turn it into behaviour

aggression
attacking

blaming
someone else's fault

delusion
lie to yourself & believe it

denial
it's not happening

disassociation
go numb

distortion
changing the story to fit

emulation
copy what you know

fantasizing
go into other worlds

idealization
over regard for others

identification
forge an alliance

internalization
holding it all in

isolation
separate off feelings

neediness
over-dependence on another

omnipotence
all powerful, no weakness

passive aggression
indirect & concealed attacks

projection
put your feelings on someone

regression
revert back to immaturity

repression
unconsciously burying it

rationalization
a false but plausible excuse

somatization
turn it into a physical illness

splitting
good/bad, love/hatred

suppression
consciously burying it

MATURER DEFENCES

altruism
efface it with good deeds

cynicism
everything is false

devaluation
it doesn't matter

displacement
find a teddy bear

eroticization
safety in sex

humour
deflect with jokes

individualism
celebrate it

intellectualization
turn it into safe concepts

perfectionism
never slip up again

power
control everyone

planning
safety in organization

reversal
do the opposite of how you feel

spiritualization
it's all a divine purpose

sublimation
make art out of it

undoing
constant acts of compensation

source: the work of Freud, Heinz Kohut, John Bradshaw and A.H.Almaas

Being Defensive
How psychotherapy works

You slowly build a relationship of trust and intimacy with the therapist. That allows you to investigate, explore and ultimately learn to drop your outer defences without feeling threatened.

Exploring your life history, you re-experience situations and relationships from childhood in slow motion with the therapist. This way you can bring adult awareness and understanding to those experiences.

Some types of therapy and their target areas

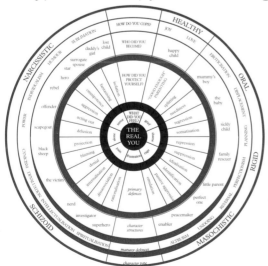

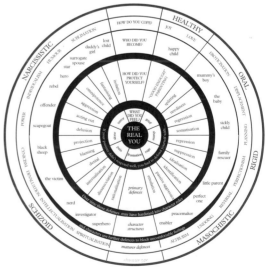

PSYCHOANALYSIS Explores the connection between (possibly "forgotten") events in early life and current disturbances and stress. Talking freely allows fantasies, feelings, dreams and memories to emerge more easily.

COGNITIVE-BEHAVIOURAL THERAPY Uncovering and understanding how inaccurate thoughts, beliefs and assumptions can lead to inaccurate interpretations of events and so to negative emotions and behaviours.

As those experiences are re-felt, digested, understood and perhaps resolved, the difficult and unbearable feelings you weren't able to feel at the time can also be felt. Deeper blocks and resistances may be revealed.

As those feelings are repeatedly felt, you learn to understand, tolerate and deal with them. The "real you", underneath all the defences, can be felt. Nothing really changes. All your defences are still there. You just feel less blocked and become more "transparent".

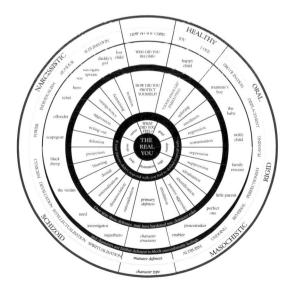

ANTI-DEPRESSANTS Reducing the intensity of symptoms of depression and anxiety and other symptoms of psychological disturbance and distress through regular use of psychiatric medicine.

Most Popular US Girls' Names

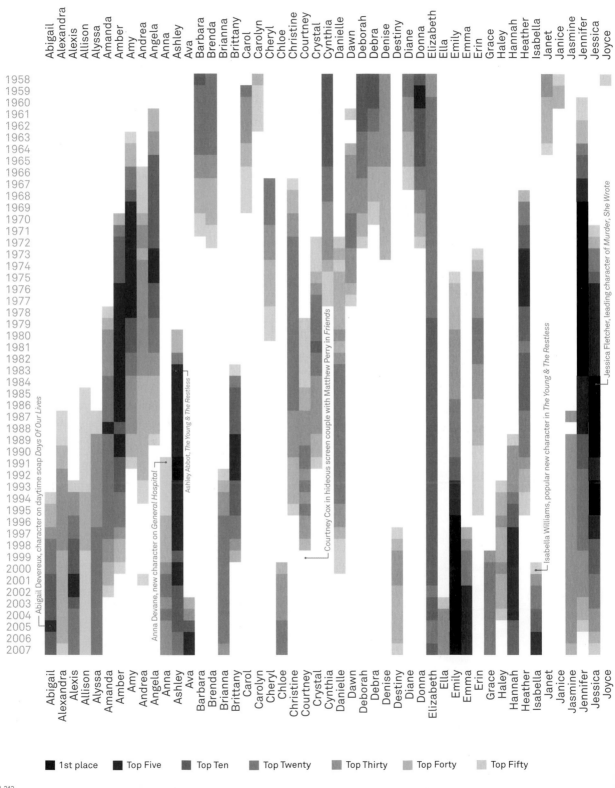

Abigail · Alexandra · Alexis · Allison · Alyssa · Amanda · Amber · Amy · Andrea · Angela · Anna · Ashley · Ava · Barbara · Brenda · Brianna · Brittany · Carol · Carolyn · Cheryl · Chloe · Christine · Courtney · Crystal · Cynthia · Danielle · Dawn · Deborah · Debra · Denise · Destiny · Diane · Donna · Elizabeth · Ella · Emily · Emma · Erin · Grace · Haley · Hannah · Heather · Isabella · Janet · Janice · Jasmine · Jennifer · Jessica · Joyce

1958–2007

Abigail Devereux, character on daytime soap *Days Of Our Lives*

Anna Devane, new character on *General Hospital*

Ashley Abbot, *The Young & The Restless*

Courtney Cox in hideous screen couple with Matthew Perry in *Friends*

Isabella Williams, popular new character in *The Young & The Restless*

Jessica Fletcher, leading character of *Murder, She Wrote*

■ 1st place ■ Top Five ■ Top Ten ■ Top Twenty ■ Top Thirty ■ Top Forty ■ Top Fifty

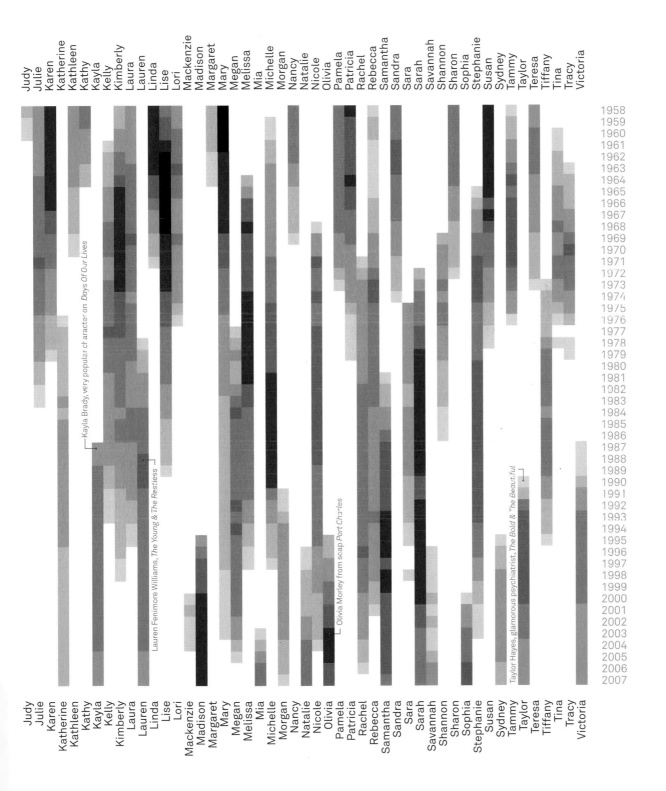

Judy Julie Karen Katherine Kathleen Kathy Kayla Kelly Kimberly Laura Lauren Linda Lise Lori Mackenzie Madison Margaret Mary Megan Melissa Mia Michelle Morgan Nancy Natalie Nicole Olivia Pamela Patricia Rachel Rebecca Samantha Sandra Sara Sarah Savannah Shannon Sharon Sophia Stephanie Susan Sydney Tammy Taylor Teresa Tiffany Tina Tracy Victoria

Kayla Brady, very popular character on *Days Of Our Lives*

Lauren Fenimore Williams, *The Young & The Restless*

Olivia Morley from soap *Port Charles*

Taylor Hayes, glamorous psychiatrist, *The Bold & The Beautiful*

1958 1959 1960 1961 1962 1963 1964 1965 1966 1967 1968 1969 1970 1971 1972 1973 1974 1975 1976 1977 1978 1979 1980 1981 1982 1983 1984 1985 1986 1987 1988 1989 1990 1991 1992 1993 1994 1995 1996 1997 1998 1999 2000 2001 2002 2003 2004 2005 2006 2007

source: US Social Security Administration @ ssa.gov

Most Popular US Boys' Names

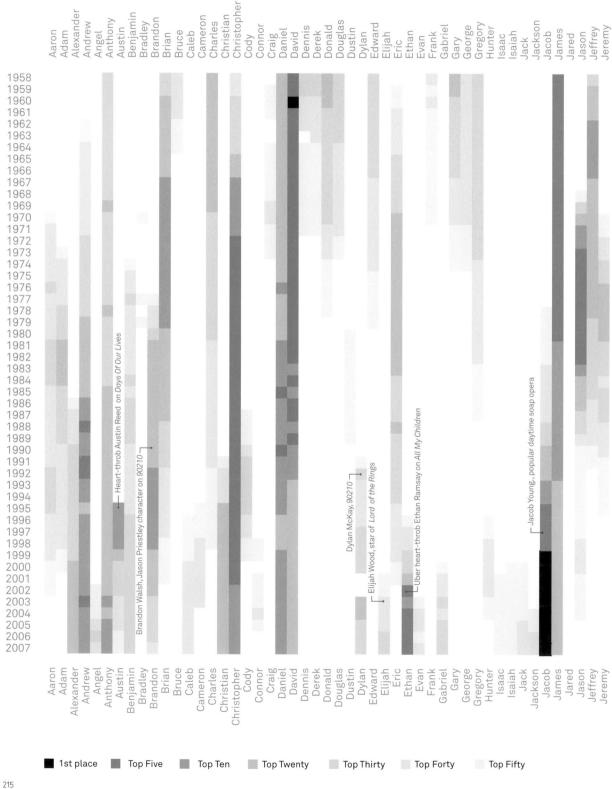

Aaron, Adam, Alexander, Andrew, Angel, Anthony, Austin, Benjamin, Bradley, Brandon, Brian, Bruce, Caleb, Cameron, Charles, Christian, Christopher, Cody, Connor, Craig, Daniel, David, Dennis, Derek, Donald, Douglas, Dustin, Dylan, Edward, Elijah, Eric, Ethan, Evan, Frank, Gabriel, Gary, George, Gregory, Hunter, Isaac, Isaiah, Jack, Jackson, Jacob, James, Jared, Jason, Jeffrey, Jeremy

1958, 1959, 1960, 1961, 1962, 1963, 1964, 1965, 1966, 1967, 1968, 1969, 1970, 1971, 1972, 1973, 1974, 1975, 1976, 1977, 1978, 1979, 1980, 1981, 1982, 1983, 1984, 1985, 1986, 1987, 1988, 1989, 1990, 1991, 1992, 1993, 1994, 1995, 1996, 1997, 1998, 1999, 2000, 2001, 2002, 2003, 2004, 2005, 2006, 2007

Heart-throb Austin Reed on *Days Of Our Lives*

Brandon Walsh, Jason Priestley character on *90210*

Dylan McKay, *90210*

Elijah Wood, star of *Lord of the Rings*

Uber heart-throb Ethan Ramsay on *All My Children*

Jacob Young, popular daytime soap opera

■ 1st place   ■ Top Five   ■ Top Ten   Top Twenty   Top Thirty   Top Forty   Top Fifty

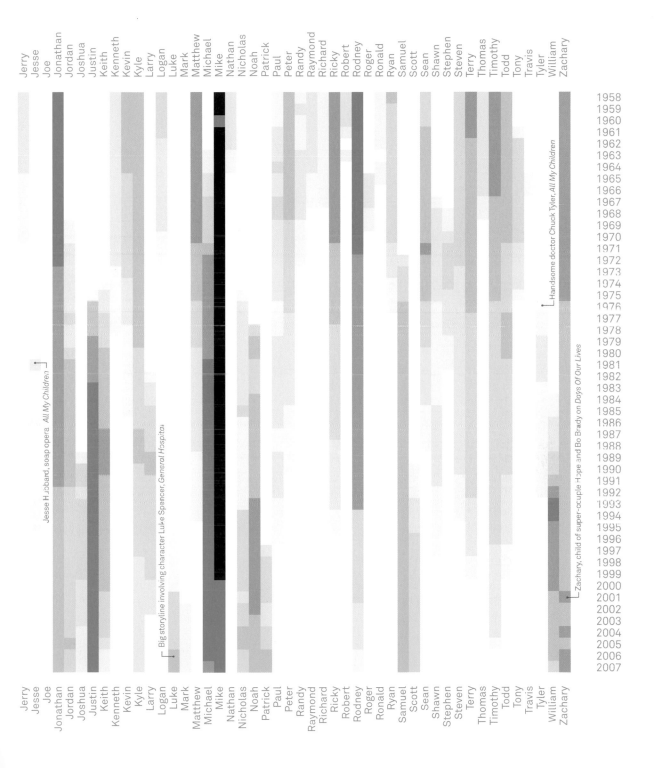

Jerry · Jesse · Joe · Jonathan · Jordan · Joshua · Justin · Keith · Kenneth · Kevin · Kyle · Larry · Logan · Luke · Mark · Matthew · Michael · Mike · Nathan · Nicholas · Noah · Patrick · Paul · Peter · Randy · Raymond · Richard · Ricky · Robert · Rodney · Roger · Ronald · Ryan · Samuel · Scott · Sean · Shawn · Stephen · Steven · Terry · Thomas · Timothy · Todd · Tony · Travis · Tyler · William · Zachary

1958
1959
1960
1961
1962
1963
1964
1965
1966
1967
1968
1969
1970
1971
1972
1973
1974
1975
1976
1977
1978
1979
1980
1981
1982
1983
1984
1985
1986
1987
1988
1989
1990
1991
1992
1993
1994
1995
1996
1997
1998
1999
2000
2001
2002
2003
2004
2005
2006
2007

Jesse Hubbard, soap opera *All My Children*

Big storyline involving character Luke Spencer, *General Hospital*

Handsome doctor Chuck Tyler, *All My Children*

Zachary, child of super-couple Hope and Bo Brady on *Days Of Our Lives*

source: US Social Security Administration @ ssa.gov

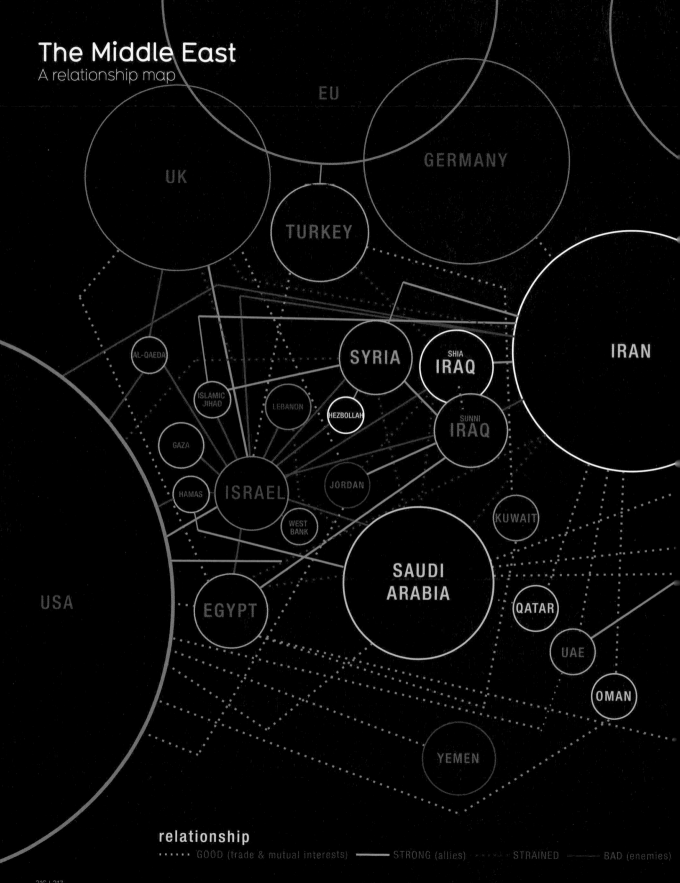

The Middle East
A relationship map

EU

UK

GERMANY

TURKEY

AL-QAEDA

ISLAMIC JIHAD

LEBANON

SYRIA

SHIA IRAQ

IRAN

HEZBOLLAH

SUNNI IRAQ

GAZA

HAMAS

ISRAEL

JORDAN

KUWAIT

WEST BANK

USA

EGYPT

SAUDI ARABIA

QATAR

UAE

OMAN

YEMEN

relationship

····· GOOD (trade & mutual interests) ——— STRONG (allies) ····· STRAINED ——— BAD (enemies)

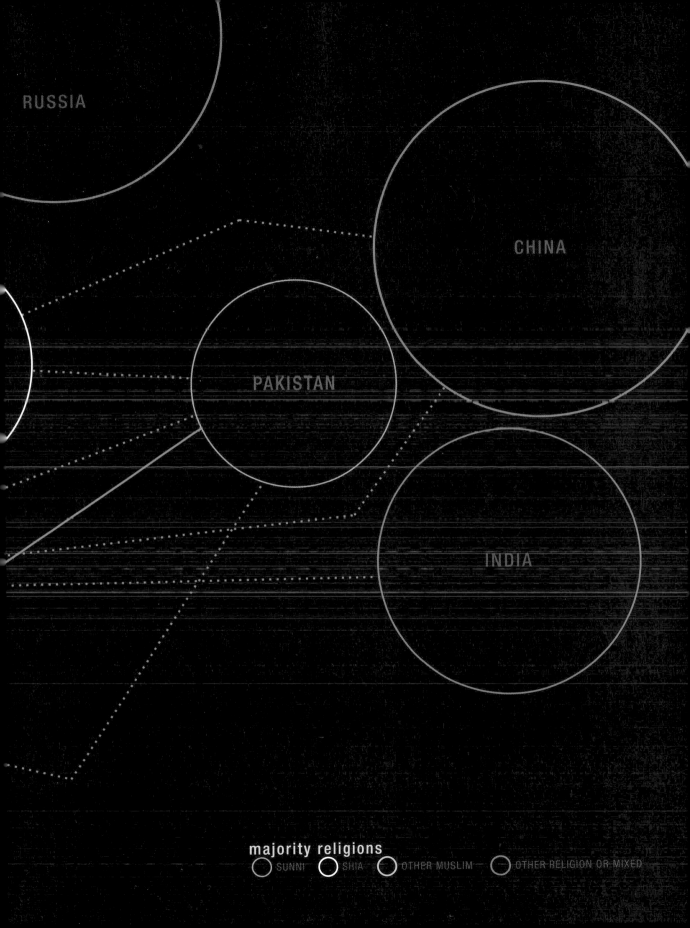

RUSSIA

CHINA

PAKISTAN

INDIA

majority religions
SUNNI   SHIA   OTHER MUSLIM   OTHER RELIGION OR MIXED

The Middle East: Some Context
Palestinian territories

1946   1947   1999   2007

MILLION

Oil States
Who has the world's oil?

2009

Oil States
Who'll have the world's oil?

2020

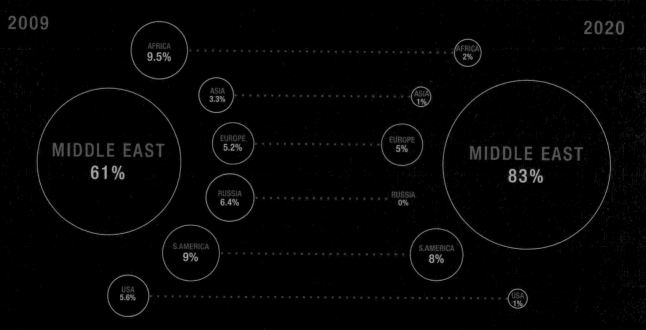

AFRICA
9.5%

AFRICA
2%

ASIA
3.3%

ASIA
1%

MIDDLE EAST
61%

EUROPE
5.2%

EUROPE
5%

MIDDLE EAST
83%

RUSSIA
6.4%

RUSSIA
0%

S.AMERICA
9%

S.AMERICA
8%

USA
5.6%

USA
1%

The Future Of Energy
Place your bets

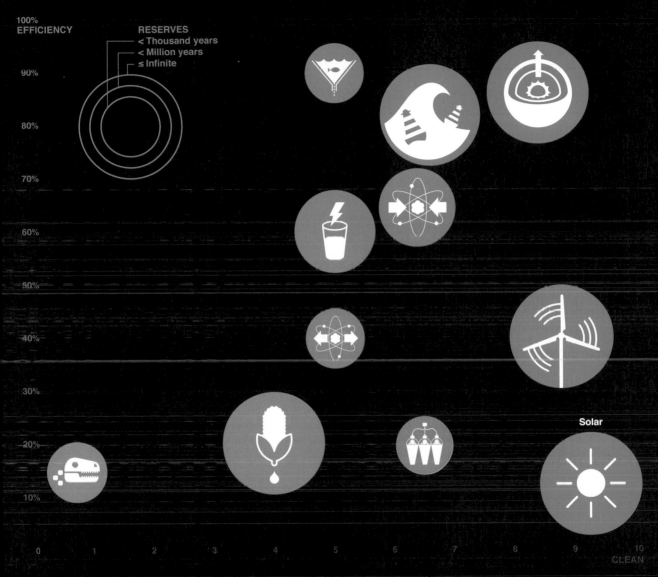

100%
EFFICIENCY

RESERVES
< Thousand years
< Million years
≤ Infinite

90%

80%

70%

60%

50%

40%

30%

20%

Solar

10%

0   1   2   3   4   5   6   7   8   9   10
CLEAN

Biofuel – To replace all of America's petrol consumption with biofuel from plants would take three quarters of all the cultivated land on the face of the Earth.

Fossil Fuel – By products: sulfur dioxide, carbon monoxide, methane, poisonous metals like lead, uranium and of course CO_2.

Geothermal – Drilling for free heat under the earth's surface has lots of advantages and is pollution free. Iceland gets 20% of its energy this way. But watch out for earthquakes!

Human Batteries – The energy in the food needed to feed human power sources is greater than the energy generated. Doh.

Hydroelectric – There's an unavoidable built-in limit to dams. There are only so many places you can put them. And space is running out...

Hydrogen – Currently 96% of hydrogen is made using fossil fuels.

Nuclear Fission – To meet the world's electricity needs from nuclear power would require 2230 more nuclear power stations. There are currently 439 in operation. They can take 5–10 years to build.

Nuclear Fusion – Recreates the temperatures at the heart of the sun. Generates much less nuclear waste than fission. But no one can work out how to do it. "At least 50 years away".

Solar – To replace all current electricity production in the US with solar power would take an area of approximately 3500 square miles (3% of Arizona's land area) covered in solar panels. In most areas of the world, solar panels would cover 85% of household water heating needs.

Tidal – Several question marks remain. Mostly related to its impact on environment and biodiversity.

Wind – Turbines covering about 0.5% of all US land would power the entire country. Around 73,000 to 144,000 5-megawatt wind turbines could power electric cars for every single American.

source: Wikipedia, USGS

Kiss

The Beatles

Black Sabbath

Red Hot Chili Peppers

Nirvana

Aerosmith

The Beach Boys

Pink Floyd

Genesis

The Ramones

AC/DC

U2

Dead members
Sacked members
Members who just gave up
Replaced drummers
Extra lead guitarists
Changes in musical direction
Classical music pretensions
Albums disowned by band
Number of concept albums

Most Successful Rock Bands
True rock success got nothin' to do with selling records

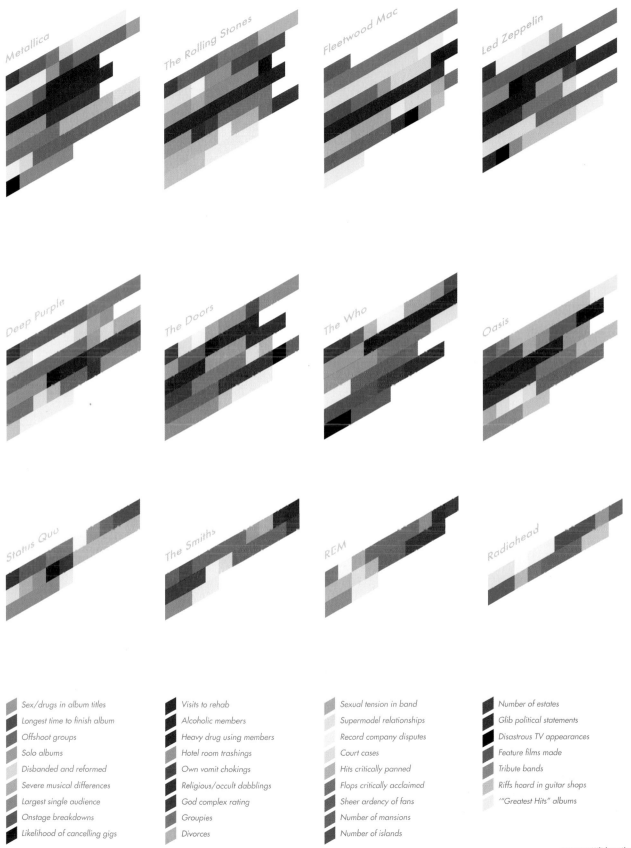

Metallica

The Rolling Stones

Fleetwood Mac

Led Zeppelin

Deep Purple

The Doors

The Who

Oasis

Status Quo

The Smiths

REM

Radiohead

Sex/drugs in album titles
Longest time to finish album
Offshoot groups
Solo albums
Disbanded and reformed
Severe musical differences
Largest single audience
Onstage breakdowns
Likelihood of cancelling gigs

Visits to rehab
Alcoholic members
Heavy drug using members
Hotel room trashings
Own vomit chokings
Religious/occult dabblings
God complex rating
Groupies
Divorces

Sexual tension in band
Supermodel relationships
Record company disputes
Court cases
Hits critically panned
Flops critically acclaimed
Sheer ardency of fans
Number of mansions
Number of islands

Number of estates
Glib political statements
Disastrous TV appearances
Feature films made
Tribute bands
Riffs heard in guitar shops
'"Greatest Hits" albums

source: Wikipedia

22 Stories

P=The Protagonist

Fish Out Of Water P tries to cope in a completely different place/time/world.
Mr Bean, Trading Places

Discovery Through a major upheaval, P discovers a truth about themselves and a better understanding of life.
Close Encounters, Ben-Hur

Escape P trapped by antagonistic forces and must escape. Pronto.
Poseidon Adventure, Saw

Journey & Return P goes on a physical journey and returns changed.
Wizard Of Oz, Star Wars

Temptation P has to make a moral choice between right and wrong.
The Godfather, The Sting

Rags To Riches P is poor, then rich.
Trading Places, La Vie En Rose

The Riddle P has to solve a puzzle or a crime.
The Da Vinci Code, Chinatown

Metamorphosis P literally changes into something else (i.e. a werewolf, hulk, giant cockroach)
Spiderman, Pinocchio

Rescue P must save someone who is trapped physically or emotionally
The Golden Compass, Die Hard

Tragedy P is brought down by a fatal flaw in their character or by forces out of their control.
One Flew Over the Cuckoo's Nest, Atonement

Love A couple meet and overcome obstacles to discover true love. Or – tragically – don't.
Titanic, Grease

Monster Force A monster / alien / something scary and supernatural must be fought and overcome.
Jaws, The Exorcist

Revenge P retaliates against another for a real or imagined injury.
Batman, Kill Bill

Transformation P lives through a series of events that change them as a person.
Pretty Woman, Muriel's Wedding

Maturation P has an experience that matures them or starts a new stage of life, often adulthood.
The Graduate, Juno

Pursuit P has to chase somebody or something, usually in a hide-and-seek fashion.
Goldfinger, Bourne Ultimatum

Rivalry P must triumph over an adversary to attain an object or goal.
Rocky, The Outsiders

Underdog Total loser faces overwhelming odds but wins in the end.
Slumdog Millionaire, Forrest Gump

Comedy A series of complications leads P into ridiculous situations.
Ghostbusters, Airplane

Quest P searches for a person, place or thing, overcoming a number of challenges.
Raiders Of The Lost Ark, Lord of the Rings

Sacrifice P must make a difficult choice between pleasing themselves or a higher purpose (e.g. love, honour).
300, 3:10 to Yuma

Wretched Excess P pushes the limits of acceptable behaviour, destroying themselves in the process.
There Will Be Blood, Citizen Kane

source: Tennesse Screenwriting Association, Robert McKee's *Story*

Most Profitable Hollywood Stories 2007

By percentage of budget recovered

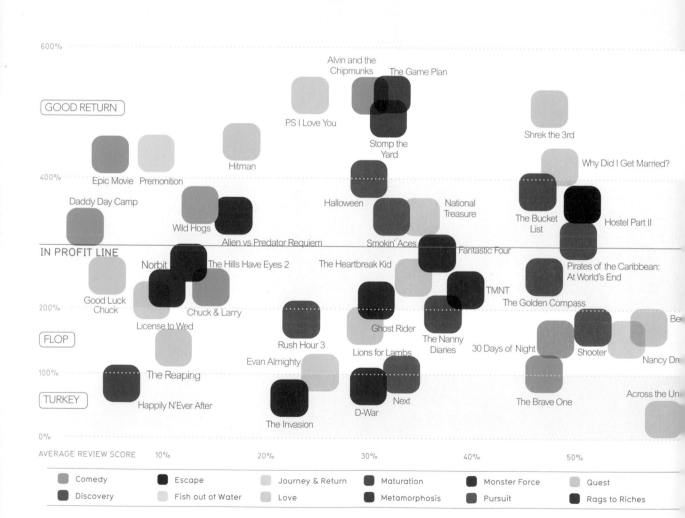

PROFITABILITY

1000%

Saw IV

MEGA HIT

800%

KERCHING!

600%

GOOD RETURN

Alvin and the
Chipmunks   The Game Plan

PS I Love You

Shrek the 3rd

Why Did I Get Married?

Stomp the
Yard

Hitman

400%

Epic Movie   Premonition

Daddy Day Camp

Halloween   National
Treasure

The Bucket
List   Hostel Part II

Wild Hogs

Alien vs Predator Requiem   Smokin' Aces

IN PROFIT LINE

Norbit   The Hills Have Eyes 2   The Heartbreak Kid   Fantastic Four

Pirates of the Caribbean:
At World's End

Good Luck
Chuck   Chuck & Larry   TMNT

The Golden Compass

200%

License to Wed

Be

FLOP   Rush Hour 3   Ghost Rider

The Nanny
Diaries   30 Days of Night   Shooter

Evan Almighty   Lions for Lambs   Nancy Dre

100%

The Reaping   Next

Across the Uni

TURKEY   Happily N'Ever After   D-War   The Brave One

The Invasion

0%

AVERAGE REVIEW SCORE   10%   20%   30%   40%   50%

Comedy   Escape   Journey & Return   Maturation   Monster Force   Quest

Discovery   Fish out of Water   Love   Metamorphosis   Pursuit   Rags to Riches

Average profitability: 316% Average quality: 47%   Most common stories: ■ Love ■ Pursuit

WORTH WATCHING LINE

1000% — Juno
Waitress

800% — Superbad

The Simpsons Movie
Knocked Up   No Country For Old Men — 600%

300

Disturbia

Sicko   The Bourne Ultimatum — 400%
Transformers
The Kite Runner
Spiderman 3   Ocean's 13   The Messengers   Enchanted   Ratatouille
Music & Lyrics   I am Legend   Into The Wild
Live Free Or Die Hard   Michael Clayton   There Will Be Blood
The Mist   American Gangster   Sweeney Todd   Hairspray
We Own The Night
Mr Brooks
Blades Of Glory — 200%
The Darjeeling Ltd
Meet The Robinsons   Surf's Up
Vacancy   Charlie Wilson's War   3:10 Zodiac
The Kingdom   Beowulf   to Yuma — 100%
Shoot'em up
Walk Hard: The Dewey Cox Story   Grind House

0%

55%   60%   70%   80%   90%   100%

■ Rescue   ■ Rivalry   ■ Temptation   ■ Tragedy   ■ Underdog
■ Revenge   ■ Sacrifice   ■ The Riddle   ■ Transformation ■ Wretched Excess

Story

source: BoxOfficeMojo.com, The-Numbers.com, Wikipedia, IMDB.com & RottenTomatoes.com. Note: reported film budgets are notoriously unreliable
(especially for flops)

Most Profitable Bollywood Stories 2007

Average profitability: 292%   Average quality: 59%   Most common stories: ☐ Love ■ Pursuit

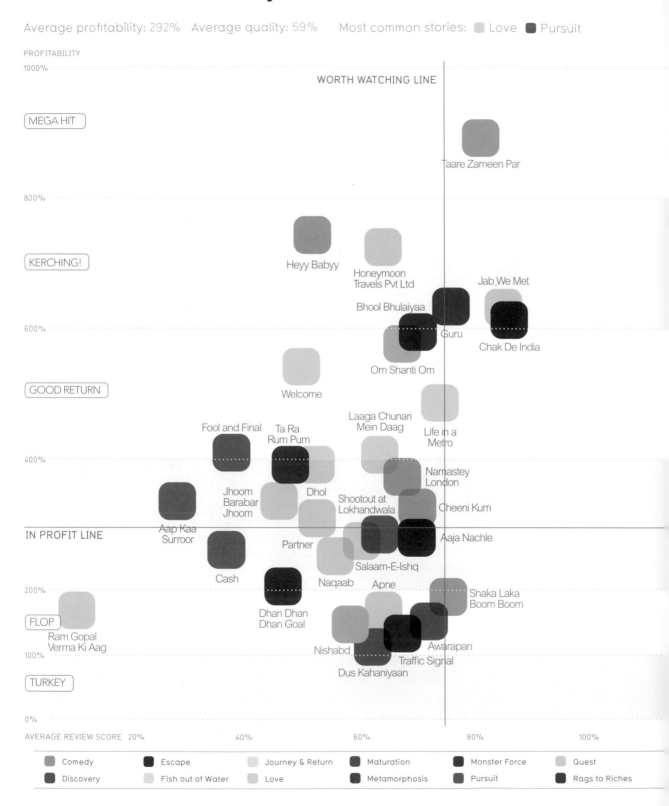

PROFITABILITY

1000%

WORTH WATCHING LINE

[MEGA HIT]

Taare Zameen Par

800%

[KERCHING!]

Heyy Babyy

Honeymoon
Travels Pvt Ltd

Jab We Met

Bhool Bhulaiyaa

600%

Guru

Chak De India

Om Shanti Om

[GOOD RETURN]

Welcome

Laaga Chunari
Mein Daag

Life in a
Metro

Fool and Final   Ta Ra
Rum Pum

400%

Namastey
London

Jhoom
Barabar   Dhol
Jhoom

Shootout at
Lokhandwala

Cheeni Kum

Aap Kaa
Surroor

IN PROFIT LINE

Aaja Nachle

Partner

Salaam-E-Ishq

Cash

Naqaab   Apne

200%

Shaka Laka
Boom Boom

[FLOP]

Dhan Dhan
Dhan Goal

Awarapan

Ram Gopal
Verma Ki Aag

Nishabd

Traffic Signal

100%

Dus Kahaniyaan

[TURKEY]

0%

AVERAGE REVIEW SCORE   20%   40%   60%   80%   100%

| ■ Comedy | ■ Escape | ☐ Journey & Return | ■ Maturation | ■ Monster Force | ☐ Quest |
| ■ Discovery | ☐ Fish out of Water | ☐ Love | ■ Metamorphosis | ■ Pursuit | ■ Rags to Riches |

Most Profitable UK Stories 2007

Average profitability: 277%   Average quality: 71%   Most common stories: ■ Comedy ■ Monster–Force

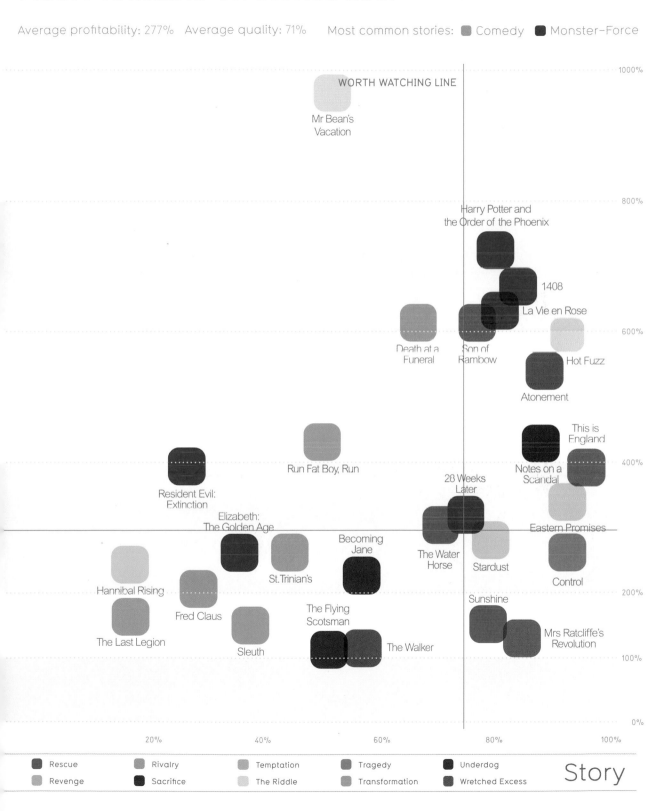

1000%

WORTH WATCHING LINE

Mr Bean's
Vacation

800%

Harry Potter and
the Order of the Phoenix

1408

La Vie en Rose

600%

Death at a
Funeral

Son of
Rambow

Hot Fuzz

Atonement

This is
England

Run Fat Boy, Run

28 Weeks
Later

Notes on a
Scandal

400%

Resident Evil:
Extinction

Eastern Promises

Elizabeth:
The Golden Age

Becoming
Jane

The Water
Horse

Stardust

St. Trinian's

Control

Hannibal Rising

Sunshine

200%

Fred Claus

The Flying
Scotsman

Mrs Ratcliffe's
Revolution

The Last Legion

Sleuth

The Walker

100%

0%

20%   40%   60%   80%   100%

| Rescue | Rivalry | Temptation | Tragedy | Underdog |
| Revenge | Sacrifice | The Riddle | Transformation | Wretched Excess |

Story

source: Naachgaana.com, BoxOfficeIndia.com, The-Numbers.com, BoxOfficeMojo.com & The British Film Institute.

Most Profitable Hollywood Stories 2008

By percentage of budget recovered

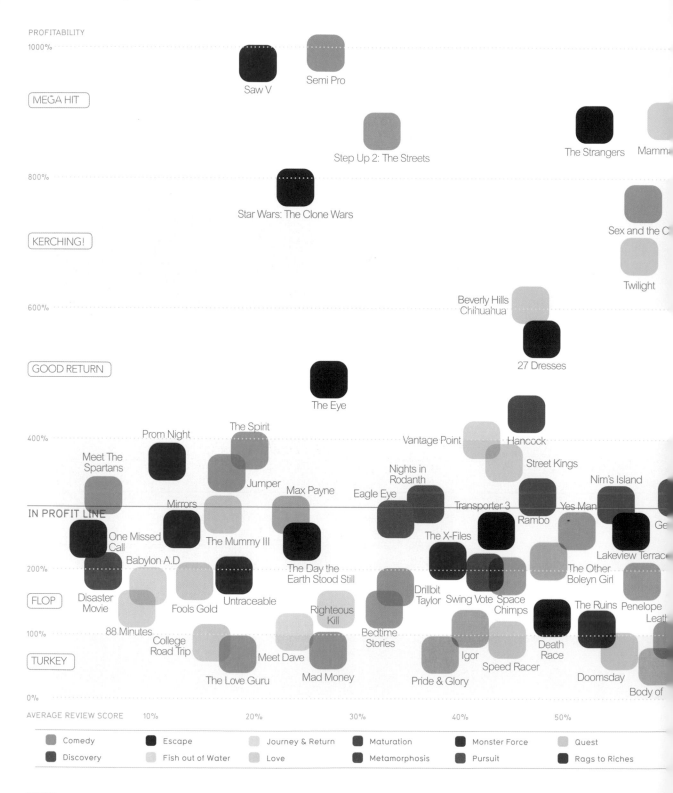

PROFITABILITY

1000%

MEGA HIT

Saw V

Semi Pro

Step Up 2: The Streets

The Strangers

Mamma

800%

Star Wars: The Clone Wars

KERCHING!

Sex and the C

Twilight

600%

Beverly Hills Chihuahua

GOOD RETURN

27 Dresses

The Eye

400%

Prom Night

The Spirit

Vantage Point

Hancock

Meet The Spartans

Jumper

Street Kings

Nim's Island

Max Payne

Nights in Rodanth

Mirrors

Eagle Eye

Transporter 3

Yes Man

IN PROFIT LINE

One Missed Call

The Mummy III

Rambo

Ge

The X-Files

Babylon A.D

Lakeview Terrac

200%

Disaster Movie

Fools Gold

Untraceable

The Day the Earth Stood Still

Drillbit Taylor

Swing Vote

Space Chimps

The Other Boleyn Girl

FLOP

Righteous Kill

The Ruins

Penelope

88 Minutes

Bedtime Stories

Leath

100%

College Road Trip

Igor

Death Race

TURKEY

Meet Dave

Speed Racer

Doomsday

The Love Guru

Mad Money

Pride & Glory

Body of

0%

AVERAGE REVIEW SCORE   10%   20%   30%   40%   50%

	Comedy		Escape		Journey & Return		Maturation		Monster Force		Quest
	Discovery		Fish out of Water		Love		Metamorphosis		Pursuit		Rags to Riches

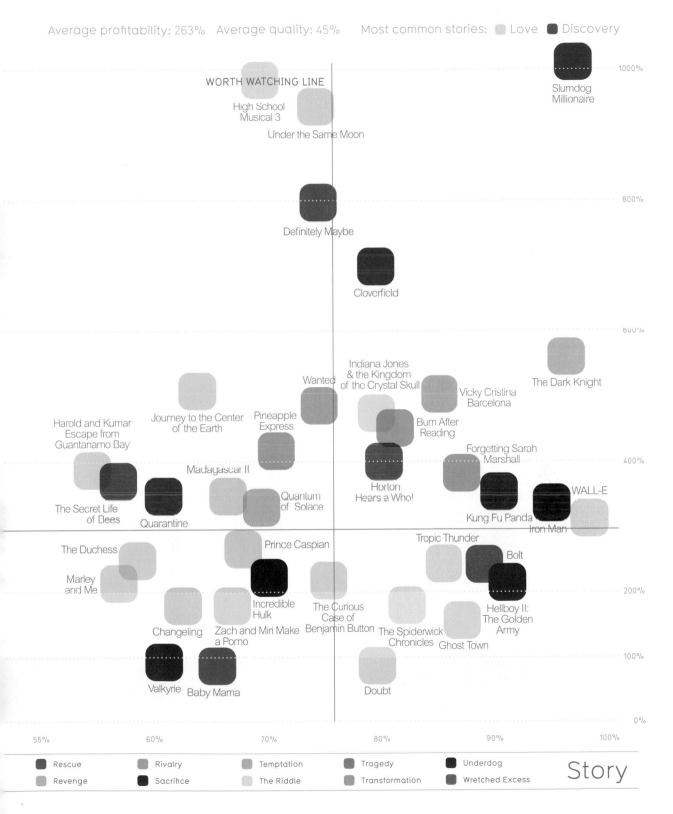

Average profitability: 263%   Average quality: 45%   Most common stories: ■ Love ■ Discovery

1000%

WORTH WATCHING LINE

Slumdog
Millionaire

High School
Musical 3

Under the Same Moon

800%

Definitely Maybe

Cloverfield

600%

Indiana Jones
& the Kingdom
of the Crystal Skull

Wanted

Vicky Cristina
Barcelona

The Dark Knight

Journey to the Center
of the Earth

Pineapple
Express

Burn After
Reading

Harold and Kumar
Escape from
Guantanamo Bay

Forgetting Sarah
Marshall

400%

Madagascar II

Horton
Hears a Who!

WALL-E

The Secret Life
of Dees

Quantum
of Solace

Kung Fu Panda

Quarantine

Iron Man

The Duchess

Prince Caspian

Tropic Thunder

Bolt

Marley
and Me

200%

Incredible
Hulk

The Curious
Case of
Benjamin Button

Hellboy II:
The Golden
Army

Changeling

Zach and Miri Make
a Porno

The Spiderwick
Chronicles Ghost Town

100%

Valkyrie   Baby Mama

Doubt

0%

55%   60%   70%   80%   90%   100%

■ Rescue   ■ Rivalry   ■ Temptation   ■ Tragedy   ■ Underdog

■ Revenge   ■ Sacrifice   ■ The Riddle   ■ Transformation ■ Wretched Excess

Story

source: BoxOfficeMojo.com, The-Numbers.com, Wikipedia, IMDB.com & RottenTomatoes.com. Note: reported film budgets are notoriously unreliable
(especially for flops)

Most Profitable Bollywood Stories 2008

Average profitability: 155%   Average quality: 62%   Most common stories: ▢ Love ▢ Temptation

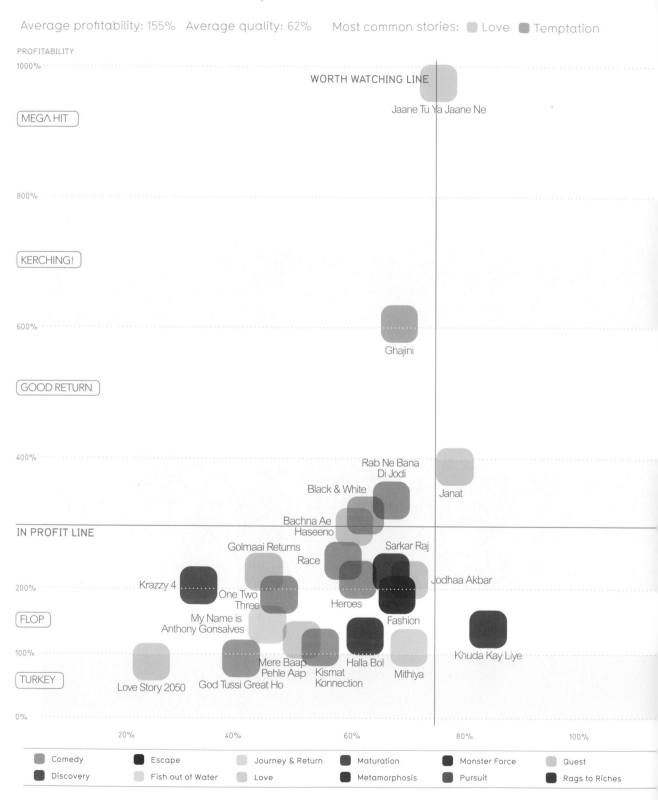

PROFITABILITY

1000% ···

WORTH WATCHING LINE

MEGA HIT

Jaane Tu Ya Jaane Ne

800% ···

KERCHING!

600% ···

Ghajini

GOOD RETURN

400% ···

Rab Ne Bana
Di Jodi

Black & White

Janat

IN PROFIT LINE ···

Bachna Ae
Haseeno

Golmaai Returns

Sarkar Raj

Race

Jodhaa Akbar

Krazzy 4

200% ···

One Two
Three

Heroes

FLOP

My Name is
Anthony Gonsalves

Fashion

Khuda Kay Liye

100% ···

Mere Baap
Pehle Aap

Halla Bol

Mithiya

TURKEY

Love Story 2050   God Tussi Great Ho   Kismat
Konnection

0% ···

20%   40%   60%   80%   100%

▢ Comedy   ▢ Escape   ▢ Journey & Return   ▢ Maturation   ▢ Monster Force   ▢ Quest

▢ Discovery   ▢ Fish out of Water ▢ Love   ▢ Metamorphosis   ▢ Pursuit   ▢ Rags to Riches

Most Profitable UK Stories 2008

Average profitability: 148%   Average quality: 57%   Most common stories: ■ Love ■ Discovery

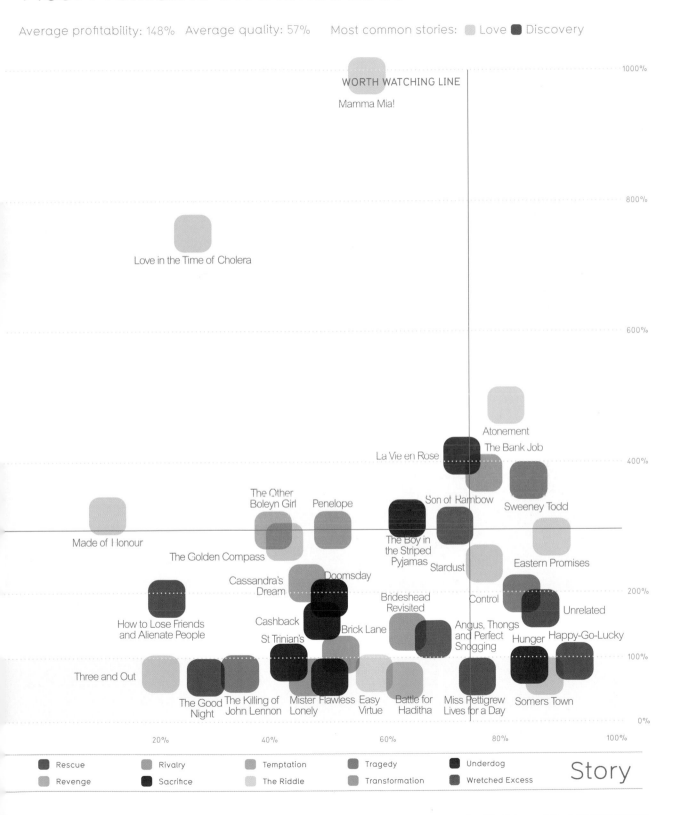

WORTH WATCHING LINE

Mamma Mia!

Love in the Time of Cholera

Atonement

The Bank Job

La Vie en Rose

The Other Boleyn Girl

Penelope

Son of Rambow

Sweeney Todd

Made of Honour

The Golden Compass

The Boy in the Striped Pyjamas

Stardust

Eastern Promises

Cassandra's Dream

Doomsday

Brideshead Revisited

Control

Unrelated

How to Lose Friends and Alienate People

Cashback

Brick Lane

Angus, Thongs and Perfect Snogging

Hunger

Happy-Go-Lucky

St Trinian's

Three and Out

The Good Night

The Killing of John Lennon

Mister Lonely

Flawless

Easy Virtue

Battle for Haditha

Miss Pettigrew Lives for a Day

Somers Town

1000%
800%
600%
400%
200%
0%

20%   40%   60%   80%   100%

■ Rescue   ■ Rivalry   ■ Temptation   ■ Tragedy   ■ Underdog
■ Revenge   ■ Sacrifice   ■ The Riddle   ■ Transformation   ■ Wretched Excess

Story

source: Naachgaana.com, BoxOfficeIndia.com, The-Numbers.com, BoxOfficeMojo.com & The British Film Institute.

Most Profitable Stories Of All Time
By percentage of budget recovered

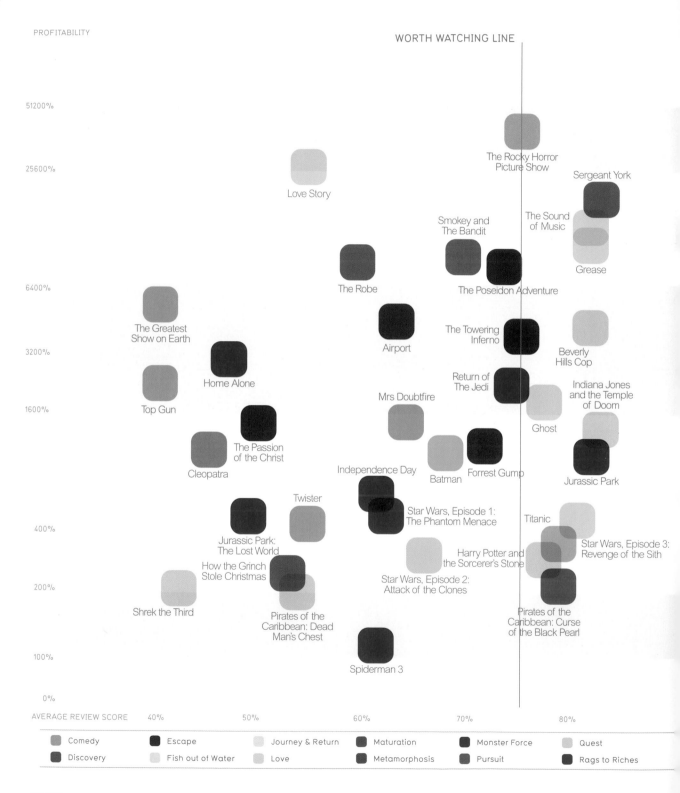

PROFITABILITY

WORTH WATCHING LINE

51200%

25600%

Love Story

The Rocky Horror
Picture Show

Sergeant York

The Sound
of Music

Smokey and
The Bandit

Grease

6400%

The Robe

The Poseidon Adventure

The Greatest
Show on Earth

Airport

The Towering
Inferno

Beverly
Hills Cop

3200%

Home Alone

Return of
The Jedi

Indiana Jones
and the Temple
of Doom

1600%

Top Gun

Mrs Doubtfire

Ghost

The Passion
of the Christ

Jurassic Park

Cleopatra

Independence Day

Batman

Forrest Gump

Twister

Star Wars, Episode 1:
The Phantom Menace

Titanic

Star Wars, Episode 3:
Revenge of the Sith

400%

Jurassic Park:
The Lost World

Harry Potter and
the Sorcerer's Stone

How the Grinch
Stole Christmas

Star Wars, Episode 2:
Attack of the Clones

200%

Shrek the Third

Pirates of the
Caribbean: Dead
Man's Chest

Pirates of the
Caribbean: Curse
of the Black Pearl

100%

Spiderman 3

0%

AVERAGE REVIEW SCORE   40%   50%   60%   70%   80%

| ■ Comedy | ■ Escape | ■ Journey & Return | ■ Maturation | ■ Monster Force | ■ Quest |
| ■ Discovery | ■ Fish out of Water | ■ Love | ■ Metamorphosis | ■ Pursuit | ■ Rags to Riches |

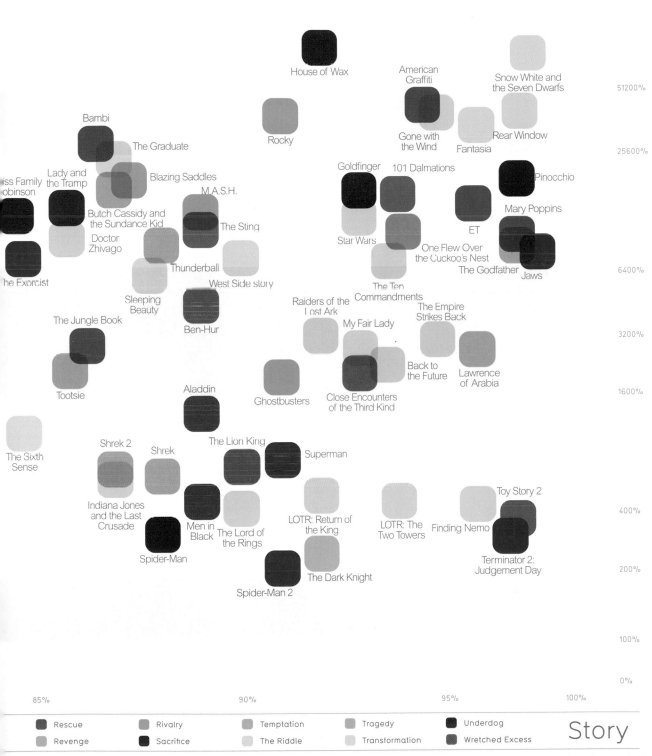

Average budget: 43m   Average quality: 83%   Most profitable stories: ◻ Quest ■ Monster Force

House of Wax

American
Graffiti

Snow White and
the Seven Dwarfs   51200%

Bambi

Rocky

Gone with
the Wind   Fantasia   Rear Window

The Graduate   25600%

Goldfinger   101 Dalmations   Pinocchio

Lady and
iss Family   the Tramp   Blazing Saddles   Mary Poppins
obinson
                        M.A.S.H.
                                                              ET
            Butch Cassidy and
            the Sundance Kid   The Sting   One Flew Over
            Doctor   Star Wars   the Cuckoo's Nest
            Zhivago   The Godfather Jaws   6400%
he Exorcist   Thunderball
                                West Side story   The Ten
            Sleeping   Commandments
            Beauty   Ben-Hur   Raiders of the   The Empire
The Jungle Book   Lost Ark   My Fair Lady   Strikes Back
                                                                              3200%

Tootsie   Aladdin   Back to   Lawrence
                        Ghostbusters   Close Encounters   the Future   of Arabia
                                            of the Third Kind   1600%

            Shrek 2   The Lion King
The Sixth   Shrek   Superman
Sense
                                                                  Toy Story 2
            Indiana Jones   400%
            and the Last   LOTR: Return of   LOTR: The   Finding Nemo
            Crusade   Men in The Lord of the King   Two Towers
                      Black   the Rings   Terminator 2:
                  Spider-Man   Judgement Day 200%

                              Spider-Man 2   The Dark Knight

                                                                              100%

                                                                              0%

85%   90%   95%   100%

◼ Rescue   ◼ Rivalry   ◼ Temptation   ◼ Tragedy   ◼ Underdog   Story
◻ Revenge   ◼ Sacrifice   ◻ The Riddle   ◻ Transformation ◼ Wretched Excess

Enneagram

A personality–type system based around an ancient symbol of perpetual motion. Each type is formed from a key defence against the world. Which one are you?

		I am...	I want to...	Virtue
1	**Reformer**	Reasonable and objective	Be good & to have integrity	Serenity
2	**Helper**	Caring and loving	Feel love	Humility
3	**Achiever**	Outstanding and effective	Feel valuable	Honesty
4	**Individualist**	Intuitive and sensitive	Be myself	Balance
5	**Investigator**	Intelligent, perceptive	Be capable & competent	Detachment
6	**Loyalist**	Committed, dependable	Have support and guidance	Courage
7	**Enthusiast**	Reasonable and objective	Be satisfied and content	Sobriety
8	**Challenger**	Strong, assertive	Protect myself	Innocence
9	**Peacemaker**	Peaceful, easygoing	Have peace of mind	Action

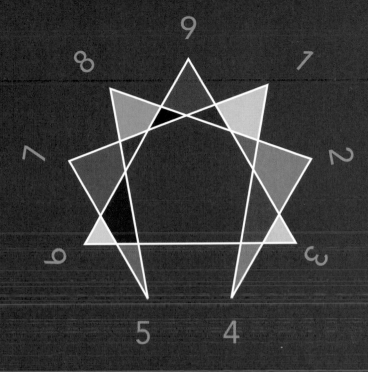

Hidden complaint	I fear being...	Flaw	Saving grace
I am usually right. Others should listen to me.	Bad, wrong	Resentment	Sensible
I'm always loving. Others take me for granted.	Unloved	Flattery	Empathic
I am a superior person. Others are jealous	Worthless	Vanity	Eagerness
I don't really fit in. I am different from others.	Insignificant	Melancholy	Self-aware
I'm so smart. Others can't understand me.	Helpless or incompetent	Stinginess	No bullshit
I do what I'm told . Others don't	Without support	Worrying	Friendly
I'm happy. But others don't give me enough.	In pain	Over-Planning	Enthusiasm
I'm fighting to survive. Others take advantage.	Harmed or controlled	Vengeance	Strength
I am content. Others pressure me to change.	Lost and separated	Laziness	Fluidity

source: Wikipedia, EnneagramInstitute.com

Bee Limit Warning

Why are they disappearing?

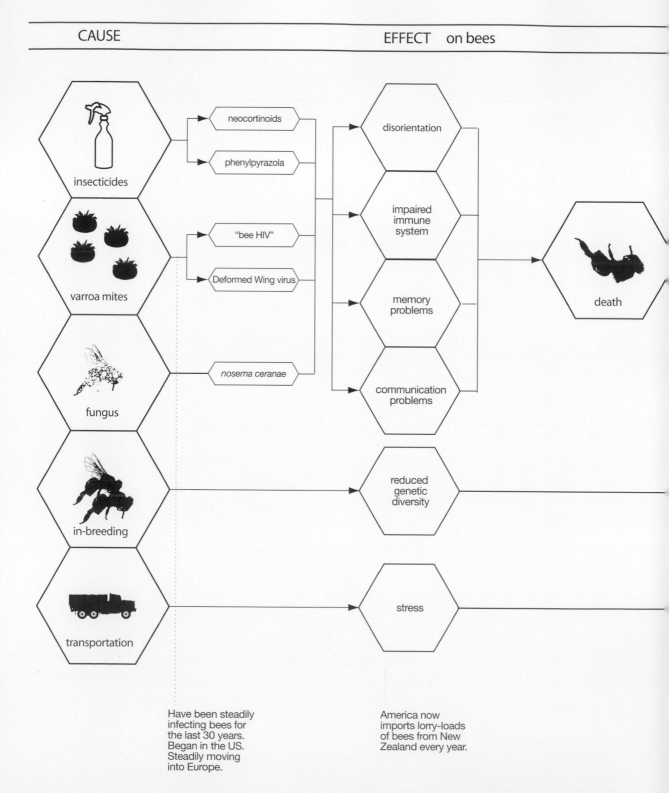

CAUSE

EFFECT on bees

insecticides

neocortinoids

phenylpyrazola

varroa mites

"bee HIV"

Deformed Wing virus

fungus

nosema ceranae

in-breeding

transportation

disorientation

impaired immune system

memory problems

communication problems

reduced genetic diversity

stress

death

Have been steadily infecting bees for the last 30 years. Began in the US. Steadily moving into Europe.

America now imports lorry-loads of bees from New Zealand every year.

on hives   on farming

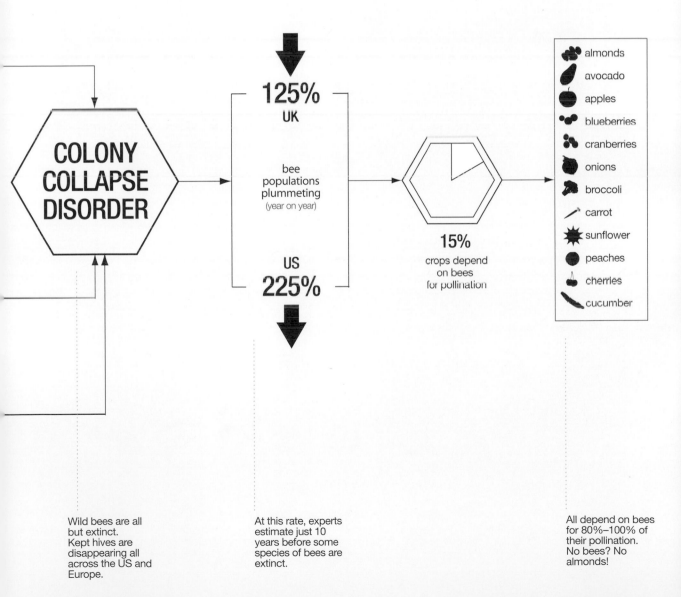

COLONY
COLLAPSE
DISORDER

125%
UK

bee
populations
plummeting
(year on year)

US
225%

15%
crops depend
on bees
for pollination

almonds
avocado
apples
blueberries
cranberries
onions
broccoli
carrot
sunflower
peaches
cherries
cucumber

Wild bees are all
but extinct.
Kept hives are
disappearing all
across the US and
Europe.

At this rate, experts
estimate just 10
years before some
species of bees are
extinct.

All depend on bees
for 80%–100% of
their pollination.
No bees? No
almonds!

source: Wikipedia, Discovery.com, New York Times

Selling Your Soul

Workers on Amazon.com's Mechanical Turk asked to draw their souls

female

Amazon's Mechanical Turk is a "cloud workforce" of people happy to do microjobs for micropayments ($0.25 and up). 200 people were asked to draw a picture of their soul for the author's ongoing collection. Muhahahahahahahaha...

source: Mturk.com. Thanks to all Turkers who took part!

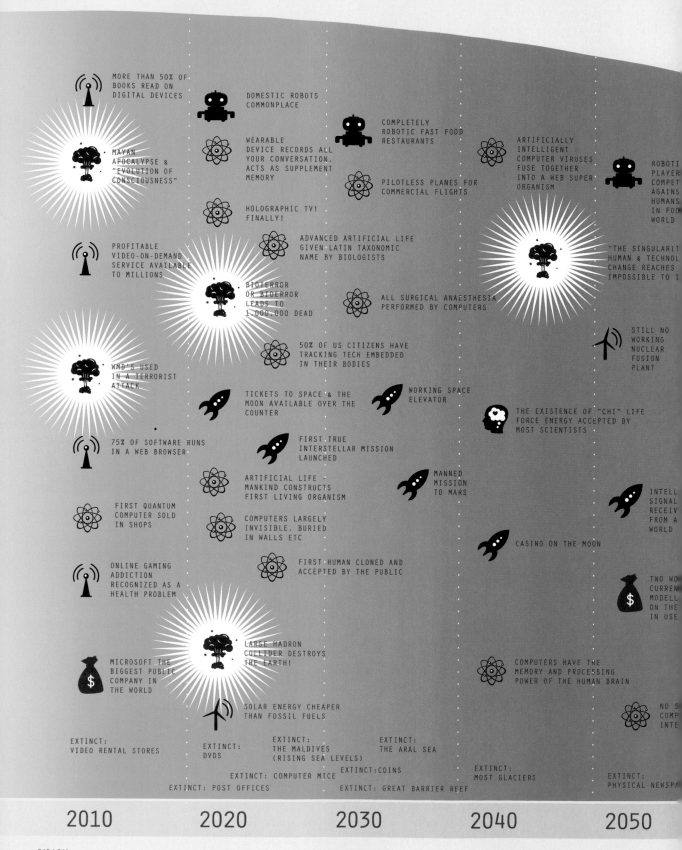

MORE THAN 50% OF BOOKS READ ON DIGITAL DEVICES

DOMESTIC ROBOTS COMMONPLACE

COMPLETELY ROBOTIC FAST FOOD RESTAURANTS

ARTIFICIALLY INTELLIGENT COMPUTER VIRUSES FUSE TOGETHER INTO A WEB SUPER ORGANISM

ROBOTI PLAYER COMPET AGAINS HUMANS IN FOO WORLD

MAYAN APOCALYPSE & "EVOLUTION OF CONSCIOUSNESS"

WEARABLE DEVICE RECORDS ALL YOUR CONVERSATION, ACTS AS SUPPLEMENT MEMORY

PILOTLESS PLANES FOR COMMERCIAL FLIGHTS

"THE SINGULARIT HUMAN & TECHNOL CHANGE REACHES IMPOSSIBLE TO I

HOLOGRAPHIC TV! FINALLY!

PROFITABLE VIDEO-ON-DEMAND SERVICE AVAILABLE TO MILLIONS

ADVANCED ARTIFICIAL LIFE GIVEN LATIN TAXONOMIC NAME BY BIOLOGISTS

BIOTERROR OR BIOERROR LEADS TO 1,000,000 DEAD

ALL SURGICAL ANAESTHESIA PERFORMED BY COMPUTERS

STILL NO WORKING NUCLEAR FUSION PLANT

WMD'S USED IN A TERRORIST ATTACK

50% OF US CITIZENS HAVE TRACKING TECH EMBEDDED IN THEIR BODIES

THE EXISTENCE OF "CHI" LIFE FORCE ENERGY ACCEPTED BY MOST SCIENTISTS

TICKETS TO SPACE & THE MOON AVAILABLE OVER THE COUNTER

WORKING SPACE ELEVATOR

75% OF SOFTWARE RUNS IN A WEB BROWSER

FIRST TRUE INTERSTELLAR MISSION LAUNCHED

MANNED MISSION TO MARS

INTELL SIGNAL RECEIV FROM A WORLD

FIRST QUANTUM COMPUTER SOLD IN SHOPS

ARTIFICIAL LIFE - MANKIND CONSTRUCTS FIRST LIVING ORGANISM

ONLINE GAMING ADDICTION RECOGNIZED AS A HEALTH PROBLEM

COMPUTERS LARGELY INVISIBLE. BURIED IN WALLS ETC

CASINO ON THE MOON

TWO WO CURREN MODELL ON THE IN USE

FIRST HUMAN CLONED AND ACCEPTED BY THE PUBLIC

MICROSOFT THE BIGGEST PUBLIC COMPANY IN THE WORLD

LARGE HADRON COLLIDER DESTROYS THE EARTH!

COMPUTERS HAVE THE MEMORY AND PROCESSING POWER OF THE HUMAN BRAIN

SOLAR ENERGY CHEAPER THAN FOSSIL FUELS

NO S COMP INTE

EXTINCT: VIDEO RENTAL STORES

EXTINCT: DVDS

EXTINCT: THE MALDIVES (RISING SEA LEVELS)

EXTINCT: THE ARAL SEA

EXTINCT: MOST GLACIERS

EXTINCT: PHYSICAL NEWSPA

EXTINCT: COMPUTER MICE

EXTINCT: COINS

EXTINCT: POST OFFICES

EXTINCT: GREAT BARRIER REEF

2010   2020   2030   2040   2050

The Future of the Future

At longbets.org leading thinkers gather to place bets on future predictions

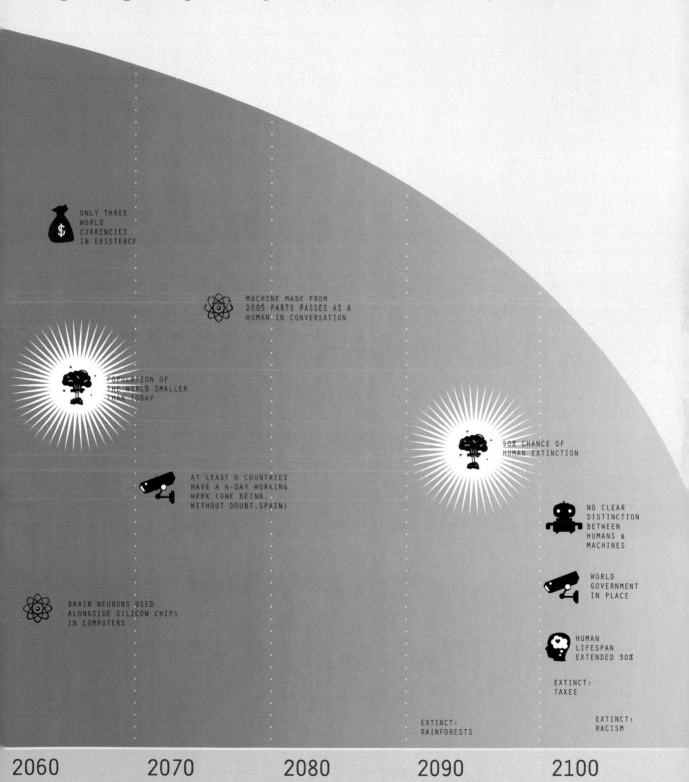

ONLY THREE WORLD CURRENCIES IN EXISTENCE

MACHINE MADE FROM 2005 PARTS PASSES AS A HUMAN IN CONVERSATION

POPULATION OF THE WORLD SMALLER THAN TODAY

50% CHANCE OF HUMAN EXTINCTION

AT LEAST 6 COUNTRIES HAVE A 4-DAY WORKING WEEK (ONE BEING, WITHOUT DOUBT, SPAIN)

NO CLEAR DISTINCTION BETWEEN HUMANS & MACHINES

WORLD GOVERNMENT IN PLACE

BRAIN NEURONS USED ALONGSIDE SILICON CHIPS IN COMPUTERS

HUMAN LIFESPAN EXTENDED 30%

EXTINCT: TAXES

EXTINCT: RAINFORESTS

EXTINCT: RACISM

| 2060 | 2070 | 2080 | 2090 | 2100 |

source: longbets.org

Making a Book

The first six months

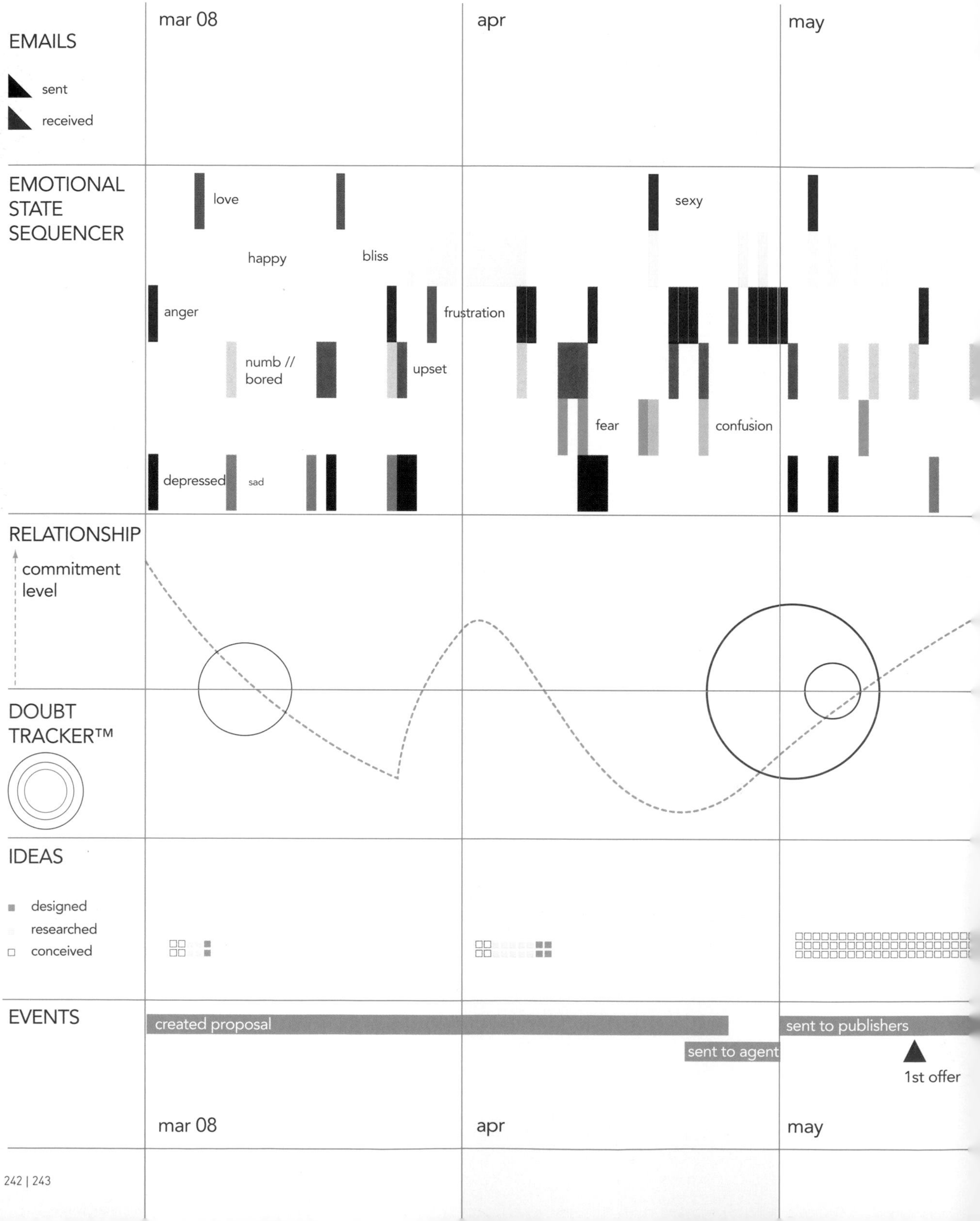

	mar 08	apr	may

EMAILS

▲ sent

◣ received

EMOTIONAL STATE SEQUENCER

love

happy   bliss

sexy

anger   frustration

numb // bored   upset

fear   confusion

depressed   sad

RELATIONSHIP

↑ commitment level

DOUBT TRACKER™

IDEAS

■ designed

□ researched

□ conceived

EVENTS

created proposal

sent to agent

sent to publishers

▲ 1st offer

mar 08	apr	may

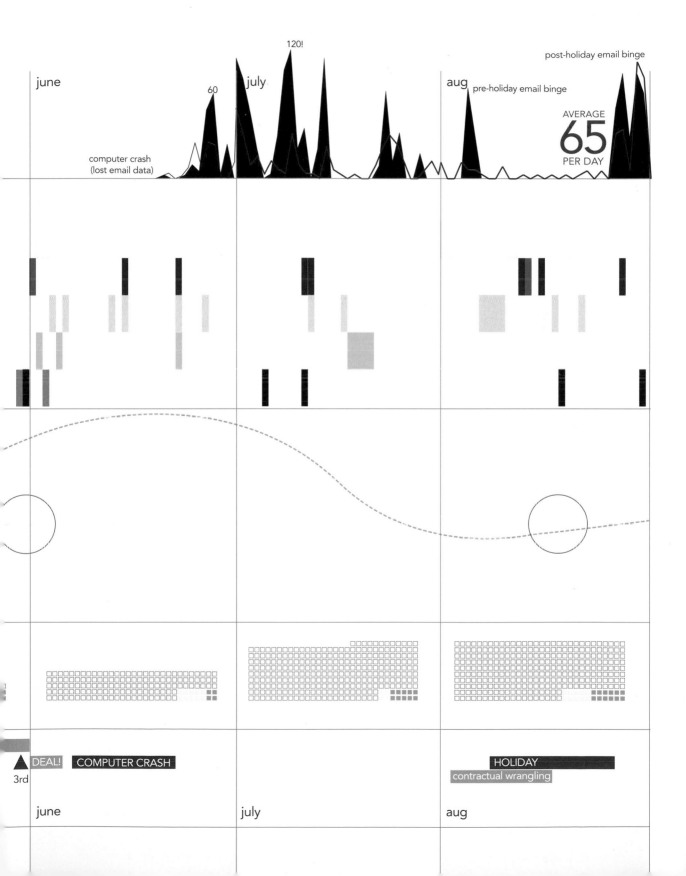

june

july

aug

120!

60

computer crash
(lost email data)

post-holiday email binge

pre-holiday email binge

AVERAGE
65
PER DAY

3rd

▲ DEAL!   COMPUTER CRASH

HOLIDAY
contractual wrangling

june

july

aug

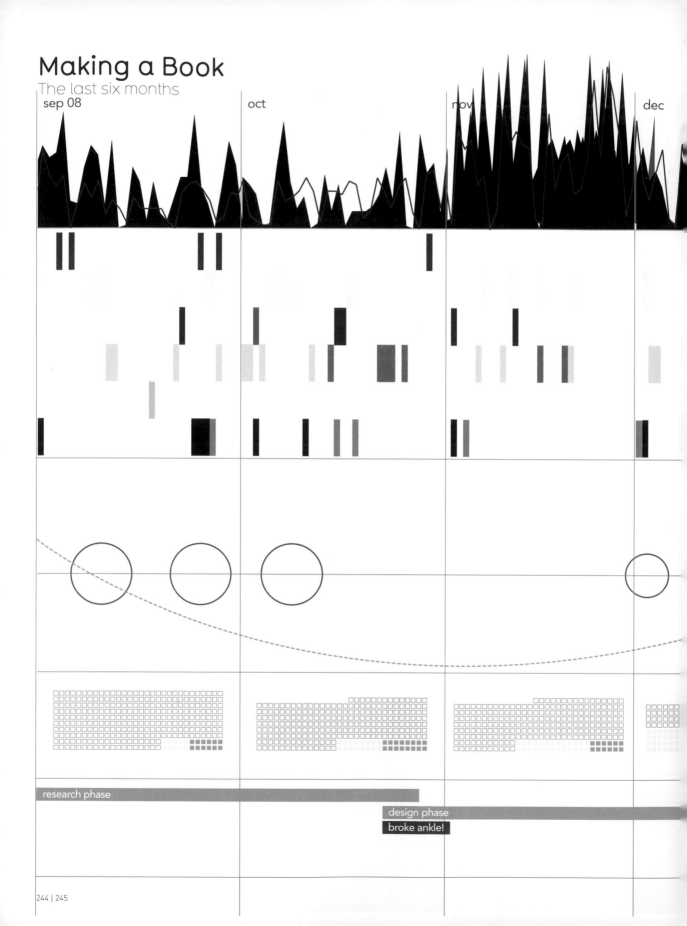

Making a Book
The last six months

sep 08

oct

nov

dec

research phase

design phase

broke ankle!

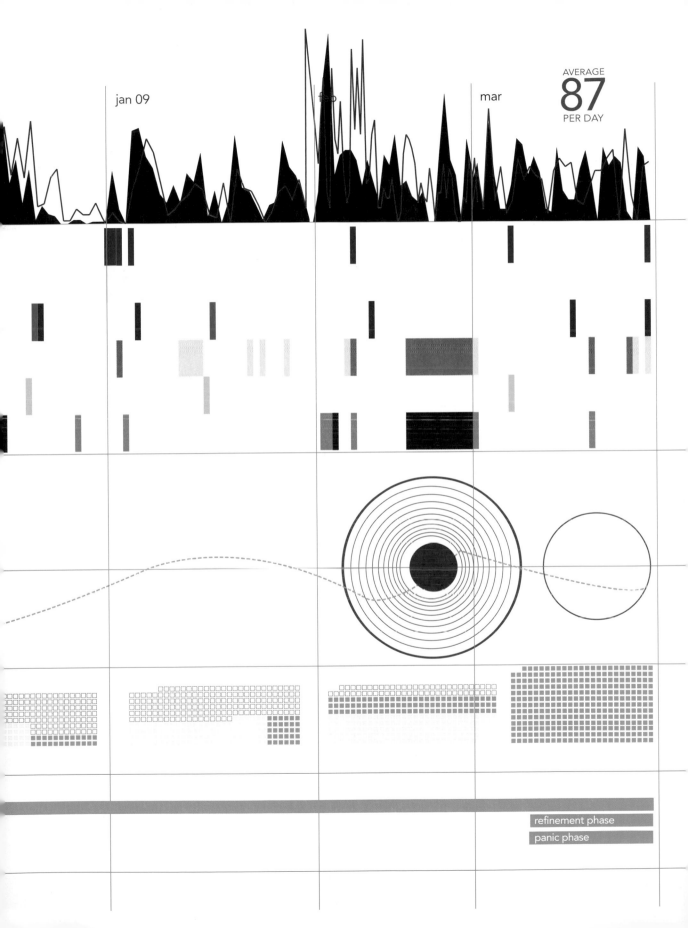

jan 09

feb

mar

AVERAGE
87
PER DAY

refinement phase

panic phase

Acknowledge Map
Thanks to all who helped and supported

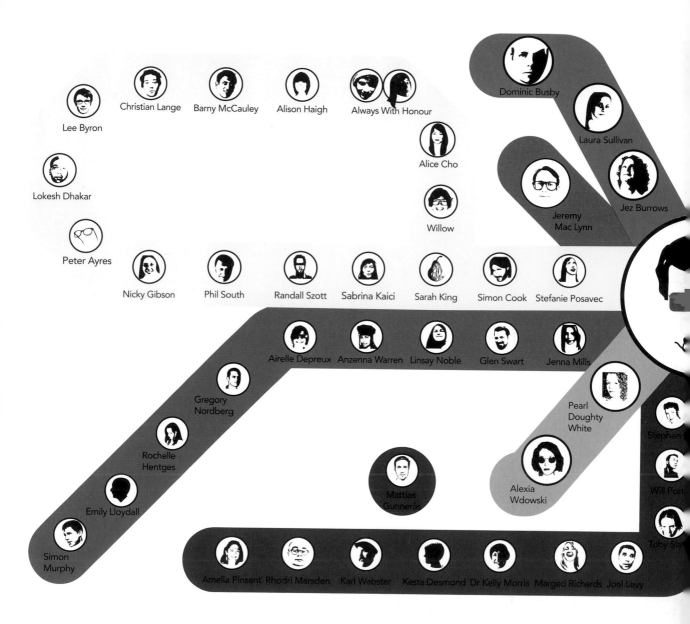

Lee Byron
Christian Lange
Barny McCauley
Alison Haigh
Always With Honour
Alice Cho
Lokesh Dhakar
Willow
Peter Ayres
Nicky Gibson
Phil South
Randall Szott
Sabrina Kaici
Sarah King
Simon Cook
Stefanie Posavec
Dominic Busby
Laura Sullivan
Jeremy Mac Lynn
Jez Burrows
Airelle Depreux
Anzenna Warren
Linsay Noble
Glen Swart
Jenna Mills
Gregory Nordberg
Pearl Doughty White
Stephen
Rochelle Hentges
Mattias Gunnerås
Alexia Wdowski
Will Port
Emily Lloydall
Toby Sla
Simon Murphy
Amelia Pinsent
Rhodri Marsden
Karl Webster
Kesta Desmond
Dr Kelly Morris
Marged Richards
Joel Levy

MANY THANKS TO: Vincent Ahrend, Dr David Archer, Steve Beckett, Delfina Bottesini, Laura Brudenell, Candy Chang, Susanne Cook Greuter, Dave Cooper, Kesta Desmond, Robert Downes, Danielle Engelman, Edward Farmer, Richard Henry, Dr Phil Howard, Claudia Hofmeister, Aegir Hallmundur, Becky Jones, Dongwoo Kim, Jenny McIvor, Priscila Moura, Mark O'Connor, Kate O'Driscoll, Dr. Lori Plutchik, Laura Price, Richard Rogers, Twitter Army, Mechanical Turkers.

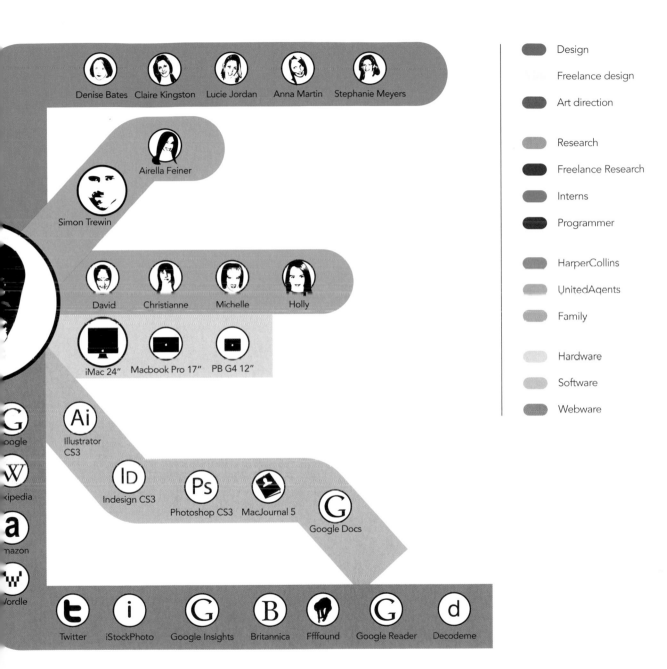

Denise Bates Claire Kingston Lucie Jordan Anna Martin Stephanie Meyers

Airella Feiner

Simon Trewin

David Christianne Michelle Holly

iMac 24" Macbook Pro 17" PB G4 12"

Illustrator CS3

Indesign CS3

Photoshop CS3 MacJournal 5

Google Docs

Google

Wikipedia

Amazon

Wordle

Twitter iStockPhoto Google Insights Britannica Ffffound Google Reader Decodeme

Design
Freelance design
Art direction

Research
Freelance Research
Interns
Programmer

HarperCollins
UnitedAgents
Family

Hardware
Software
Webware

Bibliograph
Inspiration and source material

Schott, Ben, *Schott's Almanac* 2007 (London: Bloomsbury Publishing Plc., 2007)

Tufte, Edward R., *Envisioning Information* (Cheshire, Connecticut: Graphics Press LLC, 2005)

Fry, Ben, *Visualizing Data* (Sebastopol, CA: O'Reilly Media, Inc., 2008)

Abrams, Janet and Peter Hall, *Else/Where: Mapping* (Minneapolis: University of Minneapolis Design Institute, 2006)

Bakhtiar, Laleh, *Sufi* (New York: Thames and Hudson Inc., 2004)

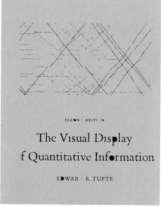

Tufte, Edward R., *The Visual Display of Quantitative Information* (Cheshire, Connecticut: Graphics Press LLC, 2006)

Levitt, Steven D. and Stephen J. Dubner, *Freakonomics* (London: Penguin Books, 2006)

Ayers, Ian, *Super Crunchers* (London: Random House, Inc., 2008)

Harmon, Katharine, *You Are Here* (New York: Princeton Architectural Press, 2004)

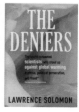

Solomon, Lawrence, *The Deniers* (Richard Vigilante Books, 2008)

Image Credits

InformationIsBeautiful.net

Visit the website for the book

 discover more
our blog covers visual journalism, unusual infographics,
far-out data visualizations

 be involved
crowdsource and help us investigate, research and
unearth facts and information for new designs

 get animated
play with interactive visuals and animations

 have a play
access all the data and research used in this book
and find editable versions of some images

 find extra stuff
tons of new diagrams, idea maps, bubble charts,
factoramas, knowledgescapes and infomaps...

twitter: @infobeautiful // facebook.com/david.mccandless

Can Drugs Make You Happy?

DRUGGIEST   Largest % of population using illegal drugs (7% or more)

Argentina, Australia, Belize, Canada, Chile, Czech Rep, Denmark, England & Wales, Estonia, France, Ghana, Ireland, Israel, Italy, Jamaica, Kyrgystan, Latvia, Lebanon, Luxembourg, Madagascar, New Zealand, Nigeria, Spain, Switzerland, Uruguay, USA, Venezuela, Zambia, Zimbabwe

source: Guardian Data blog, UN

HAPPIEST   by Happiness Index Rating (above 6.8/10)

Argentina, Australia, Austria, Belgium, Belize, Brazil, Canada, Chile, Colombia, Costa Rica, Cyprus, Denmark, El Salvador, England & Wales, Finland, Guatemala, Ireland, Ireland, Italy, Luxembourg, Malta, Mexico, Netherlands, New Zealand, Norway, Saudi Arabia, Singapore, Spain, Sweden, Switzerland, Thailand, Trinidad & Tobago, UAE, USA, Venezuela

source: Erasmus University Rotterdam, Worlddatabaseofhappiness.eur.nl

BLISSED OUT!   where happiness strongly correlates with drug use

Argentina, Australia, Belize, Canada, Chile, Denmark, England & Wales, Ireland, Italy, Luxembourg, New Zealand, Spain, Switzerland, USA, Venezuela

42%

just for fun: correlation is not cause

Ain't Nothing Going On But The Rent
money and divorce in a co-dependent relationship?

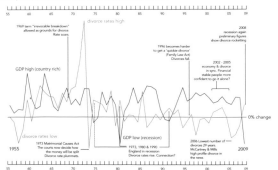

Pre-Flight Check
Reduce your odds of dying in a plane crash

Final Destination
Density of fatal accidents 1942-2009

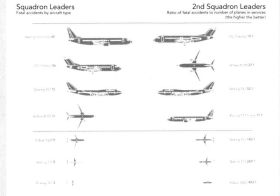

USA (2613 accidents), Russia 626, UK, India, Canada, Brazil, France, China, Colombia, Germany, Vietnam, Indonesia, Mexico, Italy, Cuba, Bolivia, Philippines, Congo, Kenya, Zaire, Spain, Argentina, Atlantic Ocean (and associated seas), the Mediterranean, Caribbean, Myanmar, Australia, Japan, Venezuela, Netherlands, Sudan, Nigeria, Iran, Peru, Angola, Papua New Guinea, Afghanistan, Poland, Egypt, Pakistan, Thailand, Turkey, Ecuador (75)

source: www.aviation-safety-aviation-safety.country

Squadron Leaders
Fatal accidents by aircraft type

2nd Squadron Leaders
Ratio of fatal accidents to number of planes in services
(the higher the better)

source: www.aviation-safety.net via the Guardian Datablog

Seating Plan
Survival rate relative to seat position

49%   56%   56%   69%

source: Popular Mechanics via Flowing Data (.com), University of Greenwich study

Bad Month
Months with the most fatal airline accidents 1942-2009

| Jan | Feb | Mar | Apr | May | June |
| Jul | Aug | Sep | Oct | Nov | Dec |

source: Wikipedia list of air disasters

The Odds
Chances of actually dying in a plane crash

source: Google

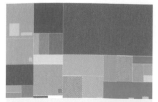

The Billion Dollar Gram
010

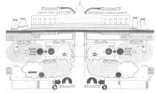

Left vs. Right
014

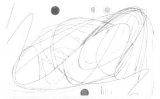

Timelines
016

Snake oil?
018

The Creationism-Evolutism
Spectrum 020

Mountains out of Molehills
022

X is the new black
024

Tons Of Carbon
026

Books Everyone Should Read
028

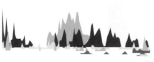

Which Fish Are Okay To Eat>
030

The 'In' Colours
032

Three's A Magic Number
036

Who Runs the World?
038

Who Really Runs The World?
040

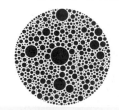

Stock Check
042

30 Years Makes a Difference
044

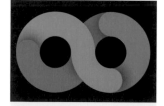

Creation Myths
046

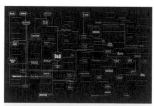

Dance Music Genre-ology
048

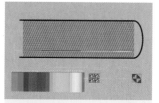

The Book Of You
050

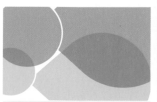

The Book of Me
052

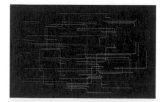

Rock Music Genre-ology
058

Simple Part I
060

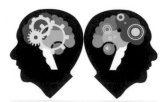

What is Consciousness?
066

Carbon Conscious
068

252 | 253

Looking for Love Online
072

Sea Level Rises
074

Colours &
Culture 076

Stages Of You
077

Personal Computer Evolution
084

The One Machine
086

Internet Virals
092

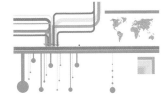

YouTubes
094

In 25 Words or Less
096

World Religions
098

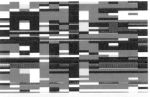

Moral Matrix
100

Carbon Cycle
102

Low Resolution
104

Taste Buds
106

Extinct
112

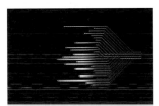

International Number Ones
114

Cocktails & Cures
116

Salad
Dressings 118

Not Nice
119

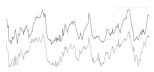

20th Century Death
120

Climate Skeptics vs The
Consensus 122

Behind Every Great Man
126

Types of Info
Viz 128

Pass The...
129

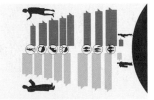

Nature vs Nuture
130

Post

Post Modernism
132

Dangers Of Death
134

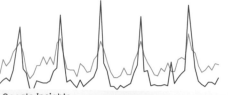

Google Insights
136

On Target?
139

The Varieties Of Romantic
Relationship 140

30 Years Makes A Difference II
142

The Great Firewall Of China
144

Better Than
Bacon 146

What Are The
Chances? 147

Some Things You Can't Avoid
148

Body By
151

Microbes Most
Dangerous 152

Cosmetic
Ingredients 153

Things That'll Give You Cancer
154

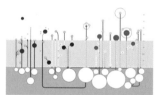

Types Of Coffee
156

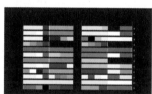

Tons Of Carbon II
158

Articles Of War
160

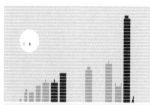

Water Towers
162

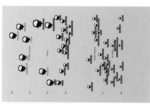

Who Clever Are You?
164

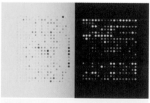

The Media Jungle
166

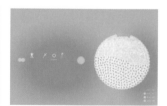

Daily Diets
168

Calories In, Calories Out
170

Types Of Facial Hair
172

Vintage Years
174

Amphibian Extinction Rates
176

Motive, Timing & Delivery
178

Good News
180

Feeding Frenzy
182

Virtual Kingdoms
184

Avatars
186

Immortality
187

Red vs Blue
188

Man's Humanity To Man
190

Fast Internet
192

Simple Part II
196

Peter's Projection
202

Alternative Medicine
204

The Cloud
206

Being Defensive
208

Most Popular Girls' Names
212

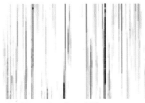

Most Popular Boys' Names
214

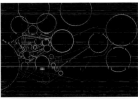

The Middle East
216

The Middle
East 218
The Future Of
Energy 219

Most Successful Rock Bands
220

Stories
222

Most Profitable Stories 2007
224

Most Profitable Stories 2008
228

Most Profitable Stories Ever
232

The Enneagram
234

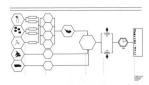

Bee Limit Warning
236

Selling Your Soul
238

The Future Of The Future
240

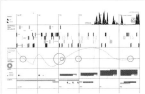

Making The Book
242

Acknowledge Map
246